YOUNG ULTRAÍSTA

the early writing of Jorge Luis Borges

Mario René Padilla

Translations by
Mario René Padilla &
Marcelino Padilla Ramos

ATOPON BOOKS

Atopon Books
907 15th Street
Santa Monica, California 90403
United States

The material in this book on Jorge Luis Borges, including his reproduced early poetry and essays, first appeared in the unpublished dissertation *Borges, Hemingway and Faulkner: Young Poets of Prose*, written by Mario René Padilla for the PhD at the University of Southern California, submitted in 1993.

Publisher's Cataloging-in-Publication data

Names: Padilla, Mario René, 1949-, author.
Title: Young ultraísta: the early writing of Jorge Luis Borges / Mario René Padilla.
Description: Santa Monica : Atopon Books, 2023.
Identifiers: LCCN: 2023939517 | ISBN: 979-8-9866907-9-7 (hardcover) | 979-8-9866907-5-9 (paperback)
Subjects: LCSH Borges, Jorge Luis, 1899-1986--Authorship. | Borges, Jorge Luis, 1899-1986--Criticism and interpretation. | Spanish poetry--20th century--History and criticism. | Ultraism (Literary movement) | BISAC LITERARY CRITICISM / Poetry | LITERARY CRITICISM / European / Spanish & Portuguese
Classification: LCC PQ7797.B635 Z79672 2023 | DDC 868/.6209--dc23

Cover image: *Ultra* ns 1, Madrid. 1921. Wood Carving by Norah Borges / Abstract red low poly background © Adobe Stock / viperagp

Printed in the United States of America

For my father:
  sabio, musician, poet, literato, historian, translator—
  and one hell of a dad

"[Writers,] someday you realize you're going to feel embarrassed about your writing. You may even think it's terrible. I don't think of it that way, I think it's really good. But you probably will, because it's a sign you're getting better at writing. Just remember, at some point in life, you have to own your words. You have to acknowledge that 'this is what I believed at the time, this is what I said at the time, this was my best at the time, and I'm okay with that.'"

Steven King

"The mature Borges tends to reject the works of youth . . . . Not only does he exclude them, he wants to literally make them invisible: he destroys any copy that he finds. . . .[But the] Borges that reflects in his stories and essays is the same one that meditates selfishly or 'fervorantly' in his poems. There are even pages of his prose that are imposing more for a certain surprise, a certain free play of thought and a certain sensibility; there exists in them so much passion as in his poetry."

Guillermo Sucre, Borges, El Poeta, 1967

"Ultraism is an abundant will that surpasses all scholastic limit. It is an orientation towards continuous and repeated evolutions, a purpose of perennial literary youth, an anticipated acceptance of all modules and of all ideas that are new. It represents the obligation to go forward with time."

Rafael Cansinos Asséns
Creator of Ultraísmo in Spain, Autumn 1918

I—and note well that I am speaking of intentions and not of fulfilled realizations—long for an art that translates naked emotion, purified of the additional data that precedes it. An art that avoids flesh and blood reality, the metaphysical, and the ultimate levels of caustic egocentricity.

Jorge Luis Borges, 21 years old,
"Anatomía de mi Vltra"

Contents

A Note on the Texts

The following books and anthologies of Jorge Luis Borges—not a complete list—are abbreviated as follows throughout this study:

Fervor – *Fervor de Buenos Aires* (1923)
Luna – *Luna de Enfrente* (1925)
Inquisiciones – *Inquisiciones* (1925)
El tamaño – *El tamaño de mi esperanza* (1926)
El idioma – *El idioma de los argentinos* (1928)
Cuaderno – *Cuaderno de San Martín* (1929)
Carriego – *Everisto Carriego* (1930)
Discusión – *Discusión* (1932 & 1964)
Historia Universal – *Historia universal de la infamia* (1935)
Historia Eternidad – *Historia de la eternidad* (1936)
El jardín – *El jardín de senderos que se bifurcan* (1941)
Poemas 43 – *Poemas, 1922-1943* (1943)
Ficciones – *Ficciones* (1944)
El Aleph – *El Aleph* (1949)
Otras inq. – *Otras inquisiciones* (1952)
Historia Infamia – *Historia universal de la infamia* (1954)
Poemas 58 – *Poemas, 1923-1958*
Hacedor – *El hacedor* (1960)
Antología personal – *A Personal Anthology* (1961)
Dreamtigers – *Dreamtigers* (1964)
El otro – *El otro, el mismo* (1964)
Obra poética 67 – *Obra poética, 1923-1967*
JLB: Selected – *Jorge Luis Borges: Selected Poems 1923-1967*
Nueva antología – *Nueva antología personal* (1968)
Obra poética 69 – *Obra poética, 1923-1969*
Obra poética 76 – *Obra poética, 1923-1976*
JLB: Antología 77 – *Jorge Luis Borges: Antología poética 1923-1977* (1981)
Obra poética 85 – *Obra poética, 1923-1985*

Preface

Jorge Luis Borges arrived in Spain at the beginning of 1919, eight months before his twentieth birthday. Although he attended the Collège de Genève in Geneva, Switzerland between 1914 and 1918, where he studied German and French literature, he came to Majorca still very much a product of the New World—a South American in his deep heart's core. Moreover, he had been educated on as much American literature found in his father's library—Twain, Stevenson, Longfellow, Poe, Whitman—as on classical European and Spanish literature from the Old World. His father also expected young Borges to worship all things Argentine: tales of the pampas-dwelling gauchos, desperadoes like Juan Moreira, dangerous barrios, knife fights, the tango, which he discovered in books by Eduardo Gutiérrez and in José Hernández's *Martin Fierro*—the culture of a rough and unrefined mixed-race territory—although he himself was raised in privilege behind a gate. The fourteen-year-old Borges even tried writing a poem about gauchos before he left for Geneva.

The Borges family sailed to Europe just before the breakout of WWI. His father's eyesight was failing due to a degenerative disease—the same disease Jorge Luis would suffer in his later years. The elder Borges was to be treated by a famous Genevan eye doctor. The family visited Paris, then crossed the Alps and toured Italy, where Borges remembers reciting aloud gaucho verses from Ascasubi in an empty amphitheater in Verona. The war caught the Borges family by surprise, and Jorge's father, Jorge Guillermo, thought it best to settle in neutral Switzerland for the duration of the war. In November 1918, with the war's end, the elder Borges decided to take his family to Spain before returning home to Buenos Aires. They passed almost all of 1919 in Majorca, spent the winter of 1920 in Sevilla, then, a year in Madrid, leaving for home in the spring of 1921. The two and one half years Borges spent among the Spanish literati, especially his fellow ultraist poets in Madrid, would prove to be transformational—for among the ultraístas, young Borges began his life in letters.

Rafael Cansino Assens, the founder of Ultraísmo, and his circle of Spanish poets discovered much to admire about young Borges. He was well-educated with a keen intelligence and an arsenal of languages—his father's mother was an educated English woman, and as such, Borges grew up speaking English in the house and Spanish in school and on the streets. In Geneva, he acquired French and German. His earliest writing efforts would consist of poetry and essays in both Spanish and French. On August 20, 1919, he published his first work, an essay in a Geneva newspaper, *La Feuille*: "Chronique des lettres espagnoles: Trois nouveaux livres." Four months later while in Sevilla, he would publish his first poem, "Himno del Mar," in the magazine *Grecia*. The poem was heavily influenced by his reading of Walt Whitman, a poet favored by the German expressionists whom he greatly admired, having studied them in Geneva. Nevertheless, it is clear that his experience among the ultraístas inspired him to become a poet and a literary man—but *not* a writer of fiction.

Indeed, it would take fifteen more years of apprenticeship in poetry, essays and reviews before Borges would begin to experiment with prose narrative, labor that would eventually make him the celebrated author of the unique tales and stories in *El jardin de senderos que se bifurcan* (1941) [*Garden of Branching Paths*], *Ficciones* (1944), and *El Aleph* (1949)—collections that have secured his international literary fame.

At the time of Borges's residence in Spain, the country's poets were vibrating with the spirit of Vanguardismo (1918-1938), the term used in Spanish-speaking countries to describe the "make it new" modern aesthetic sweeping through the Western world and which many of the young Spanish writers, the Generation of '27, enthusiastically embraced. The 1920s were exciting years of experimentation, rebellion, and change in all the arts—and this desire for change was especially felt among the poets. Literary manifestos were being penned and plastered on walls and shop windows hailing the new tenets of Ultraísmo. In the poems and essays Borges began to write and publish in Spanish magazines, he reveals his experience as an ultraist as being exhilarating. The ultraists were passionate about renewing Spanish literature. They formed a lively and energetic posse that caroused the evening streets, passed long hours in cafés and bars expounding Cansino Assens ultraist aesthetics and reading freshly penned poems to each other—often until the sun came up.

When I arrived in Spain in August 1991, some seventy-two years after Borges, I was forty-one years old, a husband and father of three. I'd already spent my twenties and thirties chasing several disparate careers: television production supervisor for CBS news and entertainment, a composer of music for theater and ballet, pianist and songwriter, an actor (with a number of credits and the possibility of a career), and a poet. But eventually—in my search for what and who I was truly meant to be—I discovered that literature eclipsed all my ambitions. Following my instincts, at thirty-three I made the difficult choice to return to school and take some English courses at Santa Monica Community College. As a young man, I had earned a B.S. degree in Business Administration at Ohio State University, so with English, I was starting at the beginning. Through UCLA's extension course program, I took the required English courses that would qualify me to enroll in Loyola Marymount University's Masters program in English, and in 1987, I earned my MA. Yet, I remained uncertain about how to make a living with literature—I had a family to feed—I even took a job as a waiter in a restaurant.

My father, Marcelino Padilla Ramos, ever the *sabio*, stepped into the middle of my confusion and convinced me to travel with him to Mexico. We traveled to his hometown, San Francisco del Rincón in Guanajuato—and for the first time, I understood what it meant to say, "I'm Mexican." I met relatives, explored other cities and towns, visited Mayan and Aztec ruins. I was a man standing precariously on a precipice peering down into a vast part of myself I'd never before identified. I had been raised in Columbus, Ohio, among my mother's Italian people; as a result, I hardly knew my father's culture or language. Most importantly, throughout our trip, my father, the consummate literato, introduced me to his favorite Latin American authors, especially poets. I can still hear his *profundo* voice reading passages to me while I drove the VW van: Paz, Neruda, Mistral, Sabines, Vallejo, Fuentes, Vasconcelos: great poets and writers who came alive in my imagination. When I asked him why he had never introduced me to any of this before, he said, "You weren't ready." Enough said.

On my return to the states, without hesitation, I applied to the University of Southern California and was accepted into their PhD program for Comparative Literature. I made my area of study Anglo American and Latin American literature of the Modernist (Vanguardismo) era. Meanwhile, throughout my PhD coursework, I continued to write my own poetry. I gave public readings and published in several magazines (I was associate editor of the poetry magazine *El Playano* while at L.M.U.). Like Borges, I discovered that I was not only meant to be a poet, but a scholar as well. While my poems were being accepted for publication, so were my essays on Latin American literature, which I delivered at conferences and colloquiums at universities across the country.

Then came the momentous day I discovered young Borges—the ultraísta—and my scholarly life altered dramatically. I found fascinating the few ultraist poems made available to me in a Spanish course on Vanguardismo—I found them as fascinating as the stories from *Ficciones* I was studying. Also interesting to me was his transition from poet to prose fiction writer. It had already formed the subject of my dissertation with Faulkner and Hemingway. Thus, I added Borges to my study: *Borges, Faulkner and Hemingway: Young Poets of Prose* (1993; unpublished dissertation). Fortuitously, in 1991, I won a Fulbright award for dissertation research that granted me ten months in Spain to search for and, more or less, recover whatever I could find of Borges's other early uncollected writing he'd published in magazines between 1919 and 1923—work he later decided not worthy enough to be collected. In the ultraist works I found, I saw a younger, passionate Borges—and it became my goal to understand his ultraist phase as well as how the young poet transformed himself into the great prose stylist of the twentieth century.

Now, I must admit, and a bit shamefacedly, that I arrived in Spain with a certain predisposition to dislike the country and its people, to tolerate my residency just long enough to complete my research. I was prepared to reject all things Spanish: the culture, the food, the music, the Spanish conquerors, colonizers, arrogant oppressors. I was not yet ready to accept José Vasconcelos's philosophy in his important essay, "La Raza Cósmica," which urged those of us with Latin American heritage to accept ourselves as *sons* of Spain. My father had taught me to value my Mexican side, as Borges's father had taught him to value Argentinian culture. Moreover, as a California chicano poet—as I was being referred to—I'd learned to value my indigenous-mestizo side more than the Spanish heritage of the Padillas who'd emigrated to the Americas from Galicia in the mid-1830s and settled in Guanajuato.

However, what actually happened was something I was not prepared for. Like Borges, who also didn't lay much claim on his Spanish and Portuguese heritage, I fell under the spell of Spanish culture—the literary, artistic, passionate, musical, and yes, sometimes violent society of Spain. And like Borges, I too was welcomed into a special posse: a group of artists, poets, Fulbright scholars and sundry literati in Madrid who, when not writing dissertations, novels or poetry, worked different odd jobs to pay the rent. But at the end of the day, we passed our evenings carousing the streets, assembling in plazas for fiestas, passing all-night veladas in bars and cafés, discussing art and literature in tertulias with tapas, olives, and wine, attending Spanish festivals wherever they occurred (thanks to Maria José who was getting her PhD on the festivals of Spain). In the company of my Spanish and American friends, I discovered Iberia. Together we travelled to Barcelona, Galicia, Madrid, Sevilla, Granada, Toledo, Santiago de Compostela, Estrema de Madura, where I discovered the dark, deeply creative, always inspiring (if also sometimes disturbing) black and red *duende* of Flamenco, strumming guitars and siguiriyas in the plazas, bull fights, fútbol, Carnaval, Entierro de la Sardina, unique food and wine, the stirring, soul-clapping rhythm of creative expression and performance that dominates the Spanish subconscious.

Fortunately, during my residency in Spain between August 1991 and July 1992, the country had just reached the zenith of its surging popularity: Barcelona would be staging the Olympics in the summer of '92; the World Exposition would take place in Sevilla from April to October '92; and that year, Madrid was voted the cultural capital of Europe—all this from a country that had spent the previous sixteen years crawling its way back from fascism after Franco's death in 1975. The *movida* ran full in the streets. It was an exhilarating, hypnotic, transformative and unforgettable time for anyone lucky enough to have experienced it.

Winning the Fulbright made all this possible, and helped me, unquestionably, to earn my PhD, yet it provided me something else as important—it helped me find my own *creative voice*. Living and travelling throughout Spain for almost a year, tracking down the early writing of young Borges in magazines, I was able to discover my own sensibilities as a poet. I came upon the poems of many other young vanguardista poets who also inspired my work, such as Garcia Lorca, Rafael Alberti and Ramón Gómez de la Serna—young men like Borges who sought recognition by publishing their first works in Spanish magazines of the early 1920s. The whole experience was life-changing.

To Borges readers and aficionados, yes, it may be hard for you to imagine, but you must accept that the introverted, half-blind, erudite author of *Ficciones* (1944) and *El Aleph* (1949) was once a young, passionate, aspiring ultraist poet reveling in the streets of Madrid with his comrades and brothers, rebellious and impulsive, conspiring with other ultraists how to direct the course of Spain's poetic consciousness. Their goal was to overturn the popularity of Ruben Dario's *Modernismo* (1888-1915)—a combination of Romanticism, French Symbolism and Parnassianism—which had exerted a heavy influence on Spanish poets of the Generation of '98. I could only imagine the twenty-one-year-old Borges posting manifestos on walls and café windows, reciting poems out loud in cafés, engaged in nightly intense literary discussions, wandering the echoing bannered streets, tipsy and boisterous, declaring Ultraísmo *the new* and Dario's Modernismo *the old*. Then, as some of the poems suggest, they'd head for a brothel seeking to expunge their youthful energy. Many even declared their fascination with the Russian socialist revolution, which Borges would later reject and which would prove to be the death sentence for Garcia Lorca during the Spanish Civil War.

Caught up in their poetic revolution, the ultraists created their own magazine, *Ultra*, so they could publish their works and disseminate their manifestos—the same *Ultra* issues I would discover some seventy years later tucked away on dusty shelves of various bibliotecas throughout Spain or in private libraries—sarcophagi, as I think of them now, holding in print young Borges's first literary efforts, to be dug up and, once again, exposed to the reading public.

As I'd suspected, I had been exposed at USC to only a small portion of Borges's early writing. In the Appendix, I have listed eighty-some works he'd published in magazines—of which I now have copies—and this is, most certainly, not a complete list. Unfortunately, Borges felt shame for his early writing, and thus, throughout his career, did his best to suppress the products of his youth. For example, from all his ultraist poetry through 1923, only four poems made it into Borges's *Fervor* and were included in later poetry anthologies. Moreover, of all the essays, reviews and manifestos he published in magazines before 1925, many of which he collected in *Inquisiciones* (1925) and *El tamaño de mi Esperanza* (1926) none were made available to the public-at-large throughout most of his career, for these collections were withdrawn from circulation. I want this book to change that record. In these pages you will discover a *young* Borges exploring how to be a poet, essayist, and literato. And if you are a fan of Borges, you will learn of a very different Borges from the mature author whose stories and tales heavily influenced the course of twentieth-century Latin American fiction.

The reason for the scarcity of Borges's juvenilia is, of course, Borges himself. He insisted that his early writing be suppressed, citing shame for once being a young man with a bountiful imagination and a healthy sense of rebellion. In his "Autobiographical Notes" (1970), he writes that he destroyed two books before leaving Spain in March of 1921: a book of essays, *Los naipes del tahur* [*The Sharper's Cards*] and a book of poems, *The Red Psalms*, which was written "in free verse and in praise of the Russian Revolution, the brotherhood of man, and pacifism." However, the poems and essays from these collections he'd published in various Spanish magazines he could not suppress, and these are the poems and essays you will find in Part Two.

To be clear, I believe all writers have the right to destroy whatever works they write and find a distaste for when they are complete. I've tossed numerous poems into wastebaskets. But the works a writer deems worthy of publication—making them available to the general public for consumption—that's a completely different matter. What I wholeheartedly disagree with are writers who attempt to hide or conceal, or even destroy what they have *published*—writers who, later in life, ridicule their youthful creations. It is a disapproval I expressed in the prologue of my first collection of poetry, *Reaching Back for the Neverendings* (1993):

> I refuse to ridicule myself for any enthusiasm for an event, an experience, an emotion, a passion for abstraction or the imaginative use of metaphor tuned way too high. Whatever we do, at whatever age, must carry some measure of pride, for the power in having seen a slight chance and taken it. To ridicule the excesses of youthful dispensation is to belittle the person you believed yourself to be, one who was probably not as immature as all the stories seem to show. . . .Being young is not an excuse, it is a predicament that is finally resolved in the end.

How unfortunate for the reader of Borges that he felt embarrassed by his young avant-garde self. Clearly, his brilliant mind and formidable imagination would take his writing far beyond his youthful extravagant ultraist excesses. But readers, I believe you will find in these pages, several early works that show definitive signs of his coming literary brilliance and imagination, and, as such, I believe they deserve to be read.

Unarguably, Borges's literary reputation falls firmly on the excellence of his ground-breaking prose fiction found in *Ficciones* and *El Aleph*. In these extremely important collections of stories, pseudo-essays, narrative sketches, pieces—all terms he himself used when referring to them—Borges conducts unique experiments in narrative technique and combines them with a poet-philosopher-metaphysician's implacable, esoteric critique of the nature and meaning of existence: how people live inside the inescapable labyrinth of time and space constraints which defines and delimits their experience as human beings. It is not surprising, then, that the majority of critical studies and university courses in twentieth-century Latin American literature focus mainly on works from these two collections. They are filled with inventive, mystifying, fabulist themes with secret references and symbolic allusions that, alongside his hyper-intellectual investigations of the truth, have long been perfect fodder for literary critics, especially deconstructionists, who thrive on the challenge of interpretation and exegesis. Although professors may pay some attention to his mature poetry—mostly poems from *El Hacedor* (1960) (*The Maker*), published in English as *Dreamtigers* (1964), and from *El otro, el mismo* (1964)—few syllabi include his ultraist poems, essays and manifestos penned and published while a young man immersed in the modern aesthetics of Vanguardismo.

This book aims to broaden Borgesian scholarship in some small way—for I believe much can be learned from studying a writer's juvenilia. Consider James Joyce's *Stephen Hero* written at the age of twenty-two which remains available to scholars today, or Herman Hesse, whose first two books were books of poetry, *Romantic Songs* (1896) and *One Hour after Midnight* (1898), which he wrote at twenty-one years of age. Another case would be Rimbaud—with whom I refuse to use the term "juvenilia" when referring to the incredible poems he wrote for *Illuminations* between the ages of seventeen and nineteen. Finally, consider Pablo Neruda's second book of poetry, *Viente poemas de amor y una canción desesperada* (1924) [*Twenty Love Poems and a Song of Despair*]. His poem, "Puedo escribir los versos. . . ["Tonight I Can Write. . ."] remains one of his most beloved poems—written when he was just twenty years old. Even his first collection, *Crepusculario* (1923) (*Book of Twilight*), written at the age of eighteen, remains available for all poetry lovers to enjoy. But then Neruda, unlike Borges, had no issue with his readers knowing him as a young, passionate and vulnerable poet.

This study reveals Borges as a young *vanguardista* poet who wanted so desperately to be considered a *true* poet, but who, subconsciously, believed—and ultimately discovered—that his poetry was not as good as the poetry of some of his contemporaries. As a result, he gradually shifted his efforts to writing prose fiction—and the rest, as they say, is history. Thus, current fiction writers who once envisioned themselves first (or *also*) as poets have much to learn from Borges's transition, from his "overlap" of the genres.

Also, be assured that Borges's early writing collected in Part Two has been carefully reproduced to reflect accurately the original typography, exactly as they appeared in the Spanish and Argentine literary magazines in which they were published: *Grecia, Baleares, Cervantes,*

Reflector, Ultra, Cosmópolis, Tableros, Nosotros, Alfar, Revista de Occidente, Proa, Martin Fierro, Prisma and *Inicial*. A few exceptions are the poems that contain unusually long, prosaic lines, which Borges himself had to "turnover" in order to fit his verse into the standard columns of most magazines. In these cases, I have tried to accommodate his original intentions by placing the turned-over verses back into one verse. With his prose poems, however, I have arranged the lines to reflect the fact that they are prose poetry, a genre which he was experimenting with at the time. I have, as well, included the initial magazine version of four of his ultraist poems which he collected in the first edition of *Fervor* in 1923. I found a rare signed copy of this collection (see plates 19 and 20), which Borges self-published with money from his father, printing three hundred copies. In his youthful desire to be recognized, he even slipped some of the staple-bound books into the pockets of overcoats hanging in the cloak room of the *Nosotros* literary magazine office. Thus, be assured that Borges's early poems in this book are not the heavily revised versions he re-published in later anthologies starting with *Poemas 1923-1943*—*only the original magazine versions* appear in these pages.

I want this book to communicate the modern age in which young Borges started his literary career. To help with this, I have included plates of some of the covers of the vanguard magazines, a few displaying the woodcuts of Borges's sister, Norah—herself a talented artist—all in an effort to bring you as close as possible to the spirit and age of Vanguardismo. How thrilling it was for me to find another of Borges's early works in print—to see at the bottom of a text "Jorge Luis Borges"— which I then carried to the copier of the Biblioteca Nacional de España, almost like an archeologist handling bone fragments. Then, after completing the exhumation, how I strode joyously up Bravo Murillo to my pensión on Calle Fernandez de los Ríos, my leather saddlebag filled with a new treasure. How good it felt to catalogue the work and engage in translating it with my father. This was one of the great creative periods of my life.

A very personal, yet secondary, purpose of this book is to examine, and perhaps explain, as a writer of both poetry and fiction, and as a creative writing instructor, the phenomenon of writers such as Borges who begin their career writing poetry (in some cases exclusively), but who ultimately turn to prose fiction to create their finest works. Writers like Borges, Faulkner, Joyce, Hemingway, Lawrence, Sitwell, Beckett, Hesse, Stein, and Maddox Ford, to mention only a few, have all made that transition. How did Borges achieve this: the overlapping of his poetry, essays, and prose fiction to create his narratives? I will offer my suppositions on how I feel writers of prose fiction, who are also poets, gain much when they incorporate aspects of their innate poetic sensibilities. Borges, the nineteen to twenty-three year-old poet, would need another decade and a half before he would attempt his first piece of prose fiction, "The Man on the Pink Corner," published in *Univeral de mí infamia* in 1935 at the age of thirty-six—nine years before he would publish his greatest story collection, *Ficciones,* in 1944.

The chronological list in the Appendix of Borges's poems, essays, reviews and manifestos published between 1919-1925 does not pretend to be complete. Regrettably, the few collections that make Borges youthful poetry available in English, such as *Jorge Luis Borges: Selected Poems 1923-1967* and the 1967 *Personal Anthology* edited by Anthony Kerrigan, as well as the 1981 edition of *Borges, A Reader* edited by Monegal and Reid, include only a few examples of his ultraist poetry, the emphasis in these books placed squarely on Borges's mature poems. Norman Thomas Di Giovanni, who edited the excellent *Selected Poems,* explains in the introduction Borges's bias against his vanguard poetry during the editing of the book:

> The choice of poems was worked out jointly. We wanted to include all the famous poems, to cover every period to represent most of the different forms and kinds of lines the poet has attempted. . . .Overall, of course, we favored the later poetry. Borges chafed and fussed a good deal over the choice of poems from his first three books which he continues to improve with revisions but which nonetheless still cause him embarrassment, but with insistence and persistence I was finally able to convince him that much of this early work is both valuable and pleasurable. (xviii)

As a result of his numerous improvements and revisions, a great portion of Borges's early poetry, when it truly could be defined as "early," remains essentially unavailable to the public.

A number of critics have even questioned whether Di Giovanni's *Selected Poems*, offering both the English and Spanish versions, can be honestly considered in a study of Spanish and Latin American Vanguardismo poetry. Paul Cheselka painstakingly develops this point in his 1987 study, *The Poetry and Poetics of Jorge Luis Borges*, when he suggests that the 1967 edition of *Obra poética*, from which the translations in Di Giovanni's *Selected Poems* were made, as well as the revised 1969 edition of the poems in four individual volumes, bears little if any of the "original spirit" of the vanguardismo poetry published in the twenties due to Borges's "incessant penchant" for cutting and revising his poetry, and for placing newly written poems into old collections:

> Despite his claims to the contrary in the preface, Borges gutted his 1964, 1966, and 1967 versions of *Fervor de Buenos Aires* with a re-publication of the work as a single, independent volume in 1969; he might have done well to give this work a new title to distinguish it from his previous work. . . .The 1969 "revision" suppressed three more poems and replaced them with two newly composed poems and one poem "plagiarized" from *El otro, el mismo.* In short, to say that the 1969 edition is a revised version of the 1964, 1966 and 1967 editions is an understatement bordering on dishonesty. for it contains only *one* unchanged poem from those editions. (56)

Furthermore, Cheselka's preferred 1964 version of *Fervor* merely contains poems previously revised in 1943, 1954 and 1958. From the original 1923 version of *Fervor*, which contained forty-six poems, fifteen were cut while all of the thirty-one remaining poems—except one—underwent complete revisions. Needless to say *Luna* (1925)—the scarcest of his early books—and, to a lesser extent, *Cuaderno* (1929) received the same treatment. Thus, it could be argued that these early poems, as they exist in anthologies today, do not truthfully represent Borges's vanguardista phase.

Moreover, for the student of Borges, I have listed in the Works Cited/Selected Bibliography all of the critical material that has made my own research more focused and which has contributed significantly to the study of his complete body of work. Regarding the reproductions here of Borges's early poems, it is important to remember, once again, that they follow rigorously the original formal layout: line length, verse and word spacing, punctuation, spelling, capitalization, indention, use of italics, and signature (this minor detail being important in considering the reasons why, in August of 1920, Borges began inserting a dash between Jorge-Luis, a change that, decidedly, coincides with his mentorship under the Spanish poet Rafael Cansinos Asséns, who, curiously enough, had begun inserting a dash in his name: "Cansinos-Asséns"). With regards to typography, a consistent criticism throughout my research has been an apparent disregard among previous critics for Borges's original spatial and formal intent. As any poet or student of poetry would attest, the way a poem is laid out on paper and the use of capitalization and punctuation (if there is any) provide important symbolic and emotional keys to the reading of any poem. This becomes even more undisputable in the study of vanguard poets, a fact Gloria Videla reinforces in her important study *Ultraísmo*:

> La original disposición tipográfica es uno de los rasgos más característicos de los poetas ultraístas. Por el uso de este procedimiento se pasan las fronteras de la poesía (comunicación de un contenido psíquico determinado por medio de meras palabras, según la definición de [Carlos] Bousoño) y se buscan efectos visuales como auxiliares de la expresión poética.

> [The originality of an ultraist poem's typographical layout is one of its most characteristic features. For the purpose such methods are used goes beyond the boundaries of the poems (a psychic communication of restrainment determined by means of mere words, according to Bousoño's definition), and seeks visual effects as auxiliary to the poetic expression.]. (*El ultraísmo* 112; Buosoño 17).

Like his fellow vanguardistas, Borges experimented with typography during his ultraísta phase, as well as with the elimination of punctuation. The poem "Fiesta" even demonstrates Borges's rare attempt at a concrete or shaped poem, perhaps following the lead of Mallarmé's work in *Un Coup de Dés*. The poem speaks of banners and flags; thus, the typography of the opening verses is shaped as such. Even with Borges's well-documented disregard for his ultraist poetry, I still contend that, if given the choice, he, like any poet, would prefer that his poems be reproduced exactly as they had originally appeared. It is for this reason I was tenacious in my search throughout Spain for all the magazines of the 1920s in which Borges's vanguard poems might have appeared.

It bothers me to think there are works by young Borges I did not find, but there will always be those works of authors that simply vanish or remain unavailable due to disinterest on the part of the author. For myself, I have kept in the attic at least one copy of every magazine in which I've had a poem, story or essay published. Still, I feel confident that I found a great portion of Borges's early works and have included them in this study. In it you will find the ignored and suppressed works—the poems, manifestos, essays and book reviews—of a young "literary genius" who, two decades later, would become one of the twentieth century's most celebrated authors.

Plates

Part One

Borges in Spain, 1919-21, 1923-24

Forty years before Jorge Luis Borges would share the Formentor Prize with Samuel Beckett in 1961, establishing him as one of the most important, innovative Latin American prose stylists of the twentieth century, he considered himself *a poet*—more specifically, an ultraísta poet. Between 1919-1923, he thoroughly embraced the modern literary tenets, the "make it new" aesthetic being expounded by the American expatriate poet Ezra Pound and spreading throughout Europe and the Americas. As such, a reading of Borges's early works, his juvenilia, as he would quickly remind people, is a passage into the exciting, rebellious, experimental world of Vanguardismo, the term used in Spain and Latin America equivalent to Modernism in European/Anglo-American literature. Borges's early writing reflects various important artistic movements of that era—German Expressionism, Spanish Ultraism, the Italian Marinetti's Futurism, Pound's Imagism, Vicente Huidobro's Creacionism, and Surrealism—while categorically rejecting the fundamental Romanticism of the popular Nicaraguan poet Ruben Darío and his Modernísmo movement (1890-1915), deridingly called by Borges "Rubenianismo" in his essay, "Ultraísmo," which explicated and detailed glories of this "brand new esthetic" (see essay in Part Two). Essentially, Darío's Modernismo was a movement heavily influenced by Romanticism, French Parnassianism and the last and poorest phase of that country's Symbolist movement. It was the same movement Pound was rejecting in London when he formed his Imagism group in 1912—poets all declaring the supremacy of the image—retaining the French spelling Imagisme as an added insult. He and fellow imagists insisted that poets discard overt symbolism and return to the image as poetry's fundamental element. For young Borges and the ultraists in Spain, the essential element they wanted poetry to embrace was image as metaphor.

I have always been drawn to the modern era—the vanguard period for literary art. Such a powerful, creative and exuberant time that period was, especially for those artists residing in Madrid, Paris, London, Rome, Berlin, New York, Mexico City, Buenos Aires, Santiago and all the main centers of art throughout the Western world where artistic experimentation was at its zenith. In fact, the year 1922 is often referred to as *annus mirabilis* for modernist literature. It is the year that saw the publication of T.S. Eliot's "The Wasteland," James Joyce's *Ulysses*, D.H. Lawrence's *Aaron's Rod*, Virginia Woolf's *Jacob's Room*, W.B. Yeats' *Later Poems*, Ezra Pound's *Hugh Selwyn Mauberley* and *Cantos 4, 5, 6 and 7*, Edith Sitwell's experimental poem *Facade*, e.e. cummings' novel *The Enormous Room* and his first collection of poetry, *Tulips and Chimney*, Katherine Mansfield's *The Garden Party*, Eugene O'Neill's *Anna Christie* and *The Hairy Ape*, Marcel Proust's death and the publication of his *Sodome et Gomorrhe*, Valéry's *Charmes*, Bertolt Brecht's *Baal* and *Trommeln in der Nacht*, Hermann Hesse's *Siddartha*, Luigi Pirandello's *The Living Mask*, Federico García Lorca's first book of poetry *Libro de Poemas*, José Juan Tablada's *El Jarro de Flores*, first Nobel Prize winner from Latin America Gabriela Mistral's first book of poetry *Desolación*, and César Vallejo's incredibly important book of poems, *Trilce*, which shattered all traditions in Latin American poetry. All of these works, and more, invariably reveal a breaking away from traditional literary style and structure. A Modern Art Week festival was held in Sao Paulo in February 1922 which reflected vanguard movements in art, music, and literature, and especially poetry, introducing the European ferment of Cubism, Futurism, and Dadaism to an entire artistic generation in Latin America.

It was during this incredible shift in literary aesthetics that Borges began writing and publishing poetry while residing in Spain between 1919–21, with a second residence between 1923–24. Most critics would agree that an investigation into Borges's development as a writer during this important time would be more fruitful if they could actually study the works Borges wrote and published during his apprenticeship. During the 1920s, Borges published three collections of poetry and three of essays, but by 1930 he had removed them all from public access; moreover, he included only a handful of his ultraist poems in his first poetry collection, *Fervor de Buenos Aires* (1923). Unfortunately, the mature writer felt ashamed of his early writing and regretted his ultraist phase. In his "Autobiographical Notes," he declared his early works youthful "excesses": "I can now only regret my early Ultraist excesses. After nearly a half century, I find myself still striving to live down that awkward period of my life."[1]

Yet, I maintain, as have a few others before me, that there is much to be learned from a detailed study of a young writer's excesses. Thus, one of the central concerns in this book is to help answer several questions: What did it mean for young Borges to envision himself a poet, an ultraist poet to be exact, during the Modernist era? And how did his poetic sensibilities—his choice of language and syntax, his overlap of genres, his use of figurative language, and his rhythmic manipulation of words to achieve the musical lyricism he so desperately wanted—figure into the development of his mature prose technique that resulted in the stories of *Ficciones*?

Indeed, the majority of literary theorists and teachers of Latin American Vanguardismo see Borges's best poetic efforts inferior to his great prose fiction of the 1940s. In truth, Latin American scholars rarely mention Borges as being on par with his contemporaries, such as Pablo Neruda, César Vallejo, Federico Garcia Lorca, Vicente Huidobro, Octavio Paz, and Gabriela Mistral. But then, so few critics have had sufficient access to his true vanguardist poetry to even consider Borges as a vanguard poet of the time.

During my PhD coursework, I was fortuitously exposed to some of Borges's rare, unrevised ultraísta poems. My first reaction was that I'd never seen anything like this kind of poetry from Borges. His youthful style was one I found fresh, invigorating, authentic and truly inspired by the modernist spirit. At that time, I was formulating my dissertation subject: studying those modernist writers who, early in their careers, considered themselves poets but who went on to become greater prose fiction writers. I decided Borges fit nicely into that subject and began searching for more of his early works, only to discover, to my great disappointment, that very few examples existed. Still, I couldn't shake the intuition that Spanish scholars had only uncovered and published a small portion of his early works written before 1923. Several Spanish critics had commented in their studies on how Borges

---

[1] I cite here and throughout the text published in *The New Yorker* in 1970; also published as his "Autobigraphical Essay" in *The Aleph and Other Stories 1933-1969*.

had published *extensively* while in Spain as well as in Argentina upon his return home. He also published in magazines of his own making in Buenos Aires, *Prisma* and *Proa*, where, through 1923, Borges became the leading voice of Ultraísmo. In fact, Borges was a co-signer of two ultraist manifestos that established the fundamental tenets of the movement. The first was published in *Palma de Majorca* in February 1921 just before he returned to Buenos Aires. The second was published in the magazine *Prisma*, December of 1921, in Buenos Aires and subsequently reprinted in *Ultra* ns 21 in Madrid, January 1922. Stephen Tapscott writes in his bilingual anthology *Twentieth-Century Latin American Poetry* that young Borges "almost single-handedly" brought Ultraism to Argentina from Spain: "Borges's avant-garde rediscovery of the Spanish language as a vehicle for literary experimentation manifested itself chiefly in a commitment to 'the greatest independence' for the metaphor as a 'primordial' mode of knowledge and connotation. Borges's early poems are the chief examples in Latin America of the effect of 'Ultraism'" (13). Tapscott goes on to declare that "the period during and just after Borges' ultraist stage is the period of Borges's *best poems*" (my italics)—a sentiment with which I wholeheartedly agree.

Indeed, I could not forget the few ultraist poems that had made such a great impression upon me—certainly a greater impression than did his post-1960s poems he penned after returning to writing poetry, which were widely available in his collections and various anthologies, specifically *El hacedor (1960) (The Maker)*, published later in English as *Dreamtigers* (1964) and *El otro, el mismo* (1964). I also discovered that Borges chose to include only four of his ultraist poems from before 1923 in his ensuing anthologies: *Poemas 43, Poemas 54, Poemas 58, Antologia personal* (1961), *Obra poética 67, Nueva antologia* (1968), *Obra poética 69, Obra poética 76*, and *JLB: Antologia poética 77, Obra poética 85*. Studying these volumes, I saw how much Borges had revised the poems over the years so that they were very different from how they appeared in the original 1923 edition of *Fervor*. For this reason, I value highly the copy I found of Borges's original, signed first edition (see plates 19 and 20).

With Borges now included in my dissertation project, I realized I would have to travel to Spain to search for his published but discarded works. To my great fortune, I won a Fulbright award for dissertation research which granted me the funds to spend a year in Madrid to research Borges's vanguard publications—little did I know the *substantial* amount of works I would find. Searching throughout Spain, I recovered over eighty of Borges's early verse poems, prose poems, essays, reviews and manifestos that he'd published in vanguard magazines through 1925, many of which he subsequently left uncollected—hoping they'd die a slow death, I suppose. It has to be noted here that my study of Borges as a young writer should be viewed solely as an exploration of his apprenticeship in poetry through 1923—how a young man expressed himself and his times through poetry and essays under the sway of Ultraism and other modernist tendencies—and not the study of his mature poetry and fiction, upon which Borges built his literary reputation. The fact that Borges failed to see value in his early writing—work all writers must create at some point in their careers— is regrettable and unfortunate for writers as well as scholars who want to study an author's entire *oeuvre*.

In this light, I want to explore here the phenomenon of notable writers during the Modernist era who, like Borges, began their writing careers as poets but who ultimately abandoned or greatly reduced their poetic efforts to focus primarily on prose fiction. Besides Borges, the same case could be made for William Faulkner, James Joyce, Ernest Hemingway, Samuel Beckett, D.H. Lawrence, Herman Hesse, Gertrude Stein, Ford Maddox Ford, to mention only a few—writers of poetry early in their careers (some even exclusively) who then began writing prose fiction or plays, some even expressing doubt about their true ability as poets. For example, James Joyce's first published book was a book of poetry titled *Chamber Music* (1906), poems he wrote between the ages of 22-24; he later claimed that he found nearly all of the poems "poor and trivial," going on to say, "I am not a poet" (Beja 28). Likewise, William Faulkner's first published book was also a book of poetry, *The Marble Faun* (1924). He later published a second volume, *A Green Bough*, (1933), comprised of poems written in the early to mid-1920s. In a 1956 interview in *The Paris Review*, Faulkner called himself "a failed poet": "maybe every novelist wants to write poetry first, finds he can't, and then tries the short story, which is the most demanding form after poetry. And failing at that, only then does he take up novel writing" (4). Interestingly, Faulkner followed the advice of Sherwood Anderson, who encouraged him to drop poetry and write a novel. Faulkner acquiesced and wrote his first novel, *Soldier's Pay* (1926), in six weeks—undoubtedly the worst prose effort of his writing career. I suggest that in his tedious plotting and labored expository sentences, he wrote prose he thought appropriate for *storytelling* but which failed to incorporate the instinctual poetic sensibilities that would characterize his greatest novels.

As for myself, a verse and prose poet exclusively for twenty years who has recently begun to write short stories, I find it fascinating how Borges and the aforementioned poets-turned-prose-writers transformed themselves from composers of lyrics and prose poems into prose fiction stylists. Although most were unsuccessful in their poetic aspirations, the poetic impulse—language that reaches beyond storytelling—remained an important asset in the formation of their distinct prose styles. They may have abandoned their versification efforts, but they retained and applied their poetic sensibilities to create the modern prose fiction that would make them famous—and, ultimately, that would characterize modern fiction itself. The present study of Borges investigates this phenomenon and, as such, should be of some service to those creative writers who themselves have moved between poetry and prose, searching for ways to be innovative in the execution of their ideas in both disciplines.

How did Borges, the poet, transform himself into the great narrador of *Ficciones* and *El Aleph*?

Borges's first published poem was "Himno del Mar." It appeared in the Spanish literary magazine *Grecia* on December 31, 1919, when he was just twenty years old; he then spent the next decade attempting to make himself a recognized poet. But after publishing three collections of poetry: *Fervor, Luna,* and *Cuaderno,* he stopped writing poetry all together. From 1929 roughly to 1959, he focused on his experimentation with prose narratives. As a precursor to this period, he published in 1925 a book of essays, *Inquisiciones.* A second collection, *El tamaño de mi Esperanza,* followed in 1926—both of which he subsequently removed from public access. Then in 1928, he published *El idióma de los argentinos,* followed by a biography of the little known turn-of-the-century

Argentine poet, *Evaristo Carriego,* in 1930. By 1932 and his publication of *Discusión,* another book of essays, it was clear to Borges that his future did not lie in his poetry but in the narrative. He would later tell Jean Milleret in an interview in 1970 that he essentially stopped writing poetry in his late twenties after the publication of *Cuaderno* in 1929 because he came to fear he wasn't a "true poet" and had "lost confidence in his poetic capacities" (40)—the same concerns Faulkner and Joyce had expressed about themselves.

Normally, by the age of thirty, most great writers have penned a number of their most memorable works. For Borges, little of his creative writing efforts before that age seems to have satisfied him—and perhaps rightly so, considering the incredible stories to come in *El jardín de senderos que se bifurcan* (1941), which he then incorporated into *Ficciones* in 1944. But that should not have made him believe that his apprentice vanguard poetry and prose wasn't worthy of inspection by future generations. It's sad that he viewed his young years as a poet in the following manner: "Summing up this span of my life, I find myself completely out of sympathy with the priggish and rather dogmatic young man I then was" ("Autobiographical Notes"). He did not share the belief that the work he created as a young man was simply that—the work of a young man, what he was capable of at that juncture in his career. Certainly, all writers grow and transform; that is the nature of artistic creation. I contend adamantly that his artistic output as a young man has value for both the literary student and for Borges aficionados alike.

Interestingly, Borges did not begin fashioning the prose fiction that would make his reputation until around 1933, while in his mid-thirties—works that would be collected in *Historia universal de la infamia* in 1935. Like so many other poets of the Modernist era who turned to prose fiction, it might be said, in hindsight, that Borges finally found in the prose narrative an arena more suitable for his enormous talent. It might even be suggested that, during the 1920s and '30s, the course of fiction was greatly transformed by writers who, early in their career, envisioned themselves first (or also) as poets, only to later turn themselves into prose fiction writers—poets of prose if you will—whose most effective and innovative works incorporated their poetic sensibilities into their prose fiction works. In Borges's case, "overlap" was the term he favored in a 1969 interview with Jean Milleret over the term "expansion," which she suggested. His correction made it clear that he incorporated both genres together as opposed to simply expanding across genre boundaries into new territory: "Hay una palabra inglesa que define muy bien este período de transición: *overlap,* cuando los limites, las fronteras no están claras en absolute (15) ["There is an English word that defines very well this period of transition: *overlap,* when the boundaries, the borders are no longer absolutely clear"]. It is a term that also represents for Borges the creative crossover between his "Apprentice years (1919-1926)," a part of which Borges envisioned himself a vanguard poet, and the period of "Literary expansion (1927-1938)," in which young Borges began transforming himself into a writer of prose narratives:

> JM: En cuanto al segundo, lo utilizo para referir su estadía en España y su regreso a Buenos Aires, donde se publican sus primeras obras.
> [With regards to the second period, I use it to relate your residency in Spain and your return to Buenos Aires, where your first works are published.]
>
> JLB: Pero ya en Suiza [1914-1918] había empezado a escribir poemas. . . .Siempre me sentí autor, incluso antes de escribir. Para mí se trataba de una especie de destino.
> [But already in Switzerland I had begun to write poems. . . .I have always felt like an author, even before I began to write. For me it was always a kind of destiny.]
>
> JM: Al tercer período lo titulé "La expansión literaria. . ."
> [I've titled the third period "literary expansion. . ."]
>
> JLB: *Expansión,* es más bien exagerado. [*Expansion,* that's a bit exaggerated.]
>
> JM: . . .que empezaría en 1927, un poco arbitrariamente puesto que, antes y después, algunas de sus obras estaban en gestación continua, por ejemplo "Hombre de la esquina rosada," uno de cuyos primeros esbozos se publicó en una revista bajo el título de "Noticia policial."

[. . .which would begin in 1927, a little arbitrary since, before and after, some of your works were in continuous gestation, for example "Man from the Slums," one of your first drafts was published in a magazine under the title "Detective News Item."] (Milleret 20-21)

More often than not, any investigation into an author's transition period from poet to prose fiction writer often reveals how the not-to-be-denied poetic self—with its use of figurative language, neologism, imagery, unconventional syntax and word choice, not to mention the liberties he takes with punctuation rules—can assert itself in the language and technical execution of the prose work. In the case of Borges, the overlap of genres proves even more complex, for it includes the overlapping of other genres as well: the prose poem, biography, historical texts, sacred texts, the parable. Once again, preferring the term overlap, Borges suggests that what occurs in the composition of his prose work during this important period of transition is the amalgamation of all his literary knowledge and efforts, a great part of which is the writing of poetry—some of which was his "ultraistic" poetry.

Clearly, during the Modernist period, poetry was experiencing a crisis that found more and more poets turning to prose, not only for experimentation's sake, but also as a means of survival—poetry wasn't selling: short story collections and novels were. For centuries, poetry had been the medium for writers whose works represented serious reflections on truth, philosophy, history and metaphysical inquiry. However, in the years leading up to the Modernist era, according to Jeffrey Kittay and Wlad Godzich in *The Emergence of Prose: An Essay in Prosaics*, prose waged a successful battle to naturalize itself by "wrestling the domain of truth away from the central vernacular signifying practice of the age—verse" (cited. in Fredman 2). Using their study as a starting point, Stephan Fredman, in his book *Poet's Prose*, discusses the significance of this tug-of-war between prose and poetry among twentieth-century writers. He points out that prose poets have waged their own battle to return to poetry the domain of truth: " [By] inviting and examining the 'prose' realms of fact and anecdote," prose poets hope to reclaim for poetry "the right to investigate the domain of truth":

> I [Fredman] have felt for a number of years that the most talented poets of my own postwar generation and an increasing number from previous generations have turned to prose as a form that, in its pliancy and its linguistic density, seems to promise a faithful reproduction of the exquisite and terrible scene that stretches around us. (1)

As writers of poetry (both verse and prose) and prose fiction know well, it is a mysterious moment—the fingers poised above the keyboard as the mind tracks images, thoughts, emotional impulses, notes on paper, journal entries—a precise, but often indefinable moment of decision when the writer ponders: do I write what I want to say in verse and subject my work to a form that demands economy, precision and brevity or do I write a prose poem or lyric (pseudo) essay (as Borges chose to do), lifting the work out of genre specific restrictions and liberating the poetic lines for a freer expression?

Charles Baudelaire, initiator of the prose poem genre in 1855, famously wrote to a friend after reading Aloysius Bertrand's book *Gaspard de la Nuit*, "Which one of us, in his moments of ambition, has not dreamed of the miracle of a poetic prose, musical, without rhythm and without rhyme, supple enough and rugged enough to adapt itself to the lyric impulses of the soul, the undulations of reverie, the jibes of conscience?" (*Paris Spleen* ix-x). Along with other French poets, such as Mallarme, Rimbaud, Verlaine and Valéry, Baudelaire's experimentation with prose poetry opened up new possibilities for literary creation—and here you will see that Borges fully embraced the genre. But how do prose poets expand their prosaic poetry into prose fiction? How do they move beyond lyric, soliloquy, description, and self-expression and enter the equally difficult terrain of the narrative—dialogue, plot and characterization—to tell a *story*? More specifically, how did Borges do it?

As it is generally understood, language and technique take on different characteristics as they move through distinct genres: verse poetry, prose poetry, lyric essay, micro-fiction, flash fiction, short story, novella, novel. In resurrecting and studying Borges's early poems and essays, I am interested in how, at the beginning of his fiction writing career, he

overlapped his poetic "prose poem" sensibilities with his pseudo-essay/
narrative experiments to create "story." Certainly, for Borges, the fundamental function of poetry—to suggest rather than to state—remained
an integral part of his prose writing strategy. As a prose fiction writer,
he went on to demonstrate how he, Borges the poet, re-discovered the
music inherent in the signs of language: a music that, over time, had
been abandoned by the ordinary person and the storyteller alike.

In focusing on Borges's first poetic efforts as well as his early essays as they relate to and influence his mature prose fiction style, this
book is as much a study of the prose sentence and its relation to verse
and prose poetry. I want to explore the standard assumption that
prose somehow lends more authenticity to philosophical and existential contemplations—that a didactic, declarative sentence is closer
to truth than the lyric poem with its visionary, personal, and soulful
expressiveness.

Some would also claim that the prose sentence lends greater weight
to "serious" historical, philosophical or existential ideas than a verse
line, which, during the Modern era, became the medium for the poet's
personal exploration of the self, love, art, and angst of modern life: T.S.
Eliot's *The Wasteland*, for example. For poets to follow Pound's edict to
"make it new" and, at the same time, stir readers' emotions, they must
engage in considerable intellection, along with some social and political
diatribing, as many key figures of modern poetry did quite successfully:
Eliot, Pound, Garcia Lorca, Neruda and Vallejo, to name only a few.

Clearly, since the beginning of the twentieth century, prose fiction,
as well as the essay, has been the preferred medium for philosophical,
sociological, political, and esoteric explorations of life, socio-po-
litical statement and existential questioning of human psychology.
Ironically, a key criticism of Borges's postmodern poems of the '60s
and '70s among his peers was that his poetry was *too* intellectual. In
Latin American poetry during the 1920s, the intellect was held subor-
dinate to passionate instincts and intuition. In fact, aspects of all the
aforementioned considerations figure into the decision of those who
abandoned poetry for fiction. Thus, a study of Borges' motivations to
turn to prose fiction, in many ways, is a study of the motivations of
every notable fiction writer of the early twentieth century who wrote

poetry first, then, due to dissatisfaction with their poetic efforts, shifted primarily to prose.

In studying the initial stages of Borges's writing career—the passionate, emotional, exuberant poems and essays written by Borges as an *ultraísta* in the early 1920s—readers can discern for themselves how, in the three decades to follow, he overlapped the genres of prose fiction, essays, biography, reviews and critical commentary, successfully turning himself into an inventive, esoteric, eclectic, even hermetic story teller—descriptors usually reserved for poets. As previously asserted, Borges will never be considered a significant Vanguardist poet as the qualification is often applied to Neruda, Vallejo, Lorca, Huidobro, Storni, Bodet, Machado, Mistral, and Drummond de Andraje. Nor will his "mature" poetry, at its best, be considered on par with his prose fiction. However, Borges is an important poet of the twentieth century and, as this study asserts, his early authentic ultraist poetry deserves some attention as well, for his vanguard poetry achieved much of the same goals of modernism as did the work of his more popular peers.

Another supposition I have long asserted is that fiction became modern when poets began to write fiction. It is a theory that asks readers to reflect on the kind of prose fiction that came immediately before the modern era: Dostoevsky, Tolstoi, Dickens, Flaubert, Hugo, Zola, Sinclair Lewis, Henry James, Evelyn Waugh, Mariano Azuela, Ricardo Guiraldes, Pio Baroja—writers of the didactic, realistic, non-lyrical, non-musical novel whose sentences followed the best rules of punctuation and exposition, and rarely deviated from proper syntax; nor did plot, narration, and characterization stray far from the standard form and purpose of storytelling. Literary history reveals that only two writers attained equal success in both prose and poetry during the nineteenth century: Edgar Allan Poe and Thomas Hardy. But then they, in fact, saw each genre—as did Emerson and Thoreau—as separate fields of endeavor demanding different artistic approaches. It's curious to note that Poe, like Borges, wrote prose poems as well—see Poe's "Eureka" from 1848—a phenomenon I will demonstrate is an important ingredient in Borges's transition to the prose narrative.

In focusing on Borges's early experimentation in verse and prose poetry between 1920-23—and considering his arduous transformation over the next fifteen years into a supreme prose fiction writer—one should recognize the great verbal artifice he possessed. Indeed, Borges's prose fiction style originates in and flows out of his intellect, his instinctive, eclectic disposition. But it originates as well from his *distinct poetic sensibilities*, which Julio Cortázar called "Mallarméan":

> Borges's great lesson was neither a lesson of themes or contents nor of technique. It was a lesson in writing. The attitude of a man who, facing each sentence, has studiously thought not which adjective he would add, but which one he would remove in a manner reminiscent of Mallarme's attitude of extreme rigor toward the written page. (Cited in Alazraki, *Critical Essays* 17)

Borges's concise and chiseled language, as with all good poets, is truly a lesson in writing itself. Whether in prose or verse, the totality of Borges's work reveals a rigorous, artistic, suggestive language that very early in his career was inextricably rooted in the undeniable passion he held for poetic expression. A contextual relationship exists between Borges's poetic "self" and his ensuing prosaic "self" during his arduous and lengthy transformation into a teller of tales. Looking back on his career, regarding the earliest phase of his attempt at writing prose *pieces*—for he could not yet call them stories—Borges labeled them a "series of sketches. . .fictional pieces. . .narrative exercises. . .hoaxes and pseudo-essays" ("Autobiographical Notes"). The prose works he collected in *Historia universal de la infamia* in 1935 were important experiments in approximating stories while applying the vanguard poet's zeal for breaking with convention. These experiments then led to his next volume of essays, *Historia de la eternidad* (1936) (*A History of Eternity*), where he finally felt confident enough to label at least one of the pieces a "story": "The Approach to al-Mu'tasim." It is a story that perfectly reflects Borges period of *overlap*, a blending of his skills as prose poet/essayist/literary critic and reviewer, resulting in a style of narrative fiction never before experienced in Latin American literature. Referring to this important story in his "Autobiographical Notes," Borges even admits he was "unfair" to call it merely a "hoax and a pseudo-essay," adding, "it now seems to me to foreshadow and even to set the pattern for those tales that were somehow awaiting me and upon which my reputation as a story teller was to be based."

Thus, in studying much of Borges's early, disregarded ultraist verse, prose poems, essays, and manifestos published in magazines between 1919-1923, I hope to demonstrate that at the beginning of his fiction writing career, Borges manipulated the distinctions between poetry and prose—much like many creative non-fiction writers do today. Of course, Borges's resurging interest in writing poetry, his so-called second phase of poetry in the 1960's and 70's, helped to strengthen his reputation as a twentieth century poet. But I contend that even his so-called mature phase of poetry begins with what are essentially prose-poetic pieces in *El hacedor* (1960). It is a curious collection that blends both verse and prose poetry.

Borges's ultraistic, sometimes nationalistic, vanguard poetry of the early 1920s should be viewed, then, in the broader context of the avant-garde spirit of that time. A reading of his Ultraísmo manifestos, as well as his early essays on the tenets of Ultraism included in Part Two, should help to define his nascent artistic approach. which most certainly had a decided influence on his mature prose.

Young Borges in the Spirit of Vanguardismo

In all of Jorge Luis Borges's prose narratives in his greatest collection, *Ficciones,* there exists descriptive imagery, metaphor, analogy, and symbolism that approaches poetry. The brevity of his pieces also approximates that of poetic expression. In his ultraist verse and prose poems, as well as his essays and manifestos, one cannot mistake the sense of anarchy, innovation, experimentation and invention of a Vanguardista. It is this same spirit that led Borges to circumvent in his fiction fifteen years later the traditional rules of narration. Borges himself proclaimed in his essay "Ultraismo" and in his ultraíst manifesto "Proclama" that it was time to see a new way forward—and both these documents were written in 1921 when he was just twenty-two years old. Ronald Christ, one of the first American scholars to study Borges in the mid-1960s in his book *The Narrow Act,* affirms that "Borges's writing, and fiction in particular, is characterized by the stylistic elements of Ultraism" (2).

Focusing on brevity and the metaphor as two key elements, Christ goes on to say,

> He [Borges] made his debut as a literary theoretician in 1921 advocating a poetry of concentrated, essential metaphor, stripped of all decoration and logical or descriptive framework. For once we have seen this, we have focused on the two stylistic concerns—concentration (or brevity) and metaphor—which inform not only the poetry of Borges's Ultraist period, but much of his later writing as well. (5)

For Borges, Ultraism, just one of numerous vanguard theories of writing he championed as a young writer, moved beyond the narrow definition of the movement, which he helped develop in Spain and then carried with him back to Argentina in March 1921. Held by the spirit of Vanguardismo, Borges embraced the rebellious reduction, deletion, and abolition of all things traditional, with an expressed interest in always going forward into unchartered territory. Keeping one eye on his countryman Huidobro's Creacionism and the other on Expressionism, Borges's central ultraistic concern was to create outside of conventional boundaries.

After returning to Buenos Aires in 1921, Borges continued to apply ultraistic aesthetics to his poetry. According to Christ, "[Borges] weighed lines from Garcilaso, restless and grave beneath the stars of the suburb, demanding a limpid art that might be as atemporal as the eternal stars." Borges and his fellow ultraístas, he goes on to assert, "abhorred the muddy hues of Rubenism [Rubén Darío] and metaphor inflamed [them] because of the precision that there is in it, because of its algebraic form of correlating remote things." Clearly, a "limpid art that might be as atemporal as the eternal stars" remained a constant ideal for Borges, and the word atemporal is a key to many of his later works (3)[2]

---

[2] Christ quotes from one of Borges's essays published in the 1925 *Inquisiciones* but which, being unpublished in a magazine, is not included in this collection. I reprint the excerpts in English as they were translated and reproduced by Christ.

With Christ's comment in mind, let's look at Borges essay on Expressionism, "Acerca del Expresionismo" ["About Expressionism"], which was published in *Inicial* ns. 3 in December 1923, and which effectively contrasts his developing theories of poetry at that time with his original conception of Ultraism in 1920. Borges, at the last outpost before his complete renunciation of Ultraism in 1923 (though not necessarily a rejection of all its goals), begins the essay by praising what the expressionists did for German literature, saying that poetry should record "intensity" rather than mere "harmony." Here he decries the verses of the "well-to-do-gentleman ...stuck in bland yearnings" with the need to "reach for some motionless beauty...with a conscience free of rhetorical schemes, that never astonish the reader." Such poems are not "thought-provoking literature but the pleasant amusement of men." Borges's ideal writer would combine disparate qualities of "the pensive, intellectual man [who] lives in the intimacy of atemporal, even metaphysical thoughts like eternity, concepts that are pure abstraction," with those of "the sensitive man, the sensual lustful man, in the continuity of the external world." He then concludes that "[b]oth types of people may obtain an elevated eminence in letters." Moreover, in the closing line of the essay, when praising the new expressionists who have "disordered with visual images the contemplative Germanic lyric," Borges approves of the arrival of intellect in versification and the *fantastic reality* it is capable of conjuring—the reason of interior logic, where reality does not collaborate" (see "Acerca del Expresionismo" in Part Two; my italics). In his essay, written at the same time as the appearance of *Fervor*, which included only four of his "ultraist" poems, young Borges has essentially begun defining the Borges of both *Ficciones* in 1944 and his much later collection of poetry and prose poems (and his best in my opinion), *Hacedor,* in 1960. In demonstrating the value of Borges's poetic sensitivities as they undoubtedly figure into the structure and language of his most innovative prose, his earliest verse poems, prose poems and literary essays during his vanguard phase indeed provide an interesting point of reference, for in several ways, they collaborate and resonate with his later works.

Borges came to Spain a young man who already believed his destiny was to be a writer. He possessed extraordinary literary tools that many of his fellow poets (a majority of the Spanish literati for that matter) in

Mallorca, Sevilla, and Madrid, did not own. Perhaps his multi-lingualism is the most important of these assets. As a polyglot, his linguistic dexterity allowed him access to and a more thorough understanding of much of Western society's great literary works. Due in part to his Argentine upper-class education, which emphasized English literature over Spanish, and his four-year education in Geneva, which emphasized French and German literature, young Borges acquired an ability to communicate and read in English, French and German as well as his mother tongue. During his residency in Spain, he was enlightened to all the classic literature his native Castellana had to offer: Gongora, Quevedo, Cervantes, Villarroel, Unamuno, among others. Moreover, he possessed a good knowledge of Latin, a linguistic code that his biographer Emir Rodriguez Monegal points out was an important ingredient in developing the tight syntactical structure of his prose:

> Latin became his fourth code [German was his fifth]. Although it was never to be one of his major languages. . .it gave Georgie [Borges] a firm syntactic structure and an awareness of etymology that were later reflected in Borges's prose style. Combined with French, Latin erased the rhetorical vagueness inherent in Spanish and the untidiness of nineteenth-century English. Learning Latin and French simultaneously gave Georgie the linguistic discipline Borges later put to such good use. (*Literary Biography* 114-15)

Young Borges's talent for languages and love of the world's great literary and philosophic works, together with a penchant for mythological and etymological research, gave his artistic/poetic sensibilities a firm foundation. It enabled him to cut an impressive figure and become a prominent intellectual force in the Spanish and Argentine literary communities of the 1920s.

As already asserted, young Borges's favored literature was not written in Castellana or by Argentina's nationalist writers—it was literature written in English. For Borges, English represented the language of the educated, while Spanish was relegated to mere communication. It was the servants' language, the language of the streets. In the prologue to the second edition of his biography of Evaristo Carriego, Borges confesses, "For years I believed I had grown up in one of the suburbs of Buenos Aires, a suburb of adventurous streets and visible sunsets. The truth is that I grew up in a garden, behind a speared railing, and in a library of unlimited English books" (*Evaristo Carriego* 9). In his "Autobiographical Notes," Borges goes on to admit, "If I were asked to name the chief event in my life, I should say my father's library. In fact, I sometimes think I have never strayed outside that library." Borges conveniently lists his early reading: *Huckleberry Finn*, *Treasure Island*, *A Thousand and One Nights*, and works by Poe, Dickens, Longfellow, Lewis Carroll—such classics that would normally be taught any young English or American scholar. Yet, it is safe to assume that, growing up in Argentina, the Buenos Aires that was teeming with rogues, knife fights, gauchos, the tango, guitars, squalid and dangerous barrios, gambling, prostitutes—all of which existed outside his garden fence—did not go unnoticed. It would also be safe to say that, although they were not a part of his boyhood experiences, these darker and more dangerous elements, or at least the fantasies they conjured, left an indelible impression on Borges's mind: see his stories "El sur" ["The South"] and "El fin" [The End"] in *Ficciones*. Indeed, the setting for his first legitimate story in 1933 will be a squalid and dangerous barrio of Buenos Aires.

In his "Autobiographical Notes," Borges also remembers entering into the Spanish literary milieu as a young man teeming with enthusiasm for German Expressionism, Schopenhauer, Walt Whitman, and the original nineteenth-century French symbolist poets, Rimbaud, Verlaine, Mallarmé—not the second generation symbolists of the early twentieth century that Pound was criticizing, as previously discussed. Undoubtedly, many of the ideals and intentions of the Expressionists and the early French Symbolist poets remain in the inner linings of Borges's creative writing, as they clearly do for many twentieth century occidental poets—consider, for example, the importance of *vers libre* right up to the present day. Through his direct exposure to German expressionist writers, who from the outset of their movement held Walt Whitman in high esteem, Borges soon became the prime proponent among the ultraists in Spain of Expressionism and Whitmanian verse. In his first essay on Expressionism, "Lírica expresionista: Sintesis," ["Expressionist Lyric: Synthesis"] published in Sevilla's *Grecia* ns 47 in

August 1920, and written when he was twenty-one, Borges defines the expressionist lyric:

> Si quisiéramos definirlo [la lírica expresionista]—y no ignoro lo carcelarias que suelen ser estas definiciones—diriamos que es la tentativa de crear para esta época un arte matinalmente intuicionista, de superar la realidad ambiente y elevar sobre su madeja sensorial y emotiva una ultra-realidad espiritual. Diríamos que el expresionismo (con los demás impulsos paralelos que accionan bajo distintas latitudes) no es otra cosa en última exégesis que el arte *subrayado*. . . .
> Su fuente la constituye esa visión ciclópea y atlética del pluriverso que rimara, Walt Whitman (partiendo a su vez de Fechte y de Hegel). (See "Lírica expresionista: Sintesis" in Part Two)

> [If we wanted to define it [the expressionist lyric]—and I'm very well aware of how confining these definitions usually are—we would say that it is the attempt to create for this era a dawning intuitionist art, to surpass the physical reality and to raise above its sensory and emotive skein, a spiritual ultra-reality. We would say that expressionism (along with other parallel impulses that act under different latitudes) is nothing more, in the final analysis, than art with a capital A underlined.
> Its source is constituted by the cyclopic and athletic vision of a pluriverse, multiple verses that rhyme, Walt Whitman (in turn, parting from Fichte and Hegel's vision).]

Of course, years later Borges's interest in a "spiritual ultra-reality" would shift to a more metaphysical one, while others might even suggest one of *realismo magico*; however, what is most important to note here is that, as early as 1921, Borges began his life-long rejection of mere realism, confessionalism, and catharsis in writing. In another one of his early essays dealing with Expressionism, "Horizontes: Reseña de la antología Die Aktions-Lyrik—1914-1916—Berlin" [Horizons: Review of *Die Aktions-Lyrics—1914-1916—Berlin*], published in *Ultra* ns 16 in October 1921, Borges discusses two different aspects of poetry using his own characteristic poetic approach:

Como una estatua jónica, o, más sencillamente, como cualquier moneda, presenta dos aspectos: el uno, documental, histórico, de apuntación inmediata de los instantes de la guerra; el otro, de muestrario del expresionismo lírico en sus albores.

El primero no debe detenernos. Eso de concederle más importancia a los escritos que reflejan la realidad visible y palpable que a los que son espejos de la emotiva y pasional, es un prejuicio ayuno de todo justificativo. Deriva de los enciclopedistas y de las teorizaciones de Zola, y se basa en el absurdo de suponer que un árbol o un tranvía son más reales que yo que los comprendo. En el fondo, lo visto, lo sufrido, lo imaginado y lo soñado son igualmente reales, es decir, existen. La objetividad no es en última exégesis más que una suerte de denominador común de muchas sensaciones subjetivas. . . . (See the essay in Part Two)

[Like an ionic statue, or, more simply, like any coin, it [the anthology] presents two aspects: one documentary, historical, of immediate wartime notations; and the other, as a sampler of lyric Expressionism in its dawning hours.

The first must not detain us. The tendency of giving more importance to writings that reflect a visible and palpable reality over those which are mirrors of what is emotional and passionate is a prejudice lacking all justification. It comes from the encyclopedists and the theorizing of Zola, and is based on the absurd supposition that a tree or a streetcar is more real than I who comprehends them. Essentially, what is seen, experienced, imagined and dreamt are equally real, that is, they exist. Objectivity in the final analysis is no more than a kind of common denominator of many subjective sensations. . . .]

What Borges also finds interesting in the Expressionist anthology are those works *expressing* emotion. Once again, using his poetic sensibilities, he writes, "Pero también hallamos emoción. Una emoción viviente que tiembla muchas veces en el fondo como una lámpara sepulta y que se expresa en frases truncadas y en un heróico barroquismo verbal." ["But we find emotion as well. A vital, living emotion that often trembles in its central core like an entombed lamp, expressing itself in truncated phrases and in a heroic verbal baroqueism"] (see essay in Part Two). As prefigured in this early essay, so much of Borges later fiction will investigate the reality, duality, or even the non-reality of the "I" who comprehends what is supposedly "real" in the world, and this metaphysical ultra-reality will elicit emotion in the reader far greater than an author's confessional, autobiographical retelling of reality. As an example, see one of his most famous stories, "Borges y yo," in his 1960 collection of poetry and prose *El Hacedor*.

From his early interest in symbolist and expressionist imitations, it is clear that verisimilar concerns of real life will not play a large role in Borges's mature literary works. Certainly, in time, his language would ultimately be purged of both Symbolism and Expressionism's worst characteristics: excessive musicality, choice of words simply for their shock effect, overloading of descriptive adjectives, wordiness, and overt symbolism, to name only a few. But in the early years, it was important for Borges to see himself as a vanguardista, and as an expert on German Expressionism. This view helped him in his self-definition as a poet—a man whose destiny was to be a writer. In fact, Borges would go on to publish five articles on the German Expressionist movement between 1920 and 1923, four of which are included in this book and have never been collected in anthologies of his essays.

Borges's admiration for Whitman has been thoroughly documented. Whitman's "bardic" voice, full of vivacious enthusiasm for life and desire for communion with eternal, spiritual forces proved a fitting contrast to the bleak atmosphere, emotional stricture, and pessimistic angst that followed World War I. Borges, who essentially grew up with books and without religion, immediately connected to this pantheistic vision that looked upon God as an "abstract principle of energy that is manifested in every living creature" (Cowley xiv). Whitman saw God in "the grass that grows wherever the land is and the water is" (*Leaves of Grass* xiv). Borges relates at the end of his life, "I cannot believe in the existence of God, despite all the statistics in the world." When the interviewer interjects, "But you said you believed some time ago," Borges responds, "No, not in a personal God. To search for the truth,

yes; but to think that there is somebody or something we call God, no"
(Barili 29). However, Whitman's God, as manifested in all living things,
falls easily into his intellectual scope of the eternal.

As one might predict, Borges's first published poem, "Himno del
mar" ["Hymn of the Sea"], from 1919, is essentially a curious mixture of
expressionist and symbolist aesthetics. In it, Borges employs Whitman's
bardic tone of voice with the descriptive brush strokes of an expressionist, the free verse of a vanguardista, and Whitman's long prosaic
lines that must be turned over to fit most magazines, while relying on
the significance of symbolic images to expand his meanings. In short,
the work demonstrates, beyond the shadow of a doubt, young Borges's
facility, like Faulkner's, in adapting or imitating aspects of an admired
author's work:

> Yo he ansiado un himno del Mar con ritmos amplios
> > como las olas que gritan;   (t/o)
> Del Mar cuando el sol en sus aguas cual bandera
> > flamea. . . ;   (t/o)

> ¡Hermano, Padre, Amado. . .!
> Antes de conocerte, Mar hermano,
> Largamente he vagado por errantes calles azules con
> > oriflamas de faroles. . . (t/o)
> Ansío aún crearte un poema. . .
> Oh proteico, yo he salido de ti.
> ¡Ambos encadenados y nómadas;
> Ambos con una sed intensa de estrellas. . . .
> > (see poem in Part Two)

> [I've longed for a hymn of the Sea with ample rhythms
> > like waves that scream; (t/o)
> > Of the Sea when the sun glimmers upon the water like
> > > a scarlet banner. . . ; (t/o)

> Brother, Father, Lover. . . !
> Before knowing thee, fraternal Sea,

Long have I wandered through blue errant streets with
                    banners of lamps. . . (t/o)
I even long to create a poem of you. . .
Oh protean, I have come out of you.
Both of us chained and wandering;
Both of us with an intense hunger for stars. . . .]

A reading of the entire poem shows a youthful effort—indeed, the mature author was very embarrassed by his "hunger for stars"—that is characterized by violent and shocking imagery in the manner of German Expressionism: waves that "scream," for example. Borges longs to hear the sea transform itself into a hymn; better still, he longs to be the one who creates the hymn of the sea which he would claim as a "lover." This exaltation of the sea parallels Whitman's love for his brother "the grass" and hints at what will be Borges's long literary affair with analogy, symbolism and metaphor. Borges's poetic strategy, as Christ asserts,

> is the transformation of a rhetorical metaphor, the staple of his *ultraist* period, into a metaphysical proposition, the staple of his mature art. . . .The point of origin for most of Borges's fiction is neither character nor plot, as considered in the traditional sense; but, instead, as in science fiction, a proposition, an idea, a metaphor, which, because of its ingenious or fantastic quality, is perhaps best called a conceit. (14-15)

Indeed, metaphor remains a central controlling element in the majority of Borges's works: both poetry and prose fiction. Part Two contains three essays where Borges asserts the supremacy of the metaphor in poetry.

A central factor in Borges's interest in and knowledge of Expressionism and other vanguard movements that characterized literature in the 1920s lies in the fact that, while he was residing in Geneva (1914-1918), the city became a haven for German, French and Italian artists fleeing the war and the subsequent artistic restrictions of their countries. At this time, young Borges arrived in Spain with the advantage of first hand exposure to contemporary Vanguard movements: the cubists, symbolists, dadaists (soon to be surrealists), and Marinetti's futurists. His subsequent participation in Ultraísmo in Spain marks the real beginning of his poetic apprenticeship, for very little, if anything, remains of the Whitmanian bard in his subsequent published poems. The spirit of Ultraism (more than its specific techniques), which his early mentor Rafael Cansinos-Assens defined as "una voluntad caudalosa que rebasa todo límite escolástico. . .una orientación hacia continuas y reiteradas evoluciones, un propósito de perenne juventud literaria, una anticipada aceptación de todo módulo y de toda idea nuevos" ["an abundant will that surpasses all scholastic boundaries. . .an orientation towards continuous and repeated evolutions, an intention of perennial literary youth, an anticipated acceptance of all new modules and of all new ideas"], inspired young Borges "al compromiso de ir avanzado con el tiempo" ["to commit to go forward in time"] (see "Ultraísmo" in Part Two). One should think here of Pound's modernist declaration to "make it new," which remains inextricably rooted in Borges's mature work and his approach to fiction. Moreover, it is the spirit of Vanguardismo that urged the poet to express a new point of view, to be innovative and work against traditional forms. Incidentally, a glance at Borges's early poem on Cansinos-Assens, published in *Proa* in 1924, then collected in *Luna de enfrente* (1925) but subsequently dropped from the collection in the 1960s, reveals how close the two writers were. It even seems reasonable to suggest that Borges went so far as to adopt the "hyphen" in his name, Jorge-Luis, as a direct result of his admiration for the writer and his guidance. The hyphen first appears in June of 1920 right after meeting Cansinos-Asséns (the writer was also using a hyphen at the time) in the spring of 1920 and Borges employs the hyphen regularly on most of his published works through September 1921, when the hyphen is suddenly dropped—although it will be used one more time on "Sabado," in September 1922, which he published in Argentina. Curiously, the hyphen appears to be an added appendage as well on Cansinos-Assens's part, for he rarely used it on his later published works.

During the time Borges was steeped in Ultraism, and in the spirit of Vanguardismo, he continued to incorporate his natural affinity for expressionist and symbolist techniques, fusing them with the terse language expected of an ultraist: lyrics reduced to "rhythm and metaphor," a strategy he encouraged in his early essay "Anatomía de mi Vultra," published in Madrid in *Ultra* ns 11 in May, 1921. In seeking "sensation itself," rather than merely dabbling with impressionistic "descriptions of space and time elements that surround it," Borges began writing poetry whose non-metrical rhythms, "undulant, free, redeemed, abruptly truncated," created a language that could "translate naked emotion, purified of the additional data that precedes it" (see essay in Part Two). This philosophical stance, primarily French symbolist in nature, played a large role in his youthful compositions. Poetry became, for Borges, an art form that avoids flesh and blood reality as well as all the configurations and considerations of the ego—in other words, no confessions of love nor romantic sighing. Indeed, Borges rarely wrote of romantic love. Erudite observations, intellectual inquiries, and symbolic metaphoric connections of the human condition were to be made rather than any revelations of one's deepest emotions and sensitive feelings.

Central to Borges's ultraist aesthetic in poetic expression was the metaphor: "that verbal curve that almost always traces the shortest path between two points—spiritual points." A reading of one of Borges's earliest verse poems, "Hermanos," published in *Grecia* ns 45, July 1, 1920, demonstrates how ultraistic and symbolistic ideas come together with figurative language. Borges's speaker and his companion—brother poets? brothers-in-arms? brothers of the human race?—want to understand and commune with the beyond, but they are held captive, restrained, nailed against the cross of time:

Crucificados en el tiempo
callábamos a lo largo de los ponientes gastados
que nos miraban con sus viejos ojos de ofidio,
y nuestros labios eran cicatrices.
                              Quien desgarró el conjuro?

[Crucified in time
we were silent throughout weary sunsets
looking at us with their old reptilian eyes,

and our lips were scars.
Who tore away the spell?]

They are motionless and silent, with sealed scarred-over lips. Observing a sunset, "asombrada de azul," the brothers are transfixed by the sunset's colors spreading over the blue: one of the important French symbols representing the "absolute" or "heaven" (see poem in Part Two). And the colors become reptile-like, transforming themselves into a serpent, an ancient symbol of treachery and deception. Heaven and eternity, that the blue sky perhaps represents, are illusions. What are the brothers looking for? Perhaps it is the desire to commune with what's eternal.

In their "awe of the blue," any reader of Mallarmé certainly recognizes the French poet's direct influence on Borges's verse. In several poems, Mallarmé dealt with "the blue," man's dream of eternity / God / heaven / the beyond" symbolized by the color of the sky, or the *cielo raso* that separates humans from it. In Mallarmé's poem "Les Fenêtres," as well as in "L'Azur" and "Les Fleurs," the poet speaks of "the blue" or the sky as a place which most humans associate with eternal beauty. Poets as mystics were once capable of ascension into the blue, the dream that is "there beyond," whether they got there via art or mysticism. But Mallarmé's speaker must remain grounded in the physical plane, his aging body, sick and dying, trapped in a hospital. At the end of "Les Fenêtres," he is unable to break his mortal tie to the "here below" and cries out in resignation:

Mais, hélas! Ici-bas est maître: sa hantise
Vient m'écoeurer parfois jusqu'en cet abri sûr,
Et le vomissement impur de la Bêtise
Me force à me boucher le nez devant l'azur.
(*Mallarmé: The Poems* 70)

[But, alas! Here below is master and it haunts me
at times even here it comes to disgust me
and the foul vomit of its Stupidity
forces me to hold my nose before the blue.][3]

---

[3] The translation from the French is mine.

Borges's speaker in "Hermanos" shares a similar despair with Mallarmé's speaker: he works in endless failure—both a failure to conquer the "blue" and the subsequent failure to block out the blue's existence. The blue, it seems, is nothing but a deception—"above us only sky," as John Lennon would suggest some fifty years later—nothing more than "the star's abode." For Borges, at twenty, the blue was a false roof to be torn away:

Asombrada de azul
el alma destechó a los astros la casa
y nuestros corazones fueron guitarras de mil cuerdas
que se desangran hoy
                        en la otra herida
de sombras y planetas. (see poem in Part Two)

[Awed by blue
the soul unroofed the star's abode
and our hearts were guitars of a thousand strings
bleeding today
                        in the other wound
  of shadows and planets.]

The poet's heart, like a guitar, sends its blood, its song, its voice into the dark open wound that is the *beyond*, the unknown, in hopes that the mystery will return some answers about the vast darkness with all its stars and planets. Borges's speaker seeks a release from the cross onto which he is nailed (as Christ's spirit was released from his tortured, crucified body and ascended into the blue heaven), away from physical pain that is human experience on earth, where humans suffer the ravages of time, disease, hunger, pain, and death. In "Hermanos," his brothers do what Mallarmé's speaker fails to do. The brothers, awed for a moment by the illusion of the blue, the spell the blue casts, experience a sudden breaking of the spell through the volition of the soul and the power of guitar music. Hearts likened to guitars, the beyond likened to a wound: these are the kinds of elaborate metaphors Borges makes throughout his early ultraist phase as a poet.

A reading of all his early poetry shows how regularly Borges reused metaphors and analogies, placing them at times, word for word, in various different works. In such a way, these objects and ideas ultimately collect symbolic importance for Borges. His poems "Prismas," "Aldea [I]," "Rusia," "Ultimo rojo sol," "Montaña," "Sabado," "Cingladura," are but a few that treat, exchange, rearrange the following images and symbols: the crucifixion, guitar music, sunsets and dawns, wounds that scar, people and things that are "yoked," propellers and drunken sprees, demons or dark angels, and so on. Invariably, these brief, terse images are very similar to Pound's imagistic experiments. Like Pound with his modernist cry to "make it new," Borges's cry to "go forward in time" reaffirms the similar goals each poet held for poetry.

Spanish Ultraísmo and the Prose Poem

Ultraísmo first exploded on the Spanish scene around 1918 spearheaded by the literary thinking of Ramón Gomez de la Serna and Rafael Cansinos Asséns, and it melded well with the already prevalent spirit for anarchy, experimentation, and vanguardism that was circulating among young Spanish writers in Madrid, Sevilla, and Barcelona; these cities offered the fertile atmosphere of modernity for the many Latin American writers fleeing the less than cosmopolitan communities of their homelands. Borges reports in his "Autobiographical Notes" that it was Cansinos Asséns who "invented the term 'Ultraism,' believing that Spanish literature "had always been behind the times." This spirit was not lost on young Borges, whose firm Latin and classical training, seasoned by an enormous intellect and hours of study, urged him toward opportunities to unfetter his own intuitive, vanguard poetic voice. He was a young man striving to break out of the mold into which his traditional upper-middle-class education had cast him.

Indeed, some claim that Ultraísmo is nothing more than Spain's version of Imagism, Pound's movement, which he began in 1912 in London as an antidote to the last, and poorest, phase of Symbolism. Imagism certainly influenced, to some degree, the literary communities of Spain; however, others would suggest that what was really taking place was a moment of *zeitgeist*, the principle of simultaneous emergence of new ideas in disparate communities. Yet, one cannot ignore the similarities that exist. The literary scholar will surely recognize the close (but not exact) resemblance between the maxims of Pound's Imagism and the following principles of Ultraism set forth by Borges in his early essay "Ultraísmo":

1. Reducción de la lírica a su elemento primordial: la metáfora.
2. Tachadura de las frases medianeras, los nexos, y los adjetivos inútiles.
3. Abolición de los trebejos ornamentales, el confesionalismo, la circunstanciación, las prédicas y la nebulosidad rebuscada.
4. Síntesis de dos o más imágenes en una, que ensancha de ese modo su facultad de sugerencia. (See essay in Part Two)

[1. Reduction of the lyric to its primal element: the metaphor.
2. The elimination of intermediating phrases, conjunctions and useless adjectives.
3. Abolition of ornamental flourishes, confessionalism, circumstantial reportage, sermonizing and nebulous pedantic affectations.
4. Synthesis of two or more images in one, thus heightening the power of suggestion.]

Here are the rules set forth for imagists by Ezra Pound and F. S. Flint, published in 1913:

1. Direct treatment of the "thing" whether subjective or objective.
2. To use absolutely no word that does not contribute to the presentation.
3. As regarding rhythm: to compose in the sequence of the musical phrase, not in sequence of a metronome. (Cited in Pratt 18)

Pound and Flint's maxims were widely published in London, Paris and in the United States, and, most certainly, they caught the attention of visiting Spanish and Latin American writers. Some suggestion is made that Huidobro perhaps introduced the theories into the Spanish literary community. Huidobro, born in Chile, resided in Paris starting in 1916 and became a key figure there in the avant-garde literary scene of which Pound, after moving to Paris from London, was an important influence. Just as Paris was a mecca for writers among Anglo-Americans seeking change, it served as well for many Latin American and Spanish writers who were seeking to break the hold Ruben Darío, with his Modernismo movement, and Leopoldo Lugones exerted over Spanish letters. Poets traveling between Paris and Madrid, such as Garcia Lorca, or returning to Latin America would announce new movements, books to read, important ideas occurring outside of Spain. Oddly enough, in the case of Dario's Modernísmo, the influence worked in reverse. Begun in Latin America circa 1890, Modernísmo was then carried by Dario to Spain. In the case of Ultraísmo, Borges himself is credited with introducing it into the literary scene of Buenos Aires in 1921, along with the Spaniard Guillermo de Torre, who accompanied Borges to Argentina and married Norah, Borges's sister, in 1923. However, the movement had little influence outside Spain and Argentina.

Like the poetry of the time, Borges's earliest poetry did indeed emphasize the "new," using the best principles of Ultraísmo. Borges became a literate voice for the movement and urged in numerous essays and manifestos an "acceptance of all modules and of all ideas that were new" (see "Ultraísmo" in Part Two). In his first manifesto, "Manifiesto del ultra," written with fellow ultraists Jocobo Sureda, Fortunio Bonanova and Juan Alomar, and published in *Baleares* ns 131 in February 1921, Borges shouts out the principles:

Esta es la estética del Ultra. Su volición es crear: es imponer facetas insospechadas al universo. Pide a cada poeta una visión desnuda de las cosas, limpia de estigmas ancestrales; una visión fragante, como si ante sus ojos fuese surgiendo auroralmente el mundo. Y, para conquistar esta visión, es menester arrojar todo lo pretérito por la borda. Todo: la recta arquitectura de los clásicos, la exaltación romántica, los microscopios del naturalismo, los azules crepúsculos que fueron las banderas líricas de los poetas del novecientos.

Toda esa vasta jaula absurda donde los ritualistas quieren apri-sionar al pájaro maravilloso de la belleza. Todo, hasta arquitectar cada uno de nosotros su creación subjetiva. (See "Manifiesto del ultra" in Part Two)

[This is the ultraist's aesthetic. His wish is to create: to impose un-suspected facets to the universe. It demands of each poet a naked vision of things, devoid of ancestral stigmas; a fragrant vision, as if the world rising up were dawning before his eyes. And, in order for this vision to be triumphant, it is imperative that all things of the past be tossed overboard. Everything: the straight architecture of the classics, the romantic exaltation, the microscopic view of naturalism, the blue twilights that were the lyric banners of the nineties poets. The entire vast and absurd cage in which the ritu-alists wish to imprison the wonderful bird of beauty. Everything, until each one of us has constructed his own subjective creation.]

Here again, Borges takes a swipe at the nineties poets of Mod-ernísmo, including Dario's major symbol of the "blue," which he had expropriated from Mallarmé and the French symbolists (as did Borges), along with the "swan." Borges ridicules the image of the swan almost as loud as the Mexican poet Enrique González Martínez did when, referring to Dario's famous poem, "El Cisne" [The Swan], he cries out, "Wring the swan's neck. . .with its deceptive plumage" (cited in Tapscott 48). In his youthful commitment to go forward in time, Borges cries out in his manifesto, "Los ultraístas han existido siempre: son los que, adelantándose a su era, han aportado al mundo aspectos y expresiones nuevas" (see this manifesto in Part Two). ["The ultraists have always existed: they are the ones that, ahead of their time, have given the world new aspects and expressions"]. The enthusiasm for all things new rings throughout the Ultraist manifesto, and, after leaving Spain in 1921 and returning to Argentina, Borges continues to proclaim loudly and insis-tently the glories of Ultraism.

In Buenos Aires, Borges's method for spreading his Ultraism's praises was most ingenious. He and his new group Guillermo Juan, Eduardo Gonzalez Lanuza, and Guillermo de Torre printed their new ultraist manifesto, "Proclama," in a mural magazine of their own creation, which they could then post on doors and shop windows, like a political protest announcement. They called the magazine *Prisma*, which Borges edited and dutifully plastered throughout the city: "Hemos tirado cinco mil ejemplares" ["We have printed five thousand copies"], Borges tells the editor of the magazine *Ultra* who was preparing to reprint the manifesto in Madrid, "con los cuales, dentro de una semana, estará empavesada la ciudad. Queremos desparramar el ultraísmo por toda la República y hemos enviado números para que sean pegados en Córdoba, en el Rosario de Sante Fe y en Corrientes. También mandamos a Chile y Montevideo. . . ." (see "Proclama" in Part Two) ["with which, within a week, this city will be decorated. We wish to broadcast Ultraism throughout the Republic and we have sent copies to be placed in Cordoba, Rosario de Sante Fe, and Corrientes. We also sent them to Chile and Montevideo. . ."]

Although a copy of the mural magazine *Prisma* could not be located, included in this study is the January 1922 version reprinted in *Ultra*. Guillermo de Torre's 1965 study, *Historia de las literaturas de vanguardia*, contains an excellent reproduction of the *Prisma* issue containing "Proclama," along with one of Norah Borges's magnificent woodcuts that accompanied the manifesto. As one can imagine, everywhere throughout the city, this poster could be found proclaiming the arrival of a new literary esthetic intended to "stir up the bowels of the sisterland" (Argentina as a sisterland to Spain). In the manifesto, words are compared to playing cards and the poet to a shuffler/philosopher so that their dealt words now become designs or figures:

En su forma más enrevesada i difícil, se intenta hasta explicar la vida mediante esos dibujos, i al barajador lo rotulamos filósofo. Para que merezca tal nombre, la tradición le fuerza a escamotear todas las facetas de la existencia menos una sóla, sobre la cual asienta las demás, i a decir que lo único verladero (sic) son los átomos o la energía o cualquier otra cosa. . .

¡Como si la realidad que nos estruja entrañalmente (sic), hubiera menester muletas o explicaciones!

[In their most complicated and difficult forms, we even try to explain life with these figures, and we label the shuffler philosopher. For him to deserve such a name, tradition forces him to do a sleight-of-hand trick with all the facets of life except the one on which the rest are based, and to say that the only real things are atoms or energy or something else...

As if reality which fundamentally twists us around needed props or explanations!]

It's hard not to recognize Borges's fascination with *naipes*, or playing cards. The image appears, perhaps for the first time in his career, in this manifesto. Once again, Borges and his fellow ultraists reiterate their rejection of Ruben Darío and his appropriated symbols: "the roses, the swans, the fauns, the Greek gods, the well-ordered and flower ornamented landscapes" and, of course, the "blue." In "Proclama," Borges, for whatever his contribution might be, is particularly cruel to his fellow Latin American Ruben Darío and the modernístas pointing out how they

> engarzar millonariamente los flojos adjetivos *inefable, divino, azul, misterioso*! Cuánta socarronería i cuánta mentira en ese manosear de ineficaces i desdibujadas *palabras*, cuánto mie?do (sic) altanero de adentrarse verdaderamente en las cosas, cuánta impotencia en esa vanagloria de símbolos ajenos!

> [string together millions of weak adjectives: *indescribable, divine, blue, mysterious*! So much cleverness and deceit in this handling of ineffective and vague words, so much arrogant fear of truly going deep into things, so much impotence in that vainglory of others' symbols!]

Borges rises up against those poets who "live within their autobiography" and reasserts the need for brevity in poetry. Finally, Borges shouts loudest when he says that Ultraísmo, in having synthesized poetry down to its primordial element, the metaphor, "has a propensity towards the formation of an emotional and variable mythology" (see "Proclama" in Part Two).

As Christ points out in his book, *The Narrow Act*, Borges's fictional work, heavily influenced by the local mythology of his native Argentina, the gaucho for example, centers itself on certain ideas developed during his ultraistic experiments, the most important of which was the supremacy of the metaphor. Christ does much to explain the evolution of Borges from the young ultraísta who championed the supremacy of the metaphor to the writer of prose fiction who "rejects the supremacy of rhetorical metaphor in favor of an absolutely metaphorical world of art" (14-15).

For Borges, Ultraism was a necessary experiment in direct connection with the changing attitude of society towards the creation of art; however, the developing brand of Ultraísmo that Borges began to spread in Argentina contained new intentions and slightly different strategies than the Ultraísmo he proclaimed in Spain. Borges's Spanish brand incorporated passages "after the manner of futurism" with "modernity and gadgets" ("Autobigraphical Notes"). Once back in Argentina, Borges rejected aspects of Futurism, as he explains in an essay published in his *Inquisiciones* (1925). In that essay, Borges wrote that "the Ultraism of Seville and Madrid was a resolution for renewal, it was the resolve of girding esthetic time in a new cycle, it was a lyric written, as it were, with florid capital letters on the leaves of the calendar, a lyric whose most eminent emblems—the airplane, antennas, and propellers—are spokesman for a chronological present. The Ultraism of Buenos Aires was the yearning to obtain an absolute art which would not depend on the prestige of the authors and which would last in the continuity of the language as a guarantee of beauty'" (cited in Christ 3).[4]

Writers and poets everywhere throughout the Spanish and Latin American world were experimenting, rejecting, deleting and rebelling by way of breaking the ties with Rubén Darío, Modernismo, and the Romantic past. Like its cousin Imagism, Ultraism ushered in a new approach to writing, a purification, if you will, of all the excesses that were overburdening the poem: prestigious words and foreign symbols,

---

[4] Not having been published in a magazine, this essay is not collected in my study. I reprint the excerpts in English as they were translated and reproduced by Christ.

rhyme, punctuation, verbosity, autobiography and confessionalism. Unfortunately, in its zeal to do so, the act of reducing verse to the primacy of the metaphor, at times, could reach for bizarre (some would say even absurd) comparisons, much like some of John Donne's unique and unexpected metaphors that were decried by many and which critics termed "metaphysical." Observe examples of Borges's unusual, if not bizarre, metaphors in "Tranvias" ["Streetcars"] and "Norte" ["North"], poems he published in *Ultra* in 1921:

Con el fusíl al hombro   los tranvías
patrullan las avenidas
Prora del imperial bajo el velámen
de cielos de balcones y fachadas

       verticales cual gritos

[With rifles on their shoulders   streetcars
patrol the avenues
Imperial prow underneath canvas sails
of balconied skies and facades

       vertical like shouts]
               from "Tranvías"

Los carteles borrachos
       saltan de las fachadas
y las proras enhiestas de las casas
van talando los años
Los edificios caen sobre mis ojos
Me lapidan los muros

[Drunken billboards
       leap from the facades
and the years continue felling
the upright prows of the houses
Buildings fall on my eyes
The walls stone me]
      from "Norte" (see poems in Part Two)

Yet, concomitantly, some very inventive lyrics come during Borges's youthful ultraístic experiment, as seen in "Montaña," published in *Tableros* in 1921, in "Cingladura" [Sculling], published in *Ultra* 1922, and in "Siesta," published in *Ultra* 1921:

De espaldas a la tierra   yo recojo la sombra vendimiaria

[My back to the earth   I gather shade like harvesting grapes
                              from "Montaña"

La neblina sosiega los ponientes
La noche rueda como un pájaro herido

[The mist pacifies the setting sun
Night falls like a wounded bird]
                              from "Cingladura"

Muchedumbres de sol
              bloquean la casa
y el tiempo acobardado se remansa
detrás de las persianas
              verdes como cañaverales

[Multitudes of sun
              blockade the house
and cowardly time slowly flows
behind green venetian blinds
              like reeds of cane]
                      from "Siesta" (see poems in Part Two)

Naturally, regarding Borges's ultraist experimentation with metaphor, readers themselves must determine the quality or the absurdity of his metaphoric imagery. Part Two provides almost all of his early verse from his Ultraismo period for your inspection.

At the height of his enthusiasm for ultraist aesthetics, during which he rejected confessionalism, romanticism and intellectualism, Borges attempted to condense expressionistic images of sunsets, campos [fields], cityscapes and landscapes into short snippets of emotionally detached observation. This sort of condensation certainly works best with verse poetry. Yet, Borges was also a fan of the prose poem. In fact, his second published poem is a prose poem, "Paréntesis passional" (January 1920). Moreover, through January 1922, he will publish five more prose poems— and beginning around the time of the writing of *Fervor* (1922-23) and extending until the late twenties, his verse becomes increasingly prosaic (see three poems collected as "Salmos" from August 1924). Concomitant with this development, Borges seems to take on more personal subjects: romance, passion and sexuality, along with the metaphysical and philosophical issues he would treat much more successfully in the short prose pieces of the 1930s: narrative pieces he would describe as pseudo-essays, articles, hoaxes, and exercises. Many of these works he would publish in *Historia universal de la infamia* (1935) and the following year in *Historia de la eternidad* (1936). An addendum to the above observation is that his prose poems from the very beginning of his writing career almost always treated themes of love, passion and sexuality. It's as if prose gave Borges the poetic license to explore these personal and emotional issues, while verse poetry, the more traditional medium for expressions of passion and love, was reserved for describing landscapes, sunsets and streetcars. Ronald Christ believes, concerning certain ultraist poems Borges included in *Fervor*, such as "Campos atardecidos," that, starting in 1923, Borges begins transcending the "actual" to commence focusing on "eternity embodied in a point of space: each scene, each object is like a rock in the stream of time, interrupting the flow and causing a deep pool to well up there. Necessarily, such a vision avoids the human individual, the complex issues of love, sex and passion, and the limitations of his chronological and spatial existence" (51).

Yet, writing his book in 1969 and not having seen the early ultraist poetry Borges published in magazines between 1920-22 (for indeed he does not comment on them), Christ is unaware that his assertions about "Campos atardecidos" from *Fervor* fits much of Borges's early ultraist poems as well. "Campos atardecidos," as collected in *Fervor* (1923), is merely an evolved product of "Aldea [II]" from 1921, to which Borges simply adds a stanza that introduces his trademark pondering of "time" and "mirrors" while moving ever so slightly towards prose narrative with the addition of a narrator, longer and more complex sentences, and proper punctuation (see the poem in Part Two). Nevertheless, by 1923, Borges begins to turn away from ultraist poetry, so fragmentary and non-prosaic, so "metaphoric" in its desire to produce the quintessential core of things, and begins writing a slightly more prosaic and intellectually stimulating prosaic verse. This shift, I submit, is the true beginning of his overlap into pseudo-essays that leads him to the doorstep of fictional stories.

By way of comparing his early poetry to his evolving narrative experiments, I offer one of Borges's early narratives from *Historia universal de la infamia*, "El asesino desinteresado Bill Harrigan" ["The Disinterested Killer Bill Harrigan"], often described as innovative, partly because, in a fundamental way, it, like most of his early prosaic poetry, crosses the boundaries between essay, prose poetry and narrative fiction, often sharing the similar look, sound and intentions of his ultraist prose poems. In this first of five short narratives using the famous American cowboy Billy the Kid as its central theme (the "gaucho" in Argentina shares a similar mythic attraction), Borges employs a curious blend of anecdote, biography and prose poem:

> La imagen de las tierras de Arizona, antes que ningun otra imagen: la imagen de las tierras de Arizona y de Nuevo México, tierras con un ilustre fundamento de oro y de plata, tierras vertiginosas y aéreas, tierras de la meseta monumental y de los delicados colores, tierras con blanco resplandor de esqueleto pelado por los pájaros. En esas tierras, otra imagen, la de Billy the Kid: el jinete clavado sobre el caballo, el joven de los duros pistoletazos que aturden el desierto, el emisor de balas invisibles que matan a distancia, como una magia.
>
> El desierto veteado de metales, árido y reluciente. El casi niño que al morir a los veintiún años, debía a la justicia de los hombres, veintiuna muertes—"sin contar mejicanos" (65)

[The image of Arizona lands, before any other image: the image of the lands of Arizona and New Mexico, lands with an illustrious foundation of gold and silver, vertiginous and airy lands, lands of the monumental meseta and of delicate colors, lands with the white resplendence of skeletons stripped by birds. In those lands, another image, that of Billy the Kid: the rider fixed upon his horse, the young man of harsh pistol shots that stun the desert, the emissary of invisible bullets that kill from a distance, as if by magic.

The metal-streaked desert, arid and gleaming. The almost-a-boy who upon dying at age twenty-one, owed the law of men twenty-one deaths—"not counting Mexicans."]

Although the piece functions as an introduction to four more individually titled pieces on the "Kid," which are more prosaic and essay-like in character, it is clear that Borges, the poet, wants this individual work to conjure for the reader a vivid and poignant comparison between the mythical west and the myth that is Bill ("Billy the Kid") Harrigan, an intention that demands from him all of his unique poetic skills. Notice the intoned "musical" cadence Borges gives to his sentences that, with the repetition of the word "*tierras*," as well as the highly inventive descriptive imagery—"tierras con blanco resplandor de esqueleto pelado" [lands with the white resplendence of skeletons stripped by birds]—invoke the immediacy of poetry. Note also how Borges, the poet, centers his piece upon a single controlling thematic metaphor: the heroic character of Billy the Kid. Much like the famous (but fictitious) Argentine Gaucho Martin Fierro, who José Hernandez immortalized in his extremely popular poem of the same name, Billy the Kid emerges out of the poetry from the freeze-framed image of the American West in the work's musicality and economy of words.

In no work is young Borges's apprentice technique of blending his ultraism with his irrepressible proclivity for prose narrative better on display than in his second prose poem, "La llama" ["The Flame"], published in *Grecia* ns 41, February 29, 1920. In "La llama," Borges employs, as he does in almost all his early prose poems, as well as in later prose sketches, such as the Billy Harrigan prose narrative, the lyric cadence of word repetition and a language that displays an expressionistic sense of scenic description. Whitman's universal spirit of brotherhood is also present in his tone of voice with symbolic allusions that draw upon the biblical description of the Holy Spirit of God, so indicative of Borges extensive reading and knowledge of the Bible:

> Bajo la larga urna del cielo—ante los mástiles del invierno que se alzan sobre las aguas sin ruido—y las luces verdes del puerto que en amplia inmóvil procesión, anilladas de rojo en la penumbra lo ciñen,—una llama torva ondula en el aire pardo y pesado a ras de la tierra—en el derrumbamiento de las cosas visibles,—en la angustiosa espera de la tormenta cercana...

> [Beneath the long urn of the sky—before the masts of winter rising silently over waters—and the port's green lights, ringed with red in the semi-darkness, that in their wide immobile procession encircle it,—a grim flame undulates in the grey and heavy air at earth level—in the collapse of visible things,—in the anguishing wait of the approaching storm...]

In his view of the sun, the speaker sees a red flame that "hops and crackles." The flame wants to speak, and knowing that it cannot, the speaker, passing by the flame, lends to it his personal voice, the bardic voice of proclamation that draws out the conceit here to metaphysical proportions:

> *Yo, latente bajo todas las máscaras,—nunca apagada y eternamente acechando,—hermana de la abierta herida de luz en el desnudo flanco del aire—hermana de lares y piras—hermana de astros que arden en los jardines colgantes cuya serenidad enorme yo envidio,—desterrada de las selvas del sol hace abismos de siglos—encarno la grande fatiga, la sed de no ser de todo cuanto en esta tierra poluta vibra, y sufriendo vive.*
> *Te siento y paso.—Sigo a lo largo de la tarde lenta—y medito el significado de tu roja palabra—y veo que en verdad eres símbolo—de nosotros que inevitablemente sufrimos—uncidos al gris yugo del día—o al enjoyado yugo de la noche...*

[*I, latent under all masks,—never extinguished and eternally
observing,—sister of the open wound of light in the naked side of air—
sister of hearths and pyres—sister of stars burning in hanging gardens
whose enormous serenity I envy,—exiled from the sun's jungles an abyss
of centuries ago—I embody the great fatigue, the thirst of not being all
of what vibrates on this polluted earth, and suffering, lives.*

*I feel you and pass by—I follow the length of the slow
evening—and ponder the meaning of your crimson word—and
see that in truth you are a symbol—of us who inevitably suffer—
hitched to the grey yoke of day—or the jeweled yoke of night.*]

One can hardly miss the comparison here of the sun with the biblical description of the Holy Spirit, which becomes not only a flame
but a fiery tongue. It is the mysterious power of God or eternity man-
ifesting in an object of nature, or in people who are then empowered
with the word of God and who speak in "tongues." Characteristically,
for Borges, it is once again the sunset that is the vehicle for the symbolic gesture which, as Borges often does, suggests a larger metaphysical
truth to be understood.

In "La llama," as he did in his verse poem "Hermanos," Borges incorporates yet another wound, but not, this time, of the dark beyond,
but of light. As the wound is in the "naked side" of air, followed by a
mention of crucifixion, readers should sense the symbolic force of the
Christ myth, a myth Borges will turn to often throughout his career:

Espoleados—deseando deslumbrarnos y perdernos en los
pasionales festines—en la crucifixión de cuerpos tremantes—
(y pienso—que tal vez no es otra cosa la vida—que el ascua de
una hoguera muerta hace siglos—que el último eco de una voz
fenecida—que arrojó el azar a esa tierra—algo lejano a este orden
de cosas del espacio y del tiempo).—Y la llama se hunde en el gran
crepúsculo enfermo—que en jirones desgarran los grises vientos.
(See poem in Part Two)

[Spurred on—desiring to dazzle and lose us in passionate
feasts—in the crucifixion of trembling bodies—(and I think—that

life may be nothing else—than a bonfire's ember from centuries ago—than the last echo of an extinguished voice—that chance hurled onto this earth—something remote from the space and time ordering of things).—And the flame sinks into the great infirm twilight—tearing the gray winds to shreds.]

On full display in these excerpts is Borges's concern with his inability to experience or burn with passion. The solitary poet, like the flame, embodies the great fatigue, "the thirst of not being all of what on this polluted earth vibrates." Here too Borges begins introducing his philosopher's concern with such intellectual issues as the meaning of time and space restrictions. Borges's speaker ponders whether life may be nothing else than a bonfire's ember from centuries ago and not a part of man's time and space consciousness of things. The flame (sun) stands as the symbol of man who inevitably suffers, imprisoned within the cycle of life and eternally "hitched to the grey yoke of day."

In another prose poem, "Paréntesis pasional" ["Passionate Parenthesis"], Borges offers readers the first example of his prosaic treatment of the theme of sexuality and passion during his ultraísta days. Borges begins the poem with an astonishing metaphor that introduces a feeling of "magic" and "sleight-of-hand" about the night:

La tarde es el divino juglar que viene danzante, rítmico y ágil, y que apaga el sol con su diestra y en su izquierda eleva la Luna. Sus pies azules leves danzan sobre una Alfombra fragante pues poco ha que huyó la lluvia y algunos viejos nubarrones maculan todavía a lo lejos la Inmensidad de púrpura donde laten áureas estrellas.

En la plaza rendida alza su ala única la Fuente. Yo voy con pecho henchido y alma feliz. Marcho al encuentro de la Amada, de la Amada del toisón fulgente y deslumbrante cuerpo.

[The evening is the divine juggler that comes dancing, rhythmic and agile, and who extinguishes the sun with his right hand and raises the Moon on his left. His airy blue feet dance on a fragrant Carpet since the rain has barely fled and some old dark clouds still in the distance, color the purple Immensity where golden stars throb.

In the exhausted plaza, the Fountain lifts its only wing. I go with a swollen chest and happy soul. I am off to meet the Beloved, the Beloved with the sparkling golden fleece and dazzling body.]

After evoking the spirits of poets and poetry, followed by a brief greeting to his brothers—the tree and the wind, in "strong and virile Germanic words"—he meets his "beloved" and they walk in the sublimity of the night to the Beer Hall. Here Borges employs a curious metaphor pushing itself towards the dimensions of a conceit: "Con su galería turbia de vidrios, esta Cervecería no es más que el ebrio Barco de los Locos con rumbo a Orión y Aldebarán y que, empujado por el cósmico oleaje, ha encallado en este promontorio alto que, chorreante, se desmorona hasta el Ródano." ["With its turbulent gallery of glass, this Beer Hall is nothing more than the drunken Boat of Madmen bound for Orion and Aldebarán and that, pushed by cosmic surf, has run aground on this high promontory that, dripping with water, is crumbling into the Rhone."]

The two lovers then go about the task of priming their sexual desires with alcohol:

¿Qué Alcohol incendiará tu Alma, oh mi Amada? Pídeme lo que quieras pues estoy rico; tengo tres Escudos sonoros en el bolsillo. . . .

En nuestras venas ríe triunfante el Vino. Una marchita vendedora ofrece flores. Otra botella. Y yo bebo en la Copa de la Amada. Y ella en la mía. ¡Cuán Bello! ¡Cuán pueril!

[What Alcohol will ignite your soul, oh my Beloved? Ask me what you want since I am rich; I have three jingling Coins in my pocket. . . .

In our veins the Wine laughs triumphantly. A wilted vendor offers flowers. Another bottle. And I drink from my Beloved's glass. And she from mine. How beautiful! How child-like!]

It is at this point that Borges scholars begin squirming in their chairs. How few of them can imagine this image of a youthful Borges uttering these passionate words of *romantic love*, perhaps the worst passages of his entire career. No wonder Borges forsook love themes later in his life; his obvious discomfort with the topic only screams out more when he attempts to over-compensate with "love" words conjured by the "intellect"—and not from an inherent instinctual impulse—as was much more natural in the young Neruda. Borges is so carried away that he is prepared to throw away the stock and staple of his later fiction—metaphysics: ("¿Qué me importa la metafísica ni el mundo? ¿Qué me importa el mohín desdeñoso de los críticos? Sólo tú existes, Dicha de mi alma victoriosa.") [("What do I care about metaphysics or the world? What do I care about the disdainful grimace of the critics? Only you exist, Great Joy of my victorious soul"). Taking his readers into the bedroom, Borges then comes as close to eroticism as he will ever get in his career; still, it is a detached sexuality, almost like retelling a story formulated in the head of what this moment of physical love must surely be like:

Mi alma deslumbrada de tinieblas vibra como una Cuerda de Guitarra al contemplar la Amada. Mañana ya seremos extraños el uno para el otro, pero ahora yo vivo sólo para ti, para el Jardín claro y excelso que es tu cuerpo nimbado de Ternura.

Hemos de soñar juntos mientras susurre esta frondosa noche hasta el instante en que se llene de cenizas la alcoba y nos quebrante el yugo de un día nuevo y los faroles se ahorquen en las esquinas. . .Tu frente surge en la media-luz como una aurora. Tu frente es el espejo esmerilado que atesora el marfil de todos los novilunios. Tu frente es la bandera de marfil que ondeará levemente, diciendo tu rendición y mi victoria.

¡Oh Amada, nuestros Besos incendiarán la Noche! (oh sica adámica). Y deja abierta la Ventana, pues quiero invitar al Universo a mis Bodas; quiero que el Aire, el Mar, las Aguas y los Arboles, gocen el febril breve Festín de tu belleza y de mi fuerza.

* * *

Ahora mi paladar es rojo yugo que unce la llama roja de tu lengua. . .La oscuridad se llena de auroras.

* * *

Ahora tu cuerpo, deliciosamente, como una estrella, tiembla en mis brazos. . .

* * *

Ya todas las tinieblas se han dormido. (see poem in Part Two)

[My soul, dazzled by the darkness, vibrates like a Guitar String when I behold my Beloved. Tomorrow we shall both be strangers to each other, but now I live only for you, for the clear and sublime Garden of your body hallowed with Tenderness.

While the luxuriant night whispers we shall dream together up until the moment the bedroom is filled with ashes and the oppressive yoke of a new day breaks upon us and the lamps on the street corners are lynched. . .our brow rises in the half-light like dawn. Your brow is the polished mirror that possesses the ivory of all new moons. Your brow is the ivory flag that will wave slightly, voicing your surrender and my victory.

Oh Beloved, our Kisses will ignite the Night! (Oh sica adámica) [Latin : Oh stabbing dagger of passion]. And leave the Window open, because I want to invite the Universe to my Weddings; I want the Air, the Sea, the Waters and the Trees, to enjoy the brief feverish Feast of your beauty and my strength.

* * *

Now my palate is a red yoke that hitches to the red flame of your tongue. . . .The darkness is full of dawns.

* * *

Now your body, deliciously, like a star, trembles in my arms. . .

* * *

All darkness now has fallen asleep.]

Yet, even in this most intimate and passionate scene, Borges does not fail to touch upon what will become the most enduring subjects of his mature prose fiction: the metaphysical question of time and his fascination with the re-creative, reflective, and duplicating qualities of mirrors. A reading of the entire poem goes on to reveal how the speaker is exalted by both a sexual and a universal/pantheistic love as expressed through his desire to embrace all the elements of the universe as he would embrace his "beloved." Despite its abundance of Baroque metaphors meant to be shocking more than revelatory or illuminating, and its overly dramatic expressions of love and sexual ecstasy, the poem already reveals Borges's penchant for metaphoric and symbolic thought that will figure so prominently in both his later poetry and his prose fiction.

Most critics would concur how little Borges deals with erotic love or sexual intimacy in his mature fiction; yet, it is curious to note how frequently young Borges explored such themes in his earliest prose poems. One might ask why, for young Borges, such topics seemed more appropriate in prose poetry as opposed to verse. Perhaps Borges felt that he could treat the issue of sexual longing and passion in prose poetry because his prose-essay writing talents would elevate the expression beyond the sentimental level and into the comforting space of "ideas." Time and again in various early essays and manifestos, Borges rejects the cliché-riddled "romantic" verse of Darío and other poets of modernismo. Prose, somehow, freed him from the fate of being yet another love-sick, ivory-tower poet writing romantic, dreamy poems in emotional and overly sentimental language.

Whatever the reason, the fact remains that, of the six prose poems he wrote between 1920 and 1922, along with the more "prosaic poems" with long verse lines, which he wrote through 1924—not to mention the two prose poems he actually identifies as such from 1934, titled "Prose Poems For I.J."—all of them except "Rusia" deal with romantic love or sexual passion (this in contrast to only two of the twenty-three ultraist verse poems he wrote between 1919 and 1923 that deal with the subject). Perhaps some excerpts from "Prose Poems for I.J." might further elaborate on the preceding discussion regarding love and sexual passion as subjects appearing more in prose poetry than in Borges's verse poems. Borges composed these poems in English and initially included them in *Poemas 1922-1943*, later republishing them as "Two English Poems" in *El otro, el mismo* (1964) These poems were written in the same period as his pseudo-essay/myth "El asesino desinteresado Bill Harrigan." The prose poems and the Bill Harrigan sketch are good examples of Borges's overlapping of his poetic and prosaic sensibilities. As the inscribed date indicates, "Prose Poems For I.J." were written in 1934 during Borges's so-called "lyrical hiatus when he was supposedly not writing poetry" (Cheselka 3).[5] A curious side note is that, when he collected them in *El Otro, El Mismo* (1964), he states in his prologue that the book is his "preferred collection" of poetry: "De los muchos libros de versos que mi resignación, mi descuido y a veces mé pasión fueron borroneando, *El otro, el mismo* es el que prefiero." ["Of all the many books of verses that my indolence, carelessness, and sometimes my passion kept drafting, *El Otro, El Mismo* is the one I prefer the most." Once again, it seems that, in deciding to deal with his feelings of love, as diffuse as they seem here—for who is he talking to? Is he talking to I.J., his lover? the night? the reader?—he naturally falls into prose rhythms. Also, notice the similar typographical layout with some of Borges's ultraist prose poems, where after the opening line, subsequent lines forming complete units of observation or thoughts are indented. Such is the case with "Escaparate," "Paréntesis Pasional" and "Aldea [I]" where each observation, expression and image is presented in separate indented prose stanzas (although with "Prose Poems for I.J.," subsequent lines are indented instead of the first line):

---

5 For a discussion of this "lyrical hiatus," see Zunilda Gertal's *Borges y su retorno a la poesía*, which first introduces the topic. Cheselka, in fact, remains skeptical and attempts to discredit her supposition.

I

The useless dawn finds me in a deserted streetcorner; I have
     outlived the night.
Nights are proud waves: darkblue topheavy waves laden with all
     hues of deep spoil, laden with things unlikely and desirable.
Nights have a habit of mysterious gifts and refusals, of things half
     given away, half, withheld, of joys with a dark hemisphere.
     Nights act that way, I tell you.
The surge, that night, left me the customary shreds and odd
     ends: some hated friends to chat with, music for dreams,
     and the smoking of bitter ashes. The things my hungry
     heart has no use for.
The big wave brought you.
Words, any words, your laughter; and you so lazily and
     incessantly beautiful. We talked and you have forgotten
     the words.
The shattering dawn finds me in a deserted street of my city. . . .
                              (*Poemas* 43, 157-58)

The poem reaches back in many ways to the themes and expressions
of many of the poems in *Fervor* (1923): wandering the streets of Buenos
Aires, street corners at dawn, isolation, loneliness. The identity of I.J.,
as well as the reason Borges chose to write the poems in English, remain
unclear, but similarities between his ultraist prose poems and his earliest prose fiction begin to emerge. Between 1934 and his publication of
El Jardin de senderos que se bifurcan in 1941, which he would incorporate
three years later into the collection *Ficciones,* Borges is clearly experimenting with elements of prose poetry and the pseudo-essay that will
turn into his peculiar brand of prose fiction. Note in "Prose Poems
for I.J." the repetition of a key word "night," enhancing the music
and lyricism of the prose piece. This is a strategy Borges used in most
of his early prose poems and in the Bill Harrigan sketch previously
discussed. Also note the unique descriptive language and rhythmic
cadence of words that are essentially presented in more or less correct
grammar— even using a semi-colon between two independent clauses

that few verse poets would do. Meanwhile, brevity is still the operative measure for the work itself. In addition, there is Borges's creation of adjectival neologisms, as in the Bill Harrigan sketch "el casi niño," in "Escaparate" the unknown word "radioso" (radiant?), and in the prose poem itself, "streetcorner," "darkblue," "topheavy." Also notice in part two of the poem the poetic cadence, the almost chant-like properties of his language:

II

What can I hold you with?
I offer you lean streets, desperate sunsets, the moon of the
    jagged suburbs.
I offer you the bitterness of a man who has looked long and long
    at the lonely moon.
I offer you my ancestors, my dead men, the ghosts that living men
    have honored in marble: my father's father killed in the frontier
    of Buenos Aires, two bullets through his lungs, bearded and
    dead, wrapped by his soldiers in the hide of a cow; my mother's
    grandfather—just twenty-four—heading a charge of three
    hundred men in Perú, now ghosts on vanished horses.
        (*Poemas 43*, 157-60)

"I offer" serves as the opening phrase of nine stanzas that follow these initial lines of verse, a repetition similar to the one used in both the "Bill Harrigan" sketch of 1935 and in "Escaparate" as far back as January 1922. Furthermore, both poems seem to collate numerous themes that Borges often addressed in both his early poetry as well as in his mature poetry: the ethereal quality of dawn and dusk, the mysterious night that, like blindness, envelopes humans in darkness, things brought in by waves, the aimless wandering and introspection in the deserted streets of Buenos Aires, reality reflected in a mirror—streets, sunsets, ancestors, moons. A reading of the early poems reveals how all of Borges's favorite images and subjects that appear in his mature work appear, as well, in the juvenilia. As Ronald Christ asserts, two of Borges's key stylistic concerns, "concentration (or brevity) and metaphor

. . .inform not only the poetry of Borges's Ultraist period, but much of his later writing as well" (5).

From the appearance of Borges's earliest prose poem in 1920 to these "mature" prose poems of 1934, one should note that the latter year saw the emergence of his first piece that Borges actually labeled a "story." I contend that his initial prose piece shows much of the same "lyrical" energy and expression as the prose poems from his ultraist days—that his poetic voice and his idea of story writing did indeed *conjoin*. Of course, what this study of Borges has been suggesting all along is difficult to scaffold into a theory and must be done carefully. But after inspecting all of Borges's early verse and prose poetry written through 1924, it appears that, as Borges moves from his ultraísta period to a period of more "prosaic" verse, and ultimately to writing "poetic" prose essays between 1925-34, he begins to move closer as well to the metaphysical, literary and intellectual issues that will primarily concern him in his most famous prose narratives of the 1940s. Ronald Christ suggests that, from *Fervor* on, Borges's involvement with the literature of his own country is the last step in his development before he enters what will prove to be the greatest, most important phase of his career. He adds that "[t]he effects of this early period on his subsequent writing cannot be overestimated" (49-50). Indeed, it is then that he begins to create for himself that peculiar literary personality which will eventually make use of the huge range of international modernist/vanguardist literature that he has assimilated before becoming, in literature at least, a full-fledged Argentine.

It might also be theorized that the mature Borges felt that prose fiction, or even in some cases his prosaic poetry or poetic prose pieces, had become the more appropriate medium for handling loftier metaphysical questions of time and of the self as well as the self as artist. Moreover, he could see that his early attempts at tackling historical, biographical and philosophical concerns were not appreciated by the reading public in Latin America, who were more responsive to poets such as Pablo Neruda, César Vallejo, Gabriela Mistral or Octavio Paz—poets more passionate, innovative and/or socially committed. Consequently, Borges moved away from writing poetry around the age of twenty-nine and did not fully return to the discipline until 1959-60, during which time he chose to focus on his prosaic experimentations: essays, pseudo-essays, sketches, narratives, and yes, a few pieces he began to call "stories."

The point can be made that it's not only Borges's early vision of himself as poet that informs the shape and character of his fiction in *Ficciones*; it is also the ensuing dissatisfaction with himself as poet—as a *failed* poet, or at least "not truly a poet"—that initiates his change from poetry to prose. As editor of the Argentine magazine *Proa*, Borges knew full well the poetry that was claiming international attention. The list of poets from Latin America and Spain staking claim to international recognition during the twenties rarely includes Borges, who came to be known rather as the great *narrador*.

Undoubtedly, while the vanguard poetry of the more popular Spanish and Latin American poets were attracting attention, Borges's poetry was growing less and less avant-garde in its execution and language, until finally it was being regarded as work less important than his highly intelligent, superbly crafted pseudo-essays, sketches and stories. In a long discussion with Jean Milleret, as reprinted in her book *Entrevistas con Jorge Luis Borges*, the elderly Borges repeats his adamant rejection of his early ultraist and nationalistic poetry—as well as the reason for his ultimate shift away from poetry. Because he had no confidence in his verse, he turned to prose: "my poems were nothing more than prose disguised by the typography of verse." I reproduce an excerpt below in great length for it is here that Borges clearly exposes the doubts he felt about his capabilities as a poet and why his poetic instincts, already prosaic in nature, seemed to him better applied to prose fiction:

JM: Su poesía de ese período [Ultraísmo] es muy difícil de traducir. [Your poetry from that period [Ultraism] is very difficult to translate.]

JLB: Pero creo que es más difícil de leer; porque en el fondo son poemas románticos. Como lo dijo Ibarra: "Borges dejó de ser ultraísta a partir del primer verso ultraísta que escribió." (Borges se ríe) [But I believe it's more difficult to read; because they are essentially romantic poems. As Ibarra said: "Borges left off being

an ultraist beginning with the first ultraist poem he wrote."
(Borges laughs)]

JM: Es un poco cierto, pero la palabra es buena. Sin embargo, usted
publicó, creo que en el 21, el *Manifiesto Ultraísta* en *Nosotros*.
¿Era suyo o de todo el equipo?
[That's not really accurate, but it sounds good. Nevertheless,
you published, I believe in '21, the Ultraist Manifesto in
Nosotros. Was it yours or the work of a group?]

JLB: De todo el equipo. [A group effort]

JM: Sin embargo, se le reprochó a usted ser casi una especie de
renegado o apóstata del ultraísmo.
[Nevertheless, you have reproached yourself for being
somewhat of a renegade or denier of Ultraísm.]

JLB: Todo aquello era tan ingenuo, y además tan tonto, esa idea de
reducir toda la oesía a un solo artificio: la metáfora. . .
[All that was so ingenious, and so foolish as well, that idea of
reducing all poetry to a single artifice: the metaphor. . . .]

JM: ¿No conservó nada de sus escritos de la época?
[You didn't preserve any of your writings from that period?]

JLB: No, todo aquello no valía nada. . .se trataba de nacionalismo
en un estilo criollo totalmente ficticio.
[No, all that had no value. . .it tried to be nationalistic in its
native-born Argentinian style, completely false.] (34, 38)[6]

It must be noted that Borges is not even considering in this discussion his ultraist poetry published in Spain from 1920-22. He is referring
to the poems he wrote for *Fervor, Luna,* and *Cuaderno*. Naturally, many
of the poems were nationalistic, having found a "fervor" for his native
land in 1923. It could very well be that, in her interview, had she shown
Borges any of his ultraist poetry written while in Spain and published
in magazines, he would not even have recognized them.

JM: Tal vez sea lamentable, y creo que ahora vuelve a caer en esta
auto-destrucción. Hace algunos meses me decía que quería
rehacer absolutamente toda su antología personal, con gran

---

6 Except where indicated, all translations throughout this study are mine.

furor por parte de su madre que decía que usted iba a destruir lo mejor de su obra. . .

[Perhaps it's regrettable, and now I believe that once again you are falling into self-destruction. Some months ago you told me that you wished to rewrite absolutely all of your personal anthology, with great rage on your mother's part who said that you were going to destroy the best part of your work. . . .(38-39).

Borges's unceasing need to destroy the evidence of his younger ultraist self, or, at the very least, rewrite it out of recognition is well documented. Regarding Borges's tendency for destroying his early work, Jean Milleret says, "Perhaps it's regrettable." Indeed, it is—for it was the work of the authentic young Borges, albeit works written at a time when he did not feel he was a *true poet*, an important and most intriguing phenomenon that Jean Milleret touches upon but, unfortunately, fails to press and fully explore in greater detail:

JM: Pero volvamos un poco atrás. En 1929, publica *Cuaderno San Martín* que es su última producción poética y durante los diez años siguientes no se conoce de usted más que seis poemas de los cuales se publican solamente cuatro. ¿Por qué este brusco silencio poético a partir de 1929?

[But let's go back a bit. In 1929, you published *San Martín Copybook* which is your last work of poetry and for the following 10 years the only thing we know of you is six poems only four of which are published. Why this abrupt silence beginning in 1929?

JLB: Resulta un poco difícil responder a esa pregunta porque en este momento he olvidado ese silencio y esas razones. Pero creo que, sin duda, no estaba satisfecho con mi producción poética; entonces, creo que escribí ensayos, ¿no?

[It is a bit difficult to respond to that question because at this moment, I have forgotten that silence and the reasons. But I think that, without a doubt, I was not satisfied with my poetic production; so, I think I wrote essays, didn't I?

JM: Sí, en efecto, durante ese decenio usted se dedica a los ensayos de los que aparecerán seis volúmenes: *El idioma de los argentinos* en 1928, *Evaristo Carriego* en 1930, *Discusión* en 1932, *Historia universal de la infamia* en 1935, *Historia de la eternidad* en 1936 y *Otras inquisiciones* en 1937. ¿Cuales son las razones determinantes de esta evolución literaria?

[Yes, actually, during that decade you dedicated yourself to essays which appeared in six volumes: *The Language of The Argentines* in 1928, *Evaristo Carriego* in 1930, *Discussion* in 1932, *A Universal History of Infamy* in 1935, *History of Eternity* in 1936 and *Other Inquisitions* in 1937. What were the reasons that determined this literary evolution?]

JLB: Tengo la impresión de que sentía yo no era verdaderam ente poeta o, tal vez, como había escrito en versos libre, no me producía ninguna pasión, entonces los dejé.

[I have the impression that I felt I wasn't truly a poet, or, perhaps, having written in free verse, it didn't produce any passion in me, so I left it.]

JM: ¿Pero por qué ensayos?" ["But why essays?]

JLB: Porque me interesaban sus temas. [Because their topics interested me.]

JM: Entonces no es por el género sino por el gusto de las ideas. [Then it wasn't for the genre but rather the pleasure from the ideas]

JLB: Sí, gusto por las ideas y al mismo tiempo una desconfianza en mi capacidad poética.

[Yes, pleasure from the ideas and at the same time a lack of confidence in my poetic capabilities.]

JM: En resumen, parece que, por un lado, dudaba de su primera manifestación poética y que, por el otro, sus lecturas y estudios que eran muy abundantes, el gusto por las ideas y por su discusión dominaban por encima de todo el resto en usted mismo.

[In short, it appears that, on one hand, you had some reservations concerning your first poetic efforts and that, on the other hand, your prolific reading and studies, your liking of ideas and their discussion, took precedence over everything else in you.]

JLB: Sí, usted lo dice mejor que yo, pero es eso, o debe ser eso; en todo caso, es la hipótesis más verosímil. Si no ¿por que hice eso? Creo que empecé a sentir, como decía Verlaine, que la poesía es "música ante todo" y que esa música estaba ausente de mis versos; mis versos no eran más que prosa disfrazada por la tipografía en verso, ¿no? Creo que debe ser así. . . .(39-40).
[Yes, you've said it better than I, but it's that, or ought to be; in any case, it is the most probable hypothesis. If not, why did I do that? I believe that I began to feel, as Verlaine said, that poetry is "above all else music" and that music was missing from my verse; my poems were nothing more than prose disguised by the typography of verse, right? I think it must be like this.]

I am convinced that all great writers know the extent of their artistic capabilities at various stages of their career, and that they instinctively know the *quality* of their work, how it fits into the contemporary scene, whether or not it stands with the best in the field, and whether or not the work is worthy of the immense talent they somehow know they possess. For Borges, his first published works were poems that appeared in magazines two years before the *annus mirabilis* of 1922, the zenith of modernism, and of these works, it's regrettable that most Anglo-American critics know little to nothing. When today's Wikipedia lists Borges as among the Vanguardist poets, alongside of Huidobro, Neruda, Lorca, Vallejo and Mistral, it's hard to imagine exactly what poems they are considering that would put him on the list. If anything, he is more a Posvanguardismo (Postmodernist) poet whose best poetry appeared post-1960s.

Yet, it remains my supposition that it was important for Borges, when writing the stories in *Ficciones,* to have seen himself *first* as a poet, failed or otherwise, during that incredibly exciting time known as Vanguardismo.

Ficciones *and the Poetic Self as Narrator*

Literary critics could list numerous reasons why Jorge Luis Borges is one of the twentieth century's most influential and revolutionary prose fiction writers; without a doubt, first on the list would be *Ficciones*. Because of this seminal collection—its unique experiments in narrative technique, his rejection of conventional storytelling, and his own brand of concise and vivid narratives—Borges is often ranked among other notable writers, such as Joyce, Kafka, Beckett and Faulkner. Others would cite his implacable philosophical critique of the meaning of existence explored within his own personal mythology, which seem unparalleled among twentieth century fiction writers. There is as well the breadth of his knowledge of other great works of literature and his critical mind that never ceased *reading and analyzing* them—in short, the sheer magnitude of his intellect. As a result, Borges's innovative treatment of the detective genre, his bending of reality which prefigures *realismo mágico* [magic realism], and his blending of genres make him a leading figure of the *nouveau roman,* a movement with which he has been associated.

All these aspects of his writing have been widely praised by critics since he shared the Formentor Award with Samuel Beckett in 1960. Thus, to say that Borges, *el narrador,* is one of the twentieth century's most fascinating prose fiction writers is a safe conclusion for any critic to make. More challenging may be demonstrating his place among the twentieth-century Latin American poets. A more interesting and useful exercise would be demonstrating the "in-textured" relationship between Borges's poetic "self" during the 1920s and his ensuing prosaic "self" from the 1930s on: his ultimate transformation into a mature writer of prose tales and short narratives. As we have seen, Borges referred to this period as "overlap," a crossing of boundaries between his different sensibilities as a poet, essayist, biographer, editor and overall *literato,* resulting in the creation of a style of prose fiction never before experienced in Latin American literature.

As with Faulkner, who, in "Tres reseñas sobre Faulkner" [William Faulkner: Three Reviews"] Borges called "the leading novelist of our time" (*Borges, A Reader* 94) some of Borges's narrative innovations owe part of their conceptual and syntactic uniqueness to the poetic proclivity he discovered early in his life—his vanguard poet's sense of verbal artifice and modern experimentation. In her essay "Poetry as Fiction," Barbara Herrnstein Smith defines her conception of poetry as "mimetic. . .or *fictive* discourse," and states that a poet, when creating his "verbal structure," will be straining to the limit all the expressive resources of language. And, beyond that limit, he will sometimes devise new ones (184). But what critics sometimes refer to as "poetic devices" (and we may include here rhythm and meter) are really the potentially expressive features of *natural* discourse. Tropes and figures of speech, distortions of idiomatic syntax, departures from idiomatic diction, lack of punctuation—all these are certainly not restricted to poetic discourse, nor can they be taken as the distinctive characteristics of poetic language. They are not what define poetry but are, rather, entailed by what does define it, namely its fictiveness.

Borges's decision to stop writing poetry at thirty and focus on prose fiction did not eliminate his early fascination and sensibility for "poetic" discourse. Borges perhaps realized in his early work what Smith suggests here—the essential "fictiveness" of poetic language. Retaining the essence of his youthful spirit of Vanguardismo, Borges felt no obligation to craft his mature prose using declarative language that early twentieth-century writers believed interfered least with the progression of story, characterization and the development of plot. It is this unique gesture that separates Borges's prose fiction from traditional twentieth-century novelists and short story writers, whose realistic and verisimilar psychological prose was primarily written both to entertain and inform readers of life's joys and ills, using real human experience and, for the most part, traditional syntax in the creation of flesh-and-blood characters. In this way, few twentieth century writers strayed far from the lessons of Dickens, Flaubert, Thackery, Tolstoy, Emile Zola, Chekhov, Henry James, among others. A few famous exceptions would be Joyce, Faulkner, Beckett, and Robbe-Grillet when considering how they experimented with the prose sentence and the evolution of plot. In Spanish and Latin America, a plenitude of "realistic" or "regionalist" fiction writers also dominated the scene in the early 1900s: Mariano

Azuela of Mexico, Ricardo Güiraldes of Argentina, Rómulo Gallegos of Venezuela and Pio Baroja of Spain—although the Mexican Juan Rulfo, with his *Pedro Paramo,* should be placed on the "famous exceptions" list. Then came Borges with *Ficciones,* stories that shattered all conventional expectations. Carlos Fuentes, the Mexican author and himself a highly respected literary figure of Latin America, categorically claims, "Without Borges's prose there simply would not be a modern Spanish-American novel" (cited in Alazraki, *Critical Essays* 6-7).

Now, from a semantic point of view, the essay-like quality of much of Borges's narrative fiction seems the more obvious point of departure, and thus, the close relationship between his engaging pseudo-essay technique and his prose fiction has been repeatedly redefined by critics in the past half-century. Latin-American writers have long embraced the essay as the favored genre for publicly discussing the political and social concerns of their often politically and socially unstable countries. This phenomenon is no less true for Borges, *el essayista*—although Borges, having preferred more literary and philosophical topics, regularly avoided direct political or social statement in his work. Nonetheless, it is unquestionable that Borges owes a debt to his skills as an essayist and scholar for the style and rhetoric of some of his prose fiction; however, the debt he owes to his young poetic "self" remains scarcely ventured territory in Anglo-American letters. In addition to this, as stated earlier, a general resistance towards the early poetry collections and essays lingers among Borges scholars due to his own denigration and repudiation of his early work, both the poems and the essays, published before *Historia universal de la infamia* in 1935. Literary critics and readers alike can easily surmise that much is being left out.

In any case, given the nature of Borges's eclectic mind, most contemporary critics prefer—and rightly so—to study the thematic and symbolic elements of his prose compositions starting with *El jardin de senderos que se bifurcan* (1941), which Borges incorporated into *Ficciones* in 1944. They are extremely puzzling themes that at once could be described as philosophical, metaphysical, mythological, even "game-like" inquiries into human existence as seen through his own unique view of reality. Robert Scholes, in his article "The Reality of Borges," supports Borges when critics argue that his aim is the destruction or conversion of reality:

> The notion that art is a mirror is not a new one. We are all familiar with the classical view that art is a mirror held up to nature. . . .a mirror being carried down a roadway, reflecting the mud below and the sky above. But Borges's mirror is more modest. And does only what ordinary mirrors do. We see in it not nature or the world but only ourselves. . . .Art is merely a map, but it is a map that points accurately to things that are there in reality. . . .Such mirroring and such mapping [of Borges's fiction] take us deeply into reality, though the images are obviously fabulations rather than transcriptions. And this is a major point. Reality is too subtle for realism to catch it. It cannot be transcribed directly. But by invention, by fabulation, we may open a way toward reality that will come as close to it as human ingenuity may come. (19)

Meanwhile, other writers have had to defend him against the critical viewpoint exemplified in the following explanation as to why *El jardin de senderos que se bifurcan* was refused Argentina's National Prize in Literature:

> Those who would venture through the pages of this book would find an explanation to the jury's decision in the dehumanized nature of its pages, in its preciosity, in the obscure and arbitrary cerebral game which cannot even be compared to chess game combinations since these respond to precise and rigorous relationships and not to a sheer whim often bordering on mystification. (Alazraki, *Critical Essays* 3)

However, as noted earlier, Julio Cortázar, defends him against this opinion, pointing out to writers of his generation that Borges's lesson is a Mallarméan lesson in writing. It is curious to me that few critics recognize the simple fact that Borges, in his careful selection of words, is merely following his nascent instincts for poetic expression. As Pound said, every word in poetry has to be just the right word, and Poe's early edict on the writing of short fiction stressed the importance of brevity and how every word must go towards the central effect, saying, "like the lyric poem, the short story should be read at one sitting" (cited in de Carlos 2). Following their judgments, Borges, too, sought brevity and exactness in both his ultraísta poetry and his best fiction.

Even more curious to me are those critics who praise the excellence of Borges's prose yet condemn him for his seeming lack of commitment to the problems of real human life. Perhaps Gabriel García Márquez expresses best this conflicting, at times ambivalent, reaction towards Borges's work among many Latin American writers. In a 1967 interview conducted by Mario Vargas Llosa, Garcia Marquez discusses how, like Vargas Llosa, he has great admiration for Borges (even though Llosa expresses difficulty in justifying it). Marquez goes on to say that he "reads him every night":

> I just came from Buenos Aires and the only thing I bought there was Borges's *Complete Works*. I carry them in my suitcase; I am going to read them every day, and he is a writer I detest. His is a literature of evasion. Something strange happens to me with Borges. He is one of the writers I read the most and whom I have read most, and yet he is perhaps the one I like least. I read him because of his extraordinary ability for verbal artifice. I am fascinated by the violin he uses to express his things. He teaches you how to tune up your literary instrument. (Cited by Alazraki *Critical Essays* 5)

For Borges, a story is more than fact or reproduction of external life, more than an attempt to represent the "truth." His fiction aspires to be an aesthetic form, a rhythmic flow of image and language, patterns of words and sounds that, though at times they seem thematically complex, draw the reader into its labyrinth of language and meaning. In short, his unique fiction could be considered as following the aesthetics of well-written poetry—*poetic* fiction, if I may, that makes him a poet of prose.

Although Borges's thematic material seems evasive, even hermetic at times, as the material of poets can be, it does not seem to be the precise aim of the author to be so. The powerful poet does not attempt to be abstract for abstraction's sake; rather, the subjects they explore may create complexity that they themselves cannot reconcile. Borges is an explorer of complex ideas and postulations; his isn't necessarily literature that seeks verisimilitude with so-called reality. For Borges, literature can often be a personal discourse on the numerous authors, poets, philosophers, historical figures and events he has at one time encountered or read—a rereading, if you will, of history as it might influence his own current thought. The difficulty in understanding certain Borgesian themes stems from the author's fervent attempt to *communicate* that thought, or the extraordinary connection that occurs inside his intellect, in all its fullness, between the material encountered and the conceit, myth, dream or symbolic sketch (call it what you will) his esoteric perceptions generate. His is quintessentially a poet/philosopher's permanent search for meaning out of the chaos that is human existence. In a *Times* interview during the last year of his life, Borges asserts the dominance of intellection in his search for both truth and meaning through literature:

> If life's meaning were explained to us, we probably wouldn't understand it. To think that a man can find it is absurd. We can live without understanding what the world is or who we are. The important things are the ethical instinct and the intellectual instinct, are they not? The intellectual instinct is the one that makes us search while knowing that we are never going to find the answer. I think Lessing said that if God were to declare that in His right hand He had the truth and in his left hand He had the investigation of the truth, Lessing would ask God to open His left hand—he would want God to give him the investigation of the truth, not the truth itself. Of course he would want that, because the investigation permits infinite hypotheses, and the truth is only one, and that does not suit the intellect, because the intellect needs curiosity. (Barili 27-28)

Borges's intellectual investigations of truth and life's meaning result in an expression of life that reflects (or, at the very least, is compatible with) his own understanding of infinite hypotheses: where humans exist inside the inescapable labyrinth of time and space constraints. For Borges, this is human existence.

It is not surprising, then, that Borges's prose fiction—the mystifying themes, mysterious protagonists, secret references, his Mallarméan verbal artifice—involves a rigorous language that very early in his career was inextricably rooted in his perception of himself as a poet.

A reading of Borges's first series of sketches in *Historia universal de la infamia* (1935) reveals how he overlaps his skills as poet and as essayist to transpose anecdotes, biographies and mythical tales into his first narratives. In his "Autobiographical Notes," Borges remembers how these first "pseudo-essays" were written:

> The real beginning of my career as a story writer starts with the series of sketches entitled *Historia universal de la infamia* [*A Universal History of Infamy*], which I contributed to the columns of *Crítica* in 1933 and 1934. The irony of this is that "El hombre de la esquina rosada" ("Streetcorner Man" or "Man from the Slums") really was a story, but that these sketches and several of the fictional pieces which followed them and which very slowly led me to legitimate stories, were in the nature of hoaxes and pseudo-essays. In my *Universal History*, I did not want to repeat what Marcel Schwob had done in his *Imaginary Lives*. He had invented biographies of real men about whom little or nothing is recorded. I, instead, read up on the lives of known persons and then deliberately varied and distorted them according to my own whims. . . .The pieces were meant for popular consumption in *Crítica* and were pointedly picturesque. I suppose now the secret value of those sketches— apart from the sheer pleasure the writing gave me—lay in the fact that they were narrative exercises. Since the general plots or circumstances were all given me, I had only to embroider sets of vivid variations..

Although Borges does not give direct credit to his poetic sensibilities, it is apparent that, for the "vivid" and somewhat stylized prose he achieves in these "pieces" (for he cannot call them stories yet), Borges plies his poetic craft in ways he had already experimented with in his early ultraistic prose poetry. Also, it is important to note that Borges is undoubtedly referring to the poems from his first three books of poetry *Fervor, Luna,* and *Cuaderno*—the majority of which are not ultraísta poems. He can't possibly be referring to the poetry he published in Spain between 1919 and 1922 while steeped in the spirit of Vanguardismo, for as readers of this study have seen, those poems stand in keeping with the key avant-garde principles of his peers: they are imagistic, metaphoric, and concise. Indeed, it is his poetic output of his mid to late twenties rather than his earlier work that would eventually harm his reputation as a poet among his peers, as well as bruise his confidence in his poetic skills, sending him to write exclusively essays and eventually prose fiction—albeit to the great fortune of the literary world.

Borges turns to the essay not for its form but as a *forum* for the display of his eclectic and esoteric ideas. From another perspective, Carlos Horacio Magis reminds us in his 1965 study, *La literatura Argentina*:

> El poeta predominó durante los años de su iniciación literaria, pero la comunicación total de su complejo espiritual le ha ido exigiendo el ejercicio de otros géneros: la crítica literaria, el ensayo y el cuento. Aunque son géneros distintos, trabaja en ellos con idéntico fervor intelectual, los mismos objetos mentales y parecida vibración lírica. (299)

> [The poet predominated during his [Borges's] initial literary years, but the complete communication of his spiritual makeup prompted him to work in other genres: literary criticism, essay and the short story. Although they are distinct genres, he works in them with the same intellectual fervor, with similar objectives and with the same kind of lyrical vibration.]

Indeed, the same "lyrical vibration" can be found in all of Borges's prose. His erudite and skillfully crafted essays often display properties of poetic technique more than "academic" syntax and rhetoric.

Even in his later years, Borges's cannot resist unique poetic language in his prose. In a 1962 prologue written for a very academic resource book, *Catalogo de la exposición de libros españoles*, Borges gives to this mere "list" of books a *prólogo* that could easily be included in either a collection of prose poems or essays:

> Así como el crepúsculo participa de la noche y del día y las olas de la espuma y del agua, dos elementos de naturaleza dispar inseparablemente integran el libro. El libro es una cosa entre las cosas, un objeto entre los objetos que coexisten en las tres dimensiones, pero es también un símbolo como las ecuaciones del álgebra o las ideas generales. Podemos así equipararlo a un juego de ajedrez, que es un tablero negro y blanco y las piezas y la cifra casi infinita de maniobras posibles. También es evidente la analogía de los instrumentos de música, la del arpa que Bécquer entrevió en un ángulo del salón y cuyo silencioso mundo sonoro compararía con un ave que duerme. Tales imágenes son meras aproximaciones y sombras: el libro es harto más complejo. Los símbolos escritos son un espejo de símbolos orales, que a su vez lo son de abstracciones o de sueños o de memorias. Quizá baste dejar escrito que el libro, como el hombre que lo creó, se compone de alma y de cuerpo. (vii)

> [Just like twilight partakes of both night and day, and waves of both surf and water, two naturally disparate but inseparable elements make up the book. The book is a thing amongst things, an object amongst objects that coexists in three dimensions, but it's also a symbol like algebra equations or general ideas. As such we can compare it to a game of chess, which consists of a black and white board, chess pieces, and an almost infinite number of possible moves. The analogy of musical instruments is clearly suitable as well, that of the harp that Bécquer spotted in the corner of a drawing room and whose resounding silent world might be compared with that of a sleeping bird. Such images are mere approximations and shadings: the book is tremendously more complex. Written symbols are mirrors of oral symbols, which in turn become mirrors of abstractions of dreams or of memories. Perhaps it is enough to state that the book, like the man who created it, is made up of body and soul.]

In this prologue, Borges mixes metaphoric language, visual imagery and his characteristic eclectic thinking in the opening two sentences alone. Granted, much more of this "overlap" exists in his earlier essays than in the later, but as far as his ultraistic poetry, specifically his prose poems and his earliest fictional pieces, are concerned, all seem to participate in the same creative arena of language, style and content, and this formula for writing seems to continue throughout his career.

Thus, features of prose poetry, pseudo-essays, sketches, narrative exercises, biography—all overlapped to help him create his first stories. It is curious to note, however, that the result of his first legitimate "story" is a narrative piece whose language is stripped of poetry, straining to relate the *events* of an anecdote about a knife fight between two infamous characters. It's as if Borges initially felt the necessity to tame his innate poetic sensibilities in favor of basic time-honored storytelling technique. "Hombre de la esquina rosada" ("Streetcorner Man") was written in 1933 and collected in *Historia universal de la infamia*. Under its original title, "Hombres de las orillas" ("Men from the Edge of Town)," the story appeared in the Saturday supplement of a yellow-press daily called *Critica* under the pseudonym, Francisco Bustos. Apparently, even as a mature man, Borges maintained a persistent fear of embarrassing himself with vanguard, unproven experimental writing. He explains and articulates the story very well and in ways that prefigure stories to come, but unlike some of his best stories in *Ficciones*, such as "El sur," "El fin," and "El jardin de senderos que se bifurcan," his first story isn't fully *sung*, for he distances himself from poetic language with a seemingly inexperienced or traditional idea that to tell a story, one simply relates plot and develops character—the work, in fact, is *too* prosaic. Monegal comments that "Borges is on record as disliking its [the story's] excesses both in slang and in local color" (*Borges: A Reader* 343). In addition, "Hombre de la esquina rosada" has the distinction of being one of Borges's longest stories—brevity, it seems, being reserved for his poetry and those "prose pieces" with which he was experimenting that would fill *Historia universal*. A reading of some of the other short prose pieces from that collection demonstrates how they, in fact, and not "Hombre de la esquina rosada," are the real link between his poetry and his future prose fiction technique.

Blending or overlapping various genres—anecdote, biography, parable, essay, short story, verse and prose poetry—Borges combines some of their traditional features into the structural and thematic composition of his prose fiction. In "El enemigo generoso" ["The Generous Enemy"] from *Historia universal*, Borges incorporates verse poetry along with the following footnote: "(Del *Anhang zur Heimskringla* (1893), de H. Gering)." It is highly doubtful that Borges copied Gering's text; it is more likely that he simply adapted the myth, perhaps arranging the ideas into a pseudo-verse. Venting his poetic skills, Borges creates a short one-page piece that is at once anecdotal, biographic, essay-like and poetic in its intention:

> Magnus Barfod, en el año 1102, emprendió la conquista general de los reinos de Irlanda; se dice que la víspera de su muerte, recibió este saludo de Muirchertach, rey en Dublín:
> Que en tus ejércitos militen el oro y la tempestad, Magnus Barfod.
> Que mañana, en los campos de mi reino, sea feliz tu batalla.
> Que tus manos de rey tejan terribles la tela de la espada.
> Que sean alimento del cisne rojo los que se oponen a tu espada. . . .

> [Magnus Barfod, in the year 1102, undertook the general conquest of the Irish kings; it is said that on the eve of his death, he received this salutation from Muirchertach, king of Dublin:
> May gold and turmoil militate in your armies Magnus Barfod.
> May your battle be happy tomorrow in the fields of my kingdom.
> May your kingly hands horribly knit the cloth of the sword.
> May those who confront your sword become feed for the red swan
> . . . .] (130)

The piece contains six more lines of verse. Emphasizing the poetic foundation of this sketch or, as he terms it, "pseudo-essay," Borges eventually includes this piece in the verse poetry section of *El hacedor* in 1960.

The above prose-poetic work with its mythical source also demonstrates the extent and depth of Borges's reading. Like another poet, W.B. Yeats, who is well-known for his incorporation of myths and legends into his work, Borges's expansive and esoteric mind never ceases to see the symbolic or dramatic possibilities of ancient myths, tales or anecdotes in the construction of his own poetry and tales. The uniqueness of the "pieces" from *Historia universal de la infamia*, however, and the reason the collection is translated and still read today when so much of his other early work has been repressed, is partly due to the vanguard approach to essay and story writing Borges begins to pursue. He begins to mix or overlap unique anecdotal and biographic material with vivid and concise poetic prose. At this phase in Borges's transition from poetry to prose, he contrasts sharply with the realistic fiction of some of his peers, heavily steeped in *realismo* or *criollismo,* the prose fiction movements that encouraged writers to focus on local color, costumes, and regional social and political concerns. Although some regional color and figures are dealt with by Borges in his prose pieces or pseudo-essays, his work also resembles, both visually and orally, the works twentieth-century readers have come to recognize as prose poetry.

Now, I do not intend an elaborate critical discussion here concerning what can or cannot be considered, or traditionally defined, as prose poetry. This subject has been thoroughly addressed in Mary Ann Caws and Hermine Riffaterre's *The Prose Poem in France*, with related information available in Robert Bly's essay "The Prose Poem as an Evolving Form" in his *Selected Poems*, Stephen Fredman's excellent discussion in *Poet's Prose: The Crisis in American Verse* and, most recently, an article by Brooke Horvath, "The Prose Poem and the Secret Life of Poetry." My interest lies more with it's twin: poetic prose. Yet, considering Borges's early experiments with the prose poem—"Paréntesis pasional," "La llama," "Rusia," "Insomnio," "Casa Elena," "Aldea [I]," and "Escaparte" as discussed earlier—references to it are valid in any broad discussion of Borges's short narratives in *Historia universal,* and especially in the later *El hacedor* (1960). Even considering his more "legitimate" stories in *Ficciones* and *El aleph,* the discerning critic can readily isolate certain passages and, at times, an overall structure that could only have been conceived and composed by someone with the instincts and sensibilities of a poet. As Guillermo Sucre writes in his important and highly acclaimed study, *Borges, el poeta,*

El Borges que reflexiona en sus relatos y en sus ensayos es el mismo que medita ensimismada o fervorosamente en sus poemas. Incluso hay páginas de su prosa que se imponen más por cierto arrebato, cierto juego libre del pensamiento y de la sensibilidad; hay en ellas tanta pasión como en su poesía. (17)

[The reflective Borges in his stories and essays is the same one that pensively or passionately meditates in his poems. There are even pages of his prose that are impressive more for a certain impulse, a certain free play of thought and a certain sensibility; there is as much passion in them as in his poetry.]

And more specifically concerning *El hacedor,* Sucre adds, "De todos sus libros, por el que siente más predilección es *El hacedor*, libro fundamentalmente poético tanto por los poemas como por las parábolas en prosa que lo integran" (18). ["Of all his books for which he feels more predilection is *El hacedor*, a fundamental poetic book so much for the poems as for the parables in prose that make up the book."]

In discussing *El hacedor* in his "Autobiographical Notes," Borges contradicts himself, as he is often wont to do, when he states: "Around 1954, I began writing short prose pieces—sketches and parables." As evidenced by published works, Borges had already attempted prose "sketches" and "parables," in his earliest fictional pieces twenty years earlier with *Historia universal.* As Borges continues to explain, he, once again, fails to address the fundamental value of his early work, his youthful attempts at both poetry and prose fiction—which included many prose poems as listed above—nor does he address the poetry at the foundation of many of his prose pieces:

One day, my friend Carlos Frías, of Emecé, told me he needed a new book for the series of my so-called complete works. I said I had none to give him, but Frías persisted, saying, "Every writer has a book if he only looks for it." Going through my drawers at home one idle Sunday, I began ferreting out uncollected poems and prose pieces, some of the latter going back to my days on *Crítica* [the 1930s]. These odds and ends, sorted out and ordered and published in 1960, became *El hacedor* [*The Maker*]. Remarkably, this book, which I accumulated rather than wrote, seems to me my most personal work and, to my taste, maybe my best. The explanation is only too easy: the pages of *El hacedor* contain no padding. Each piece was written for its own sake and out of an inner necessity. ("Autobiographical Notes")

The lyrical impulse, often the choice of poets driven by an "inner necessity" to express themselves personally, is certainly present in the collection, but the "prose pieces" in *El hacedor* are more than prose sketches and parables, a fact Zunilda Gertel first explores as early as 1967 in *Borges y su retorno a la poesía*, when she writes, "En *El hacedor*, plenitud de la obra borgiana, se logra la fusión de la teoría y la creación en verdaderos poemas en prosa" (64). ["In *El hacedor*, the pinnacle of Borgesian work, a fusion of theory and creation is achieved in genuine prose poems."] Several works from *El hacedor* firmly demonstrate a poet's fundamental approach to language and idea that merit at least some attention as poetry.

In the piece entitled "Dreamtigers," the work that lends its name to the English edition of *El hacedor* in 1964, Borges employs a poetic cadence of words and well-defined images on a theme that could be described as essentially a lamentation over the "act of creation." In it Borges desires to recreate a "real" tiger from his dreams, but the recreation of an ideal is impossible:

En la infancia yo ejercí con fervor la adoración del tigre. . . .
Pasó la infancia, caducaron los
tigres y su pasión, pero todavía están en mis sueños. . . .
y así: Dormido, me distrae un sueño cualquiera y de pronto sé que
es un sueño. Suelo pensar entonces: éste es un sueño, una pura
diversión de mi voluntad, y ya que tengo un ilimitado poder, voy
a causar un tigre.

   ¡Oh, incompetencia! Nunca mis sueños saben engendrar la
apetecida fiera. Aparece el tigre, eso sí, pero disecado, o endeble,
o con impuras variaciones de forma, o de un tamaño inadmisible,
o harto fugas, o tirando a perro o a pájaros.
                                    (*El Hacedor* 17-18)

[In my childhood I was a fervent worshiper of the tiger. . . .
Childhood passed away, and the tigers and my passion for them
grew old, but still they are in my dreams. . . . And so, as I sleep,
some dream beguiles me, and suddenly I know I am dreaming.
Then I think: this is a dream, a pure diversion of my will; and
now that I have unlimited power, I am going to cause a tiger.

Oh, incompetence! Never can my dreams engender the wild
beast I long for. The tiger indeed appears, but stuffed or flimsy,
or with impure variations of shape, or of an implausible size, or
all too fleeting, or with a touch of the dog or the bird.]

(*Dreamtigers* 24)

The author's persona speaks of what he assumes to be his unlimited
creative power as a "*diversión*" (or translated better still: a "re-creation
or pastime") of the will; however, the speaker's repeated attempts only
prove the poet's inability to artistically recreate from memory the
real tiger—to extract reality from a dream. In his long opening sentence, the reader clearly senses something of "poetry" in the elaborate
and stylized language that suggests more than the writer's desire to
inform, as in an essay or the development of plot in a short story. With
his dense and highly figurative language, Borges reveals the speaker's
desire to identify with the imaginary world of conquerors, embracing
the exotic tiger of, shall we say, the land of Attila the Hun, as opposed
to those tigers found in abundance in the jungles of his own continent.

The rich images of this extremely personal topic suggest that the
speaker longs to recreate in his dreams (in his poetry perhaps) the
real tiger he has only seen in cages or known to exist in books, and it
is a longing that supersedes all other desires, even the desire to have
a woman. Borges's protagonists are rarely men of passionate love or
action, except perhaps in the state of unconscious dream, or at the
mystical moment of death as in "El Sur" from *Ficciones*. The speaker of
"Dreamtigers" resembles more the *literato*, a man of letters, a poet, one
who is devoted to language and ideas, especially figurative or symbolic
ideas, but who suffers nevertheless the ineffectiveness of both memory
and language, regardless of how powerful and compelling they both
may be, to recreate the thoughts and interior visions of the intellect.

Thus, as a writer and a literato, Borges concerned himself with style, grammar and the distinct power of words. He, like earlier writers he admirers, such as Browne, Quevedo, De Quincey, Menard, Mallarmé and Valèry, possesses the extensive vocabularies of "vast encyclopedias" and etymological dictionaries, searching for exotic words that might create a rich beauty (along with an inevitable ambivalence) in his language. As such, the conclusion of "Dreamtigers" bears repeating, for it draws specific attention to Borges's interest in language. His speaker's experience is that of the poet—the frustrating attempt to find the "pure" word—concept or notion—that still retains its primal significance and which can translate pure emotion or sensation that often gets lost in language: "¡Oh, incompetencia! Nunca mis sueños saben engendrar la apetecida fiera" (*El hacedor* 18). ["Oh, incompetence! Never can my dreams engender the wild beast I long for" (*Dreamtigers* 24).

In "Dreamtigers," Borges also suggests the liabilities of language and the impoverishment of memory or dreams. Borges's poem is only one of his many treatises on the act of creation using the medium of words. Perhaps Borges's first treatment of the subject appears in an early ultraist essay from 1921, "Anatomía de mi 'Vltra,'" in which the young ultraísta, in enunciating the intentions of his "lyrical efforts," states,

> Yo busco en ellos la *sensación en sí*, y no la descripción de las premisas espaciales o temporales que la rodean. Siempre ha sido costumbre de los poetas ejecutar una reversión del proceso emotivo que se había operado en su conciencia, es decir, volver de la emoción a la sensación, y de ésta a los agentes que la causaron. Yo—y nótese bien que hablo de intentos y no de realizaciones colmadas— anhelo un arte que traduzca la emoción desnuda, depurada de los adicionales datos que la preceden. Un arte que rehúyes a lo dérmico, lo metafísico y los últimos planos egocéntricos o mordaces. (See essay in Part Two)

> [In them I am seeking *sensation itself* and not the description of the space or time premises that surround it. It has always been the habit of poets to carry out a reversal of the emotional process that

had taken effect in his conscience; that is to say, to come back from emotion to sensation, and from there to the agents that caused the emotion. I—and note well that I am speaking of intentions and not of fulfilled realizations—long for an art that translates naked emotion, purified of the additional data that precedes it. An art that avoids flesh and blood reality, the metaphysical, and the ultimate levels of caustic egocentricity.]

To accomplish this, Borges proposes "two indispensable means: rhythm and metaphor." Very few critics would deny that in this statement at the age of twenty-one, Borges prefigures by several decades much of the artistic intentions behind his mature work: the avoidance of reality-based, confessional or autobiographical material, and the expression of his life-long affair with metaphor and rhythmic manipulation of language to achieve a poetic affect—although, curiously enough, the metaphysical approach to literature would come to play a major part in his work. It seems, then, that thirty-some years later, Borges, in "Dream-tigers," continues his probing into the subject: the act of creating images through language. He's explored it in pseudo-essay formats, in a story such as "Las ruinas circulares," from *Ficciones*, and here in prose poetry. Whether or not Borges chooses to call it a prose poem does not change the fact that the skills and temperament of a poet were required for the rich suggestiveness in the sketch and for the essentially metaphoric and symbolic results in his expression of erudite and deeply felt ideas.

Borges, the Ideal Literary Man

As with all writers, a look into the type of writers Borges admired is another way of understanding, more or less, the style of writing he himself aspired to achieve. In a little known early essay, "Sir Thomas Browne," published in the magazine *Proa* ns 7, in February 1925 and then collected in *Inquisiciones* (1925), Borges characterizes the ideal literary man as exemplified by Browne. What seems important about the essay is the suggestion that Borges's ideal characterization, prefigured by Ben Jonson, prefigures Borges himself:

En Sir Thomas Browne se adunaron el literato y el místico: el *vates* y el *gramaticus*, para expresarlo con Latin fijeza. El tipo literario--prefigurado por Ben Jonson, en quien campean ya todos los signos de su clase: el atarearse con la gloria, la reverencia y la preocupación del lenguaje, la urdidura prolija de teorías para legitimar la labor, el sentirse hombre de una época, el estudio de otros idiomas y hasta la presidencia de un cenáculo y el organizar banderías--es manifiesto en él. Su belleza es docta y lograda. . . . Fue novador, pero no a semejanza de los que siguen el asombro y el sacar de quicio al leyente; fué clásico, pero sin mimetismo apasionado ni rigideces de ritual. El gigantesco vocabulario de Shakespeare cayó sobre él como una capa y su ademán fué fácil y noble bajo la blasonadora riqueza. (4-5)

[In Sir Thomas Browne the literary man and the mystic merge: the *vates* and the *grammaticus* to express it with Latin certainty. The type of literary man—prefigured by Ben Jonson, in whom already abound all the signs of his class: an obsession with glory, the reverence for and preoccupation with language, the prolix plotting of theories in order to legitimize the work, the sense a man has of belonging to a period, the study of other languages and even the organizer of a coterie and movements/parties—is manifest in him. The beauty of his work is erudite and well executed. . . .He was an innovator, but not like those whose aim is to astonish or to make the reader go wild. He was a classicist, but without impassioned mimicry nor without ritual rigidity. The huge vocabulary of Shakespeare draped over him like a cape and his style was simple and noble under the boasting richness.]

Taken one step further, Christ, in his study of the text, draws upon this detailed description to list those writers who Borges not only admired but "tried himself to approximate":

The leading concerns of Borges's life—literature, learning, metaphysics—are here ascribed to Browne, but we can go a step further by seeing that as Jonson prefigured Browne, so Browne prefigures Borges, and therefore, it is exactly the trinity of roles—*grammaticus, vates, poeta doctus*—which defines the literary figure for Borges, whether that man be called Sir Thomas Browne, Pierre Menard, Herbert Quain, Paul Valéry, or Jorge Luis Borges. Writers evincing a predilection for any one of these three roles always interest him; writers combining all three stimulate him most and are who we would ordinarily call influences. For my purpose it is enough to see that this last group provides the largest source of all his allusions. (142)[7]

I must emphasize here, with regards to my study, that from the list of writers Christ identifies, the key figures Valéry and De Quincey, writers who have proven to figure the most as influences on Borges, are as much poets as they are prose writers. Each writer, I might add, has experimented extensively with the writing of prose poetry.

In most studies of the philosopher-poet Valéry, the discussion revolves around the essential relationship between his prose writing and his poetry. As Alice Coléno states in reference to Valéry's prose poetry: the "multiplicity of meanings" in his work signifies that, for Valéry, "poetry in contradiction to prose is not written to communicate a definite idea, but a shock, an emotion, of almost mystical quality which lives for its own sake and not as an intellectual expression" (280). Of course, this supposition is not to imply that an excellent short story written under the influence of realism cannot claim a multiplicity of meanings, but for writers like Borges and Valéry, who are essentially poets, the plot, topic, characterization and continuity of a story often yield to figurative language, image, allusion and mysticism in the expression of an idea—ideas often incapable of being expressed using techniques of literary realism. Moreover, Harold Watts could just as easily be writing about Borges when, in his study of Valéry's prose essays—that do not "pretend to come from any desk but that of a poet"—he adds,

---

7 See Christ's *The Narrow Act* for an intriguing, extensive discussion of the influential connections between De Quincey and Borges.

In England and America, we are more used to the poet who, when he expresses himself in prose, speaks simply as a man of sense. Therefore, we must not forget, when we read Valéry's essays on literature, painting, and politics, that here speaks a *poet* of sense. . . .Should one not hesitate to say that Valéry's prose exhibits a central concern for the creative activity of the poet of sense? (292)

For Borges, perhaps, an even more accurate title might be: the poet of ideas.

By way of completing the equation, when the great Italian writer Italo Calvino speaks out on Borges in an article entitled "La fortuna de Borges," he too finds occasion to point out the influential link between Borges's prose and poetry, as well as to discuss how Borges's work, governed by the intellect, is comparable to that of Valéry:

Sólo puedo responder apelando a mi memoria, tratando de reconstruir lo que ha significado para mí la experiencia de Borges desde los comienzos hasta hoy. Experiencia cuyo punto de partida y punto de apoyo son dos libros, *Ficciones* y *El aleph*, es decir, ese género literario particular que es el cuento borgiano, para pasar después al Borges ensayista, no siempre bien separable del narrador, y al Borges poeta, que contiene a menudo núcleos de cuentos y en todo caso un núcleo de pensamiento, un diseño de ideas.

Empezaré por el motivo de adhesión más general, es decir, el haber reconocido en Borges una idea de la litertura como mundo construido y gobernado por el intelecto. Esta idea va contra la corriente principal de la literatura mundial de nuestro siglo, que toma en cambio una dirección opuesta, es decir, quiere darnos el equivalente de la acumulación magmática de la existencia en el lenguaje, en el tejido de los acontecimientos, en la exploración del inconsciente. Pero hay también una tendencia de la literatura de nuestro siglo, ciertamente minoritaria, que ha tenido su sostenedor más ilustre en Paul Valéry--pienso sobre todo en el Valéry prosista y pensador—que apunta a un desquite del orden mental sobre el caos del mundo. (viii, par. 4-5)

[I can only respond by calling upon my memory, trying to reconstruct what the experience of Borges has meant to me from the beginning until now. It's an experience whose point of departure and base are two books: *Ficciones* and *The Aleph*, in other words, that particular literary genre which is the Borgesian story, in order to move on to Borges, the essayist, not always easily separable from the narrator, and Borges the poet, which often contains the nucleus of stories, and in any case the nucleus of thought, an outline of ideas.

I will start with the most general reason for adherence, which is to say, having recognized in Borges an idea of literature as a world constructed and governed by the intellect. This idea goes against the main current of world literature in our century, which on the contrary takes an opposite direction, in other words, it wants to give us the equivalent of the magmatic accumulation of existence in language, in the weaving of events, in the exploration of the unconscious. But there is also a literary trend in our century, certainly not widespread, which has had its most celebrated proponent in Paul Valéry—I'm thinking above all of Valéry the prose writer and thinker—which points to the intellect's revenge on the chaos of the world.]

Calvino recognizes that, in effect, through the amalgamation of various genres, Borges has created his own personal genre that does not fit squarely in poetry, essay or prose fiction but is, in fact, an "overlap" of genres.

Undoubtedly, poets like Valéry and Mallarmé figure greatly in any discussion of influences with respect to Borges's mystical and intellectual approach to writing. Evelyn Fishburn and Psiche Hughes in their *A Dictionary of Borges* point out that

[l]ike Mallarmé, from whom he [Borges] derived many of his artistic views, Valéry regarded poetry as the result of a long and patient intellectual process. In an essay dedicated to Valéry ["Valéry como símbolo" in *Otras inquisiciones* (1952)], Borges referred to the intricacy and sensitivity of his work by describing him as a "personification of the labyrinths of the spirit" (253).

Fishburn and Hughes then cite Valéry's poem "Le Cimetière marin" that draws further similarities, both in theme and in style, between Borges and Valéry, suggesting the possibility that even Pierre Menard himself was influenced by Valéry. Like Valéry, the intellectual process of "literaturizing" requires as much a search through language, thought and ideas as through the subconscious images and emotions of the heart.

As a literary man, Borges's greatest asset is language. Yet, in applying it, in seeking that obscure, primal word from his erudite readings, in seeking a word that, with all its rich ambivalence, might take the place of the real thing and express raw, naked emotion, he knows he runs the risk of achieving just the opposite effect: vagueness and obscurity. But Borges also knows that words carry within themselves the insistence of meaning, or at least the possibility of it, and that language—spoken, written or silent—offers the only chance for self-knowledge. In another early essay on Francisco Gómez de Quevedo, "Menoscabo y Grandeza de Quevedo," published in *Revista de Occidente* ns 17 in November 1924, Borges praises the "verbal dexterity" and multifarious talent of the great Spanish writer, and draws attention to his "apparent multitude of intentions," while promptly pointing out as well his concomitant "austere distrust in the efficiency of language." Of course, once again Borges could be speaking of himself here, and, as with his essay on Sir Thomas Browne, one might appropriate Borges's discussion of Quevedo's multi-genre talents and use it to describe Borges himself:

> La artimaña de quien lo despedaza según la varia actividad que ejerció no es apta para concertar la despareja plenitud de su obra. Desbandar a Quevedo en irreconciliables figuraciones de novelista, de poeta, de teólogo, de sufridor estoico y de eventual pasquinador, es empeño baldío si no adunamos luego con firmeza todas esas vislumbres. Quevedo a mi entender, fué innumerable como un árbol, pero no menos homogéneo. (50)

> [The ruse of he who pieces him [Quevedo] together according to the varied activities he practiced is not apt to determine the un-

even fullness of his work. To disperse Quevedo into irreconcilable suppositions of novelist, poet, theologian, of suffering stoic and eventual epigrammatist, is an empty effort if we don't straightaway unite with resolve all those appearances. Quevedo, to my way of thinking, was immeasurable like a tree, but no less homogeneous.

What Borges focuses on throughout the essay is the "tenacious intellectualism that was in Quevedo's mind:

> Fue perfecto en las metáforas, en las antítesis, en la adjetivación; es decir, en aquellas disciplinas de la literatura cuya felicidad o maladanza es discernible por la inteligencia. El ejercicio intelectual es hábil para establecer la virtud de esas artimañas retóricas. ("Menoscabo" 252)

> [He was perfect in the use of metaphors, in antithesis, in employing adjectives; that is, in those disciplines of literature whose felicity or misfortune is discernible by the intelligentsia. Intellectual exercise is handy to establish the virtue of those rhetorical tricks.]

Yet, it is in this concluding comment, in speaking of Quevedo's mistrust of "la inconsecuente virtud de las palabras prestigiosas," ["the consequent virtue of prestigious words"], that Borges most closely approximates his own attitude towards creative writing:

> El poeta no puede ni prescindir enteramente de esas palabras que parecen decir la intimidad más honda, ni reducirse a sólo barajarlas. Quevedo las menudeó en estrofas galantes y el no poder echar mano a ellas en sus composiciones jocosas motivó tal vez el raudal de metáforas y de intuiciones reales que hay en su burlería. Le atareó mucho lo problemático del lenguaje propio del verso. ("Menoscabo" 253-54)

> [The poet cannot dispense entirely with those words that seem to express the deepest intimacy, nor limit himself to only shuffle

them. Quevedo repeated them in flirtatious strophes and not having them available for his waggish compositions, perhaps motivated a stream of metaphors and royal intuitions found in his mockery. The problematic of the language proper to verse kept him busy.]

Perhaps Borges's approach towards the "problematic" of language is best represented in the poem "Los espejos" ["Mirrors"] and collected both in *El hacedor* and the English version of the collection *Dreamtigers*. If Borges's poems and stories, as many contend, "mirror," at times, the chaotic state of the universe, it is due as much to the "design of ungraspable architecture" that is reality itself as to the impossibility of unifying words with essences, dreams with reality:

Dios (he dado en pensar) pone un empeño
En toda esa inasible arquitectura
Que edifica la luz con la tersura
Del cristal y la sombra con el sueño

Dios ha creado las noches que se arman
De sueños y las formas del espejo
Para que el hombre sienta que es reflejo
Y vanidad. . . .(*El hacedor* 83)

[God (I keep thinking) has taken pains
To design that ungraspable architecture
Reared by every dawn from the gleam
Of a mirror, by darkness from a dream.

God has created nighttime, which he arms
With dreams, and mirrors, to make clear
To man he is a reflection and a mere
Vanity. . . .] (*Dreamtigers* 60)

Citing "Mirrors" in his book *Borges and the Kabbalah*, Jaime Alazraki includes an excellent and thorough study of the importance of mirrors in Borges's literary universe. He concludes that, for Borges, the "illusory reality that mirrors produce becomes in turn a profound mirror of our own universe since our image of the world is just a fabrication of the human mind" (109). The universe, one might say, is only a reflection of our intellect. But the more a learned and inquisitive intellect, *a poet*, Borges might say, tries to capture in the glass a more complex illusion of reality, the more he comes closest to revealing the secrets and mysteries that make up human existence.

Like Valéry, Borges has once again proven himself to be, first and foremost, a poet—not one that works best in verse, but rather, one whose refined poetic skills are better showcased in his erudite prose fiction. Some claim that his elaborate, hyper-intellectual themes weigh too heavy on his verse, resulting in a "lack of music," but there is as well the Borges that simply enjoys words, a poet who can poeticize and find meaning even in a subject as basic as toenails—though I find the philosophic implications of mortality in "Las uñas" {"Toenails"] acutely unnerving. In this prose poem, he also prefigures the great Chilean poet Pablo Neruda's poems "Ode to my Socks" and "Ode to Salt":

Dóciles medias los halagan de día y zapatos de cuero clavetea
dos los fortifican, pero los dedos de mi pie no quieren saberlo.
No les interesa otra cosa que emitir uñas: láminas córneas,
semitransparentes y elásticas, para defenderse ¿de quién?
Brutos y desconfiados como ellos solos, no dejan un segundo
de preparar ese tenue armamento. Rehúsan el universo y el
éxtasis para seguir elaborandó sin fin unas vanas puntas,
que cercenan y vuelven a cercenar los bruscos tijerazos de
Solingen. A los noventa días crepusculares de encierro
prenatal establecieron esa única industria. Cuando yo esté
guardado en la Recoleta, en una casa de color ceniciento
provista de flores secas y de talismanes, continuarán su
terco trabajo, hasta que los modere la corrupción. Ellos, y la
barba en mi cara. (*El hacedor* 21)

[Soft stockings coddle them by day and nail-bossed leather
shoes buttress them, but my toes refuse to pay attention.

Nothing interests them but emitting toenails, horny plates, semitransparent and elastic, to defend themselves—from whom? Stupid and mistrustful as they alone can be, they never for a moment stop readying that tenuous armament. They reject the universe and its ecstasy to keep forever elaborating useless sharp ends, which rude Solingen scissors snip over and over again. Ninety days along, in the dawn of prenatal confinement, they established that singular industry. When I am laid away, in an ash-colored house provided with dead flowers and amulets, they will still go on with their stubborn task, until they are moderated by decay. They—and the beard on my face.] (*Dreamtigers* 26)

As simple as Rimbaud's investigation of colors, here is Borges, the philosophical poet deferring to the seeming superiority of the base functions of the body. In this singular prose sketch or prose poem, it is evident to the critical eye and ear that Borges does not wish to segregate by genre his poetic impulses, but wishes to blend and to extend into prose his ingrained and instinctive "poetic" tendencies, much, I might add, as he did in his earliest works during his flirtation with Ultraísmo.

Brooke Horvath provides a good technical and textual criterion for discerning when a prose author like Borges overlaps with poetry and vice versa:

For like a child whose mother is for obvious reasons known but whose father is not, the prose poem is so manifestly an off-spring of prose (just look at it) that its poetic parentage is liable to be questioned or forgotten.

As for the form's inheritance from its poetic father, one might simply say, "just listen to it!" Because, really, don't we know poetry when we hear it, read it, experience it? (11-14)

Borges himself has taken a similar stand in an essay "Ejercicio de análisis" ["Analytical Exercise"] published in December 1925 in *Proa*. There he says,

Ni vos ni yo ni Jorge Federico Guillermo Hegel sabemos definir la poesía. Nuestra insapiencia, sin embargo, es sólo verbal y podemos arrimarnos a lo que famosamente declaró San Agustín acerca del tiempo: *¿Qúe es el tiempo? Si nadie me lo pregunta, lo sé; si tengo que decírselo a alguien, lo ignoro.* Yo tampoco sé lo que es la poesía, aunque so diestro en descubrirla en cualquier lugar: en la conversación, en la letra de un tango, en libros de metafísica, en dichos y hasta en algunos versos. (46)

[Neither you nor I nor George Frederick William Hegel know how to define poetry. Our inability, however, is only verbal and we can approach Saint Augustine's famous declaration concerning time: *What is time? If no one asks, I know it; if I must tell it to someone, I am ignorant.* Neither do I know what a poem is, although I'm an expert at discovering it any place: in conversation, in the words of a tango, in metaphysical books, in sayings and even in some verses.]

Does the reader not see and hear in certain works by Borges the subtle amalgamation of poetic sensibilities taking place, even when that which is perceived remains undefinable? Sucre writes in his study that when Borges was asked "si se consideraba escritor o más bien poeta" ["whether he considered himself a writer or more a poet"], Borges answered, "Un poeta, claro está. Creo que no soy más que eso. Un poeta torpe, pero un poeta, espero" (25). ["Of course, a poet. I don't believe I'm more than that. A clumsy poet, but a poet, I hope."]

With this direct, personal recognition that Borges has always considered himself a poet, the reader of this study might simply say, "Enough said." However, a little more needs to be presented to reinforce the connection between his poetic self and the prose fiction writer that the literary world celebrates. It has been this study's contention that, precisely, Borges's poetic "self"—which includes his youthful ultraist poetic "self"—brings to his prose a concise syntax, an economy of speech characterized by repetition of key words and images, assonance, a poet's penchant for closure and figures of speech, and an overall manipulation of language to achieve a lyrical aim. For example, look how repetition, or "recurring figures of sound," play a dominant role in one of Borges's earliest prose poems, "Escaparate" ["Shop Window"], published in the Spanish magazine *Tableros* in January 1922. In the work, Borges speaks of another "heroic figure" who loves (instead of kills like Billy the Kid) from a distance:

> Semejante a ese guerrero chino que encima de las olas espumosas y malvas saluda la mansión donde los gestos de su hijito florecen.
> Semejante al guerrero chino que se dirige, gracias al dragón monstruoso y pueril, hacia la costa adorable.
> Y su esposa le tiende el cuerpito radioso y vivo del niño.
> Pero siempre el espacio dorado los separa, siempre el héroe venera los suyos sin lograr abrazarlos.
> Así yo ignoraré mis amores.
> Así yo deberé desconocerte. (see poem in Part Two)

> [Like that Chinese warrior that on the mauve and foaming waves salutes the mansion where the gestures of his little son flourish.
> Like the Chinese warrior that heads, thanks to the monstrous and puerile dragon, towards the venerable coast.
> And his wife extends to him the small and radiant living body of the child.
> But always the golden space keeps them apart, the hero always honors his own unable to embrace them.
> Like this I shall never know my loves.
> Like this I must disown you.]

The poem wants to be both metaphysical conceit and mythical tale. Notice the decidedly prosaic lines that push the poem beyond verse but also the unique choices of adjectives—"flowering gestures," a dragon both "monstrous and childlike"—that, like the unique adjectival phrases in the Billy Harrigan sketch, push the prose full circle towards poetic statement.

Moreover, here, too, is Borges's characteristic closure—thought provoking, abruptly shocking in its allusive and symbolic overtures—which can be found in much of his work. In "Escaparate," the closure is an abrupt and discomforting analogy between the Chinese warrior and the solitary, loveless speaker (the writer?); it is, perhaps, an ending that first introduces one of Borges's recurring themes: the lonely and isolated man—the writer—who is unable to love or be loved in his solitary struggle to create art. Borges once wrote, "La vida del escritor es una vida solitaria" (Ferrer 89). ["A writer's life is a solitary life"]. It is a theme that, later in his career, will come to be treated more metaphysically and philosophically in his prose fiction, in works such as "Borges y yo," itself a very short "piece" that one could argue is more prose poem than narrative—or perhaps prose sketch? It is collected in *El Hacedor* (1960) which is often described as a collection of poems, short essays, and literary sketches and divided fairly evenly between prose and verse.

Indeed, closure is central in identifying many of Borges's prose sketches for their poetic intentions. As is the case with most of his work, Borges's closures are often surprising, emotionally charged, and intellectually (if not aesthetically) provocative. Traditionally, closure remains central to the emotional power of poetry, and in a prose poem it is a key sign that poetic energy is at work. In *The Prose Poem in France: Theory and Practice*, Mary Ann Caws and Hermine Riffaterre discuss the importance of closure in identifying poetry written in prose: a text can be poetic without being closed, but it will become a poem—something quite different—only if it has a well-marked beginning and end that turn it into an organized whole" (100). In addition to closure, any definition of the prose poem also insists on the need for brevity, as Michel Beaujour writes: "Shortness presents at least a presumption of lyrical energy at work, a presumption which may be confirmed by the presence of specifically lyrical features, such as broken rhythm and imagery" (cited by Caws and Riffaterre in *The Prose Poem in France* 42).

Borges confirmed as early as 1921 in his Ultraísmo manifesto "Proclama" his predilection for brevity in all his writing efforts. There he denounces "señoritos de la cultura Latina. . ." ["young dandies of the Latin culture"]:

todos quieren realizar obras apelmazadas i perennes. Todos viven en su autobiografía, todos creen en su personalidad esa mescolanza de percepciones entreveradas de salpicaduras de citas, de admiraciones provocadas i puntiaguda lirastenia. . . .Escriben dramas i novelas abarrotadas de encrucijadas espirituales, de gestos culminantes i de apoteosis donde se remansa definitivamente el vivir . . . .Idiotez que les hace urdir un soneto para colocar una línea, i decir en doscientas páginas lo cabedero en dos renglones. (Desde ya puede asegurarse que la novela esa cosa maciza engendrada por la supostición (sic) del yo va a desaparecer, como ha sucedido con la epopeya i otras categorias dilatadas.) (See poem in Part Two)

[they all want to produce stodgy and everlasting works. All of them live within their autobiography. All of them believe in their personality, that jumble of perceptions intermingled with spattered quotations of provoked admirations and pointed "lirastenia" [elaborately beautified lyricism]. . . .They write dramas and novels crammed with spiritual dilemmas, with lofty gestures and grand finales that absolutely stagnate life. . . .Stupidity forces them to weave a sonnet in order to create one line and to say in two hundred pages what can be said in two lines. (As of now we can already declare that the novel, that massive thing engendered by the assumed "I," will disappear, as happened with the epic and other drawn out genres.)

True to his passionately expressed, youthful conviction, Borges never wrote a play, a very long story, nor a novel, and the majority of his stories and other prose pieces remain extremely brief—most often a page or two. Of course, simply because a piece of prose is brief doesn't necessarily mean that poetic energy is at work, but Borges's dense meditations are so highly wrought into language, so precise in their construction, that the combination of subject, language, brevity and closure strongly suggest Borges's poetic proclivity is influential in the fabrication of the prose work—and, I might add, the same energy Borges demonstrates to be at work in much of his juvenile poetry. Italo Calvino dwells at length upon this aspect of succinctness in Borges's work in his article "La Fortuna de Borges."

> Borges es un maestro del escribir breve. Consigue condensar en textos siempre de poquísimas páginas una riqueza extraordinaria de sugestiones poéticas y de pensamiento: hechos narrados o sugeridos aperturas vertiginosas sobre el infinito, e ideas, ideas, ideas. Cómo se realiza esta densidad, sin la más mínima congestión, en los párrafos más cristalinos, sobrios y airosos; cómo esa manera de contar sintéticamente y en escorzo lleva a un lenguaje de pura precisión y concreción, cuya inventiva se manifiesta en la variedad de ritmos, en los movimientos sintácticos, en los adjetivos siempre inesperados y sorprendentes: este es el milagro estilístico, sin igual en la lengua española, del cual sólo Borges posee el secreto. (8)

> [Borges is a master of the art of succinct writing. He manages to condense in texts of very few pages an extraordinary richness of poetic suggestion and thought: narrated or suggested events vertiginous insights (openings) regarding infinity, and ideas, ideas, ideas. How does he achieve this density, without the slightest congestion, in the most crystalline, serious, and airy paragraphs; how does that synthetic narration and foreshortening lead to a language of pure precision and concreteness, whose inventiveness appears in the variety of rhythms, in the syntactic movements, in the always unexpected and surprising adjectives: This is the stylistic miracle, without equal in the Spanish language, of which only Borges possesses the secret].

Of course, this study contends that Borges's stylistic miracle is no secret at all, but owes much of its poetic resonance to the fact that, at the core of his creative talents, he is fundamentally and spiritually a poet of prose.

Yet clearly, a study of Borges's early disregarded ultraist poetry has no stake in the argument for Borges's inclusion in the ranks of twentieth-century vanguard prose poets, for, fundamentally, his work stands slightly apart from "classic" examples of Modern Latin American poetry. The focus in this study has been squarely on Guillermo Sucre's suggestion that perhaps all of Borges's creations are "essentially poetic." Considering Borges's inclination towards the short poetic prose tale which extends through his mature collection, *El oro de los tigres* (1972), Sucre concludes that the poetry

> encierra profundas correspondencias con toda la obra de Borges. Leer al Borges de los ensayos y de las ficciones es también leerlo a partir de sus poemas. Toda la creación borgiana, por otra parte, ¿no es essencialmente poética? La concentración, la intensidad verbal, el juego libre de la imaginación, la lucidez que es también rapto, la proyección de figuras míticas son, en todo caso, rasgos comunes y dominantes in los tres campos de su escritura. (22)

> [contains deep connections with all the works of Borges. Reading Borges of the essays and the fictions is also to read him beginning with his poems. On the other hand, aren't all of Borges's creations essentially poetic? The concentration, the verbal intensity, the free play of the imagination, the lucidity that is also rapture, the projection of mythical figures are, in any case, common and dominate features in the three areas of his writings.]

Yet, Borges's early involvement with the prose poem is often overlooked in studies of his later fictive works; as already suggested, this choice is perhaps because critics have not seen much of his true ultraist poetry. But his early quasi-attempts at the prose poem clearly substantiates what some critics insist to be his great admiration for French writers—all of whom were prose poets: Rimbaud, Verlaine, Mallarmé and Valéry. The greatest poets of nineteenth-century French literature have traditionally approached the writing of prose with the same passion for language, invention and expression they employ in their verse. Still, this study wants to suggest his work's *relationship* to the prose poem genre in so far as it highlights the debt owed to his poetic "sensibilities" in the creation of his short fictive pieces. It tries to show how Borges's "short prose pieces, sketches and parables" share some basic features of the French creation—*le poème en prose.*

Indeed, Emir Rodriquez Monegal, in his 1978 biography of Borges, strongly emphasizes the often overlooked importance of French literature on Borges's writing. He devotes a whole chapter tracing Borges's close affinity with certain French writers, most specifically the special importance Mallarmé had on the young writer's artistic persona:

> In later years, Borges quoted Mallarmé occasionally and always in an important context. His persona (the poet who is totally dedicated to writing and to whom the world makes sense only in a book) influenced Borges's own concept of literature and of the literary mind. Traces of Mallarmé can be detected in the invention of Pierre Menard. (*A Literary Biography* 122)

Of course, Borges already spoke best for himself when he revealed to Jean Milleret in 1970 his appreciation of the French:

> It was especially Rimbaud whom I loved to recite, and a forgotten poet, Ephraim Michael. I read them all in a yellow-covered book published by the *Mercure de France*, an anthology of French modern poetry where you could find Stuart Merrill, obviously Mallarmé, Rimbaud, Verlaine of course, and several minor poets of the symbolist movement. I read, I reread all that. . . .I knew many poems by heart. (20-21)

Monegal summarizes the debt Borges owes to his reading of French writers in the following manner:

> French literature became the second most important of his youth. Critics have followed Borges's lead in underplaying the importance of French literature in shaping his writings, but the truth is that, in spite of his preference for England and English letters, and without ever publicly admitting it, Borges was influenced by the concept of logical discourse and the subtle reasoning of French essayists. He also learned from France's poets and short-story writers. (*A Literary Biography* 117)

Throughout the 1920s and '30s, as Borges was completing his transition from poetry, pseudo-essays and critical reviews towards prose pieces, narratives and story, his youthful readings of French poets, provided for him at least one of the various roads on which to travel. Already working in *vers libre* in all his poetry and prose poems and steadily working in the essay format, Borges's characteristic poetic prose or poetic "pseudo-essays" became the logical stepping stones towards the development of his fiction. Prose works by French poets like Mallarmé or Valèry—not to slight the prose of DeQuincey or Chesterton—displayed for him all the poetic possibilities in prose. They showed how a writer could crystallize his thoughts into fewer sentences while retaining a portion of the "music" so essential to poetry. Borges's achievement was a tightly wrought prose that has all the metaphoric and symbolic concentration of poetry—a poetic prose, if you will—that made him one of the most admired prose stylists of his day.

Part Two
The Early Writing

The Early Verse and Prose Poetry, 1919 to 1923

Presented in chronological order is the early verse and prose poetry of Jorge Luis Borges written between the ages of 20 and 24 and published in Spanish and Argentine literary magazines of his time. Few English language readers of Borges have ever seen these poems for only a handful have been reprinted in English and American studies of the author. The majority of these poems have remained lost, buried in libraries and private collections since their initial publication. Borges disregarded them and included only four of his ultraist poems in his first collection of poetry and in his later poetry anthologies. I have indicated those he did ollect, along with the record of their many alterations through the years rendering them almost completely different poems from the original magazine version you will find here. The English translations are by myself and my father, Marcelino Padilla Ramos. Borges wrote the following poems during the exciting time of Vanguardismo, when he felt impassioned by the discovery of his creativity, his gift of self-expression, and his need to give voice to both his intellectual and emotional ideas. They reflect accurately the creative aesthetics of a young Borges, the ultraísta poet, who embraced Ultraísmo with enthusiasm during his time in Spain, even helping to introduce and perpetuate its principles in Argentina upon his return in 1921. The poems should give the reader some idea of his developing aesthetic as both a writer of poetry and eventually, prose while residing in Spain, most importantly Palma de Majorca, Sevilla, Madrid, as well as in Buenos Aires. To help demonstrate the Ultraísmo spirit of the time, I have interspersed plates showing the covers of some of the magazines of the time and even a few of the poems themselves as they appeared in the magazines. The initial poem is Borges's first published poem written at the age of nineteen while still under the sway of Walt Whitman. Like Whitman, who often wrote verses too long to fit the standard publication pages of magazines and books, some of Borges's poems require turnovers [t/o] of lines. However, when the work is clearly a prose poem, a genre with which young Borges experimented, turnovers are not inserted in the prose passage.

HIMNO DEL MAR

Para Adriano del Valle

Yo he ansiado un himno del Mar con ritmos amplios como las
        olas que gritan; [t/o]
Del Mar cuando el sol en sus aguas cual bandera escarlata
        flamea; [t/o]
Del Mar cuando besa los pechos dorados de vírgenes playas
        que aguarda sedientas; [t/o]
Del Mar al aullar sus mesnadas, al lanzar sus blasfemias los
        vientos, [t/o]
Cuando brilla en las aguas de acero la luna bruñida y
        sangrienta; [t/o]
Del Mar cuando vierte sobre él su tristeza sin fondo
    La Copa de Estrellas.

Hoy he bajado de la montaña al valle
y del valle hasta el mar.
El camino fué largo como un beso.
Los almendros lanzaban madejas azuladas de sombra sobre
        la Carretera [t/o]
y, al terminar el valle, el sol
gritó rubios Golcondas sobre tu glauca selva: ¡Mar!
¡Hermano, Padre, Amado. . .!
Entro al jardín enorme de tus aguas y nado lejos de la tierra.
Las olas vienen con cimera frágil de espuma,
En fuga hacia el fracaso. Hacia la costa,
con sus picachos rojos,
con sus casas geométricas,
con sus palmeras de juguete,
que ahora se han vuelto lívidos y absurdos como recuerdos
    yertos!
Yo estoy contigo, Mar. Y mi cuerpo tendido como un arco
lucha contra tus músculos raudos. Sólo tú existes.
Mi alma desecha todo su pasado
Como en nórtico cielo que se deshoja en copos
    errantes!
Oh instante de plenitud magnífica;
Antes de conocerte, Mar hermano,

Largamente he vagado por errantes calles azules con oriflamas de
                                        faroles   [t/o]
Y en la sagrada media noche yo he tejido guirnaldas
De besos sobre carnes y labios que se ofrendaban,
Solemnes de silencio,
En una floración
Sangrienta. . .
Pero ahora yo hago don a los vientos
de todas esas cosas pretéritas,
pretéritas. . .Sólo tú existes.
Atlético y desnudo. Sólo este fresco aliento y estas olas,
y las Copas Azules, y el milagro de las Copas Azules.
(Yo he soñado un himno del Mar con ritmos amplios como las
                                    olas jadeantes.)   [t/o]
Ansío aún crearte un poema
Con la cadencia adámica de tu oleaje,
Con tu salino y primeral aliento,
Con el trueno de las anclas sonoras ante Thulés ebrias de luz
                                        y lepra,   [t/o]
Con voces marineras, luces y ecos
De grietas abismales
Donde tus raudas manos monjiles acarician constantemente a
                                    los muertos. . .   [t/o]
Un himno
Constelado de imágenes rojas, lumínicas.
Oh mar! oh mito! oh sol! oh largo lecho!
Y sé por que te amo. Sé que somos muy viejos.
Que ambos nos conocemos desde siglos.
Sé que en tus aguas venerandas y rientes ardió la aurora de
                                    la Vida.   [t/o]
(En la ceniza de una tarde terciaria vibré por vez primera
                                    en tu seno).   [t/o]
Oh proteico, yo he salido de tí.
¡Ambos encadenados y nómadas;
Ambos con una sed intensa de estrellas;
Ambos con esperanza y desengaños;
Ambos, aire, luz, fuerza, obscuridades;
Ambos con nuestro vasto deseo y ambos con nuestra grande
                                    miseria!   [t/o]

Grecia ns 37, Sevilla, 31 Dec. 1919   Jorge Luis Borges.

HYMN OF THE SEA

For Adriano del Valle.

I've longed for a hymn of the Sea with vast rhythms like waves
that scream; [t/o]
Of the Sea when the sun glimmers upon the water like a scarlet
banner; [t/o]
Of the Sea when it kisses the golden breasts of virgin beaches
waiting thirsty and dry; [t/o]
Of the Sea at the howling of its forces, as the winds hurl their
blasphemes, [t/o]
When the bloody and polished moon shines in the steel-colored
waters; [t/o]
Of the Sea when upon it is spilled the fathomless grief of
The Cup of Stars.

Today I have come down from the mountain to the valley
and from the valley to the sea.
The road was long like a kiss.
The almond trees cast skeins of bluish shade over the highway
and, at the end of the valley, the sun
screamed blond Golcondas over your sea-green jungle: Sea!
Brother, Father, Lover. . .!
I enter the enormous garden of your waters and swim far from
the land. [t/o]
The waves come with fragile crests of foam,
In flight towards destruction. Towards the shore,
with its red peaks,
with its geometric houses,
with its toy palm trees,
that now have turned pale and absurd like rigid
memories!
I am with you, Sea. And my body stretched like a bow
struggles against your swift muscles. Only you exist.
My soul discards all its past
Like a Nordic sky that defoliates in errant
flakes!
Oh instant of magnificent plenitude;

Before knowing thee, fraternal Sea,
Long have I wandered through blue errant streets with banners
                                             of lamps   [t/o]
And in the sacredness of midnight I have woven garlands
Of kisses over flesh and lips that were offered,
Ceremonies of silence,
In a bloody
Flowering. . .
But now I make a present to the winds
of all those things that are past,
past. . .Only you exist.
Athletic and naked. Only this fresh breath and these waves,
and the Blue Cups, and the miracle of the Blue Cups.
(I've dreamed a hymn of the Sea with vast rhythms like the
                                    panting waves.)   [t/o]

I even long to create a poem of you
With the adamic cadence of your surf,
With your saline and primal breath,
With the thunder of sonorous anchors before Thulés, drunk with
                                    light and leprosy   [t/o]

With sailor's voices, lights and echoes
Of abysmal fissures
Where your swift nun-like hands constantly caress the dead. . .
A hymn
Constellated by luminous red images.
Oh sea! oh myth! oh sun! oh wide resting place!
And I know why I love you. I know that we are both very old.
That we have known each other for centuries.
I know that in your manantial laughing waters burned the dawn
                                             of Life.   [t/o]
(In the ashes of a tertiary evening I vibrated for the first time
                                    in your womb).   [t/o]

Oh protean, I have come out of you.
Both of us chained and wandering;
Both of us with an intense hunger for stars;
Both of us with hopes and disappointments;
Both of us air, light, strength, obscurities;
Both of us with our vast desire and both of us with our great
                                             misery!   [t/o]

GRECIA

En la angustia de la ignorancia de lo porvenir, saludemos la barca llena de fragancia que tiene de marfil los remos

RUBÉN DARÍO

| AÑO II. | Revista Decenal de Literatura
REDACCIÓN: AMPARO, 20.
Sevilla 31 de diciembre de 1919. | NÚM. XXXVII. |

MARGINALIA

Visa et ventres

Desfilaban las mujeres, en su eterna teoría, nunca interrumpida ante mis ojos atónitos, repitiéndose en la contemplación, como si sólo fuesen una sola mujer innumerable. Y las primeras, las que parecían bañadas en una claridad matutina, mostraban erguido el rostro, el rostro terso y resplandeciente, enjuto como si nunca por él hubiesen corrido lágrimas corrosivas ni otra cosa que rocíos refrigerantes y leves. Nos mostraban sus caras como espejos ávidos de deslumbrarnos para que no viéramos nada más, como si sólo por ellos quisieran ser admiradas, como si aspirasen a ser sólo semblantes en el recuerdo y en el sueño.

Y verdaderamente toda su seducción estaba en los semblantes, que eran sobre sus cuerpos como preseas absolutas puestas sobre oscuras consolas. Las mujeres que venían detrás parecían opacas y marchitas, caminando en la sombra de aquellas luminarias.

Tenían las cabezas bajas y escondían el rostro avergonzadas bajo velos o bajo sus cabelleras, como un talismán en cuya virtud no se confía. Pero en cambio, todavía, mujeres dotadas aún de seducción, mostraban otra belleza comparable a la de los rostros. Y mientras ocultaban las caras, erguían los vientres y nos conjuraban con ellos.

Toda su belleza, retraída de las caras, como la leche se retira de un seno, había bajado a sus vientres, a sus vientres maravillosos, henchidos como lunas llenas, maduros y expresivos y sin embargo tersos, combados como escudos pesados y trémulos, como si en ellos alentasen reuni-

PLATE #1 – Cover of *Grecia* ns 37, Sevilla, 1919

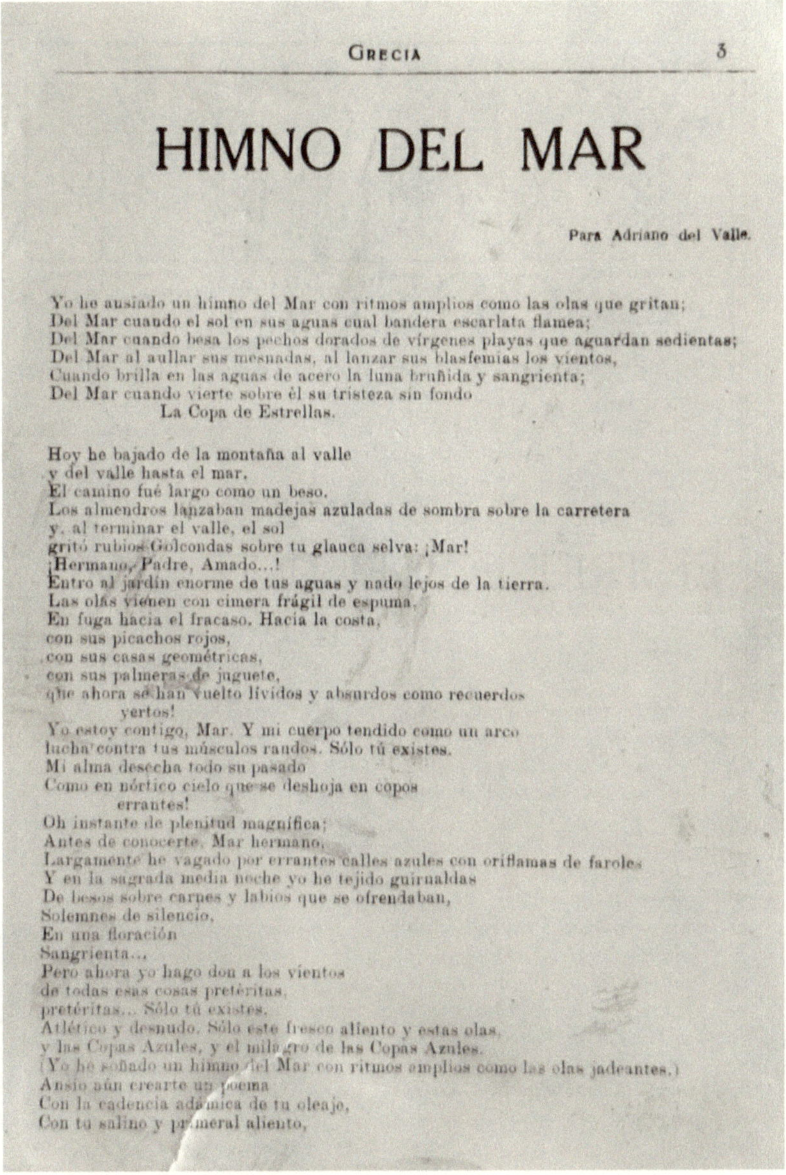

HIMNO DEL MAR

Para Adriano del Valle.

Yo he ansiado un himno del Mar con ritmos amplios como las olas que gritan;
Del Mar cuando el sol en sus aguas cual bandera escarlata flamea;
Del Mar cuando besa los pechos dorados de vírgenes playas que aguardan sedientas;
Del Mar al aullar sus mesnadas, al lanzar sus blasfemias los vientos,
Cuando brilla en las aguas de acero la luna bruñida y sangrienta;
Del Mar cuando vierte sobre él su tristeza sin fondo
　　　　La Copa de Estrellas.

Hoy he bajado de la montaña al valle
y del valle hasta el mar,
El camino fué largo como un beso.
Los almendros lanzaban madejas azuladas de sombra sobre la carretera
y, al terminar el valle, el sol
gritó rubios Golcondas sobre tu glauca selva: ¡Mar!
¡Hermano, Padre, Amado...!
Entro al jardín enorme de tus aguas y nado lejos de la tierra.
Las olas vienen con cimera frágil de espuma.
En fuga hacia el fracaso. Hacia la costa,
con sus picachos rojos,
con sus casas geométricas,
con sus palmeras de juguete,
que ahora se han vuelto lívidos y absurdos como recuerdos
　　　　yertos!
Yo estoy contigo, Mar. Y mi cuerpo tendido como un arco
lucha contra tus músculos raudos. Sólo tú existes.
Mi alma desecha todo su pasado
Como en nórtico cielo que se deshoja en copos
　　　　errantes!
Oh instante de plenitud magnífica;
Antes de conocerte, Mar hermano,
Largamente he vagado por errantes calles azules con oriflamas de faroles
Y en la sagrada media noche yo he tejido guirnaldas
De besos sobre carnes y labios que se ofrendaban,
Solemnes de silencio,
En una floración
Sangrienta...
Pero ahora yo hago don a los vientos
de todas esas cosas pretéritas,
pretéritas... Sólo tú existes.
Atlético y desnudo. Sólo este fresco aliento y estas olas,
y las Copas Azules, y el milagro de las Copas Azules.
(Yo he soñado un himno del Mar con ritmos amplios como las olas jadeantes.)
Ansio aún crearte un poema
Con la cadencia adámica de tu oleaje,
Con tu salino y palmeral aliento.

PLATE #2 – "Himno del mar" in *Grecia* ns 37

GRECIA

En la angustia de la ignorancia de lo porvenir, saludemos la barca llena de fragancia que tiene de marfil los remos

RUBÉN DARÍO

| AÑO II. | Revista Decenal de Literatura
REDACCIÓN: AMPARO, 20.
Sevilla 12 de octubre de 1919. | NÚM. XXIX. |

EL TRIUNFO DEL ULTRAISMO

GRECIA cumple su primer aniversario.

Si algún día me preguntasen cuál había sido el día más feliz de mi vida, sin vacilar respondería: ¡Oh, el día de la Fiesta de la Raza!

Porque en ese día memorable, ¡cómo es bello recordarlo! unos cuantos poetas llenos de fe y de entusiasmos en nuestros ideales, como los escultores que descorren la tela que oculta la hermosura de su obra, nosotros, descorrimos la cortina fantástica y anónima que nos cubría, para mostrar nuestro arte balbuciente, lleno de misteriosos temblores y colmado de augurios.

Y la acogida que se nos hizo no pudo ser más espléndida ni halagadora, más aún de lo que nosotros esperábamos...

¡Nunca, en verdad, salió de las bocas profanas de los vendedores de diarios, un nombre tan claro, dulce y evocador:

¡Grecia! ¡Grecia! ¡Grecia!

Parecía real y verdaderamente que nuestra modesta Revista era el vaso divino donde se conservara taumatúrgicamente el néctar del espíritu ático a través de los tiempos, y nosotros, alborozados, lo escanciábamos con la prodigalidad inefable de nuestra juventud

PLATE #3 – "El triumfo de ultraismo" in *Grecia* ns 29, Sevilla, 1919

✳

Borges's next two published poems, "Paréntesis pasional" and "La llama," are the young writer's first attempts at writing the prose poem. Also note that, in "Parénthesis pasional," his use of the latin phrase "o sica adamica" is an early demonstration of his broad reading and his language skills. With this phrase, Borges, perhaps, is intending a double entendre. The Latin dictionary defines "sica" as an assassination or murder with a small dagger, while "adamica" could refer to "adamas": hardest steel, hard as adamant; "adamica" can even be related to "adamo" which translates: to love passionately. Of course, a stabbing or piercing with the penis is analogous to the stabbing to death of one's lover, as traditionally, poets, such as Shakespeare have equated having sexual intercourse with dying. Then again, typos may exist and "adamica" should perhaps be "adanica" referring to Adam's love and the first sexual encounter between man and woman implying the ultimate experience (being the first). This would make more sense if "sica" should read "sic" which in latin means "such is," or "in this manner." With this definition the line would imply: "such was Adam's first passionate encounter with Eve." I have assumed, however, that no typing errors exist and have translated the phrase, given the obvious sexual encounter suggested here by a young Borges, as "sica adámica."

PARÉNTESIS PASIONAL

La tarde es el divino juglar que viene danzante, rítmico y ágil, y que apaga el sol con su diestra y en su izquierda eleva la Luna. Sus pies azules leves danzan sobre una Alfombra fragante pues poco ha que huyó la lluvia y algunos viejos nubarrones maculan todavía a lo lejos la Inmensidad de púrpura donde laten áureas estrellas.

En la plaza rendida alza su ala única la Fuente. Yo voy con pecho henchido y alma feliz. Marcho al encuentro de la Amada, de la Amada del toisón fulgente y deslumbrante cuerpo.

¡Evohé! (salve, amigos lejanos. Whitman, Isaac, Adriano, Abramowicz, Johannes Becher. . .).

Yo paso junto a un Arbol. Mi mano cóncava acaricia la rugosa corteza y murmuro: Heil Dir Freund Baum. . .Yo lo saludo con vocablos germánicos, pues creo que un gran árbol fuerte y viril comprenderá aquellas palabras fuertes y viriles. Y el otro hermano, el Viento, al tañer las Hojas infinitas que me doselan, me transmite la respuesta fraterna y fuerte del Arbol.

Y ahora me ilumina la Amada. Sus verdes Ojos ríen. Sus dientecitos ríen y de mis labios manan palabras de Ternura.

Y mi brazo rodea el rítmico talle. Ella charla de cosas Absurdas e Importantes; me habla de sus hermanas, de una Gatita enferma, de nimiedades, del Taller.

Gentes. . .Colores. . .Risas. . .

Hay algo de Alcahuetesco en la Noche. La Noche es cómplice. La Noche es buena. En los excelsos reverberos hay milagros palpitantes de Luz. Escalamos la larga cuesta hasta la Cervecería.

La Cervecería es un edificio vulgar y Magnífico. En la calle, al pie de sus fogosos ventanales, ruedan bruñidas Placas amarillas. Entramos. Extáticos Surtidores que son verdes palmeras vierten Frescura.

Gentes. . .Colores. . .Risas. . .

Una orquesta Ramplona exuda un Aquelarre de notas. Los músicos de frac y rígida pechera parecen Dibujos malos a Pluma. Pero los rostros congestionados y rojos son apopléjicos.

Con su galería turbia de vidrios, esta Cervecería no es más que el ebrio Barco de los Locos con rumbo a Orión y Aldebarán y que, empujado por el cósmico oleaje, ha encallado en este promontorio alto que, chorreante, se desmorona hasta el Ródano.

Bastas y azules Humaredas bailan en los cigarros y en las pipas. Los estudiantes charlan y ríen y comen con voracidades famélicas de camposanto y algunos que están Ebrios pretenden abrazar a las camareras. La Cervecería es de un alto Mirador. A mis pies vibran la Ciudad y las Montañas y el Río de Plata que Siete Puentes cicatrizan.

Las cafeteras vierten Insomnio en las tazas boquiabiertas y cándidas. ¿Qué Alcohol incendiará tu Alma, oh mi Amada? Pídeme lo que quieras pues estoy rico; tengo tres Escudos sonoros en el bolsillo.

¡Vino, vino fulgente como el reír del Sol, rojo como las Crenchas rojas que enguirnaldan tu cabeza inviolada!

Música. . .Risotadas. . .

El vino ya ha llegado; la Botella lacrada yace entre Témpanos de Hielo en un gran Cubo de Plata con dos Argollas que muerden dos testas rudas de Leones.

Y cantan roja Luz las Copas.

—¡A la tienne!

En nuestras venas ríe triunfante el Vino. Una marchita vendedora ofrece flores. Otra botella. Y yo bebo en la Copa de la Amada. Y ella en la mía. ¡Cuán Bello! ¡Cuán pueril!

(¿Qué me importa la metafísica ni el mundo? ¿Qué me importa el mohín desdeñoso de los críticos? Sólo tú existes, Dicha de mi alma victoriosa.)

Un reloj vierte la Media Noche Sagrada. Contorsiones violentas de los Músicos; un violinista se degüella rítmicamente. Acordes múltiples.

La oscuridad nos brinda su Frescura. Salimos. Afuera, un gran Perro negro aulla a la Luna de Marfil. Divino Grial inasequible. Ficha eternamente apostada en los tapetes verdes del cielo.

Descendemos la cuesta, y atravesando el Puente veo que la Noche siembra de Estrellas el Río. Amada, yo sembraré mil Besos sobre tu cuerpo.

¡Cuán sumisas y quietas, cuán sonoras y quedas, están las calles! Diríase que se han arrodillado todas las casas. Todo parece azul. Diríase que la noche se ha arrodillado sobre las calles azules.

Bésame. Bésame. . .Ya las dudas han muerto. Ya las penas han muerto y contigo a mi lado me siento fuerte como un Dios. Yo soy un Dios. Yo puedo crear la Vida.

El borroso zaguán. La escalera indecisa. Luego, la Alcoba. La Alcoba es íntima y discreta. Hay profundos espejos y Alcatifas de Persia y hondos Divanes y un amplio Lecho sumiso.

La vida es un gran Himno de Goce.

Mi alma deslumbrada de tinieblas vibra como una Cuerda de Guitarra al contemplar la Amada. Mañana ya seremos extraños el uno para el otro, pero ahora yo vivo sólo para ti, para el Jardín claro y excelso que es tu cuerpo nimbado de Ternura.

Hemos de soñar juntos mientras susurre esta frondosa noche hasta el instante en que se llene de cenizas la alcoba y nos quebrante el yugo de un día nuevo y los faroles se ahorquen en las esquinas. . .Tu frente surge en la media-luz como una aurora. Tu frente es el espejo esmerilado que atesora el marfil de todos los novilunios. Tu frente es la bandera de marfil que ondeará levemente, diciendo tu rendición y mi victoria.

¡Oh Amada, nuestros Besos incendiarán la Noche! (oh sica adámica). Y deja abierta la Ventana, pues quiero invitar al Universo a mis Bodas; quiero que el Aire, el Mar, las Aguas y los Arboles, gocen el febril breve Festín de tu belleza y de mi fuerza.

* * *

Ahora mi paladar es rojo yugo que unce la llama roja de tu lengua. . .La oscuridad se llena de auroras.

* * *

Ahora tu cuerpo, deliciosamente, como una estrella, tiembla en mis brazos. . .

* * *

Ya todas las tinieblas se han dormido.

Grecia ns 38, Sevilla, 20 Jan. 1920   Jorge Luis Borges

PASSIONATE PARENTHESIS

The evening is the divine juggler that comes dancing, rhythmic and agile, and who extinguishes the sun with his right hand and raises the Moon on his left. His airy blue feet dance on a fragrant Carpet since the rain has barely fled and some old dark clouds still in the distance, color the purple Immensity where golden stars throb.

In the exhausted plaza, the Fountain lifts its only wing. I go with a swollen chest and happy soul. I am off to meet the Beloved, the Beloved with the sparkling golden fleece and dazzling body.

I Evoke you! (greetings, distant friends, Whitman, Isaac, Adriano, Abramowicz, Johannes Becher. . .).

I pass by a Tree. My concaved hand caresses the wrinkled bark and I murmur: Hail Tree Dear Friend. . .I greet him with Germanic words, because I believe a strong and virile tree will understand those strong and virile words. And the other brother, the Wind, as it strums the infinite canopy of Leaves above me, transmits the strong and fraternal answer of the Tree.

And now the Beloved illuminates me. Her green Eyes laugh. Her little teeth laugh and from my lips flow words of Tenderness.

And my arm surrounds her rhythmic waist. She chats of things Absurd and Important; she speaks to me of her sisters, of a sick female Kitten, of trifles, of the Workshop.

People. . .Colors. . .Laughter. . .

There is something Solicitous about the Night. The Night is an accomplice. The Night is good. In the sublime reverberations there are throbbing miracles of Light. We climb the long slope to the Beer Hall.

The Beer Hall is a vulgar and Magnificent building. On the street, at the foot of its large fiery windows, run polished yellow plaques. We enter. Ecstatic Spouts shaped like green palm trees pour Coolness.

People. . .Colors. . .Laughter. . .

A Vulgar orchestra exudes Orgies of notes. The musicians in their formal tails and starched shirts appear like bad Pen Sketches. But their red congested faces are apoplectic.

With its turbulent gallery of glass, this Beer Hall is nothing more than the drunken Boat of Madmen bound for Orion and Aldebarán and that, pushed by cosmic surf, has run aground on this high promontory that, dripping with water, is crumbling into the Rhone.

Coarse blue clouds of smoke dance on the cigars and pipes. The students chat and laugh and eat with famished voraciousness as if they've come out of cemeteries, and some who are Drunk try to embrace the waitresses. The Beer Hall's Mirador has a high vantage point. At my feet vibrates the City, the Mountains and the Plata River that is scarred by seven bridges.

The coffee pots pour Insomnia into the white open-mouthed cups. What Alcohol will ignite your soul, oh my Beloved? Ask me what you want since I am rich; I have three jingling Coins in my pocket.

Wine, sparkling wine like the Sun's laughter, red like the two red Braids that wreath your inviolate head.

Music. . .Guffaws. . .

The wine has arrived; the lacquered Bottle lies among Icebergs, in a large Silver Bucket with two Rings that two unpolished Lion's heads have clamped between their teeth.

And the Wine Glasses sing red Light.

—Cheers!—

In our veins the Wine laughs triumphantly. A wilted vendor offers flowers. Another bottle. And I drink from my Beloved's glass. And she from mine. How beautiful! How child-like!

(What do I care about metaphysics or the world? What do I care about the disdainful grimace of the critics? Only you exist, Great Joy of my victorious soul.)

A clock spills the Sacred Midnight. Violent contortions of Musicians; a violinist rhythmically slits his throat. Multiple chords.

Darkness offers us its Coolness. We exit. Outside, a large black Dog howls at the Ivory Moon. Inaccessible Holy Grail. A chip eternally wagered on the green felts of heaven.

We descend the hill, and crossing the Bridge I see that Night has seeded the River with Stars. Beloved, I shall sow a thousand Kisses over your body.

How quiet and submissive, how sonorous and still, are the streets! One could say that the houses have all knelt. Everything seems blue. One could say that the night has knelt on the blue streets.

Kiss me. Kiss me. . .My doubts have already died. My pains have already died and with you at my side I feel strong like a God. I am a God. I can create Life.

The blurred foyer. The indecisive stairway. Then, the Bedroom. The Bedroom is intimate and discreet. There are deep mirrors and Carpets from Persia, low cushioned Sofas and an ample submissive Bed.

Life is a great Hymn of Joy.

My soul, dazzled by the darkness, vibrates like a Guitar String when I behold my Beloved. Tomorrow we shall both be strangers to each other, but now I live only for you, for the clear and sublime Garden of your body hallowed with Tenderness.

While the luxuriant night whispers we shall dream together up until the moment the bedroom is filled with ashes and the oppressive yoke of a new day breaks upon us and the lamps on the street corners are lynched. . .Your brow rises in the half-light like dawn. Your brow is the polished mirror that possesses the ivory of all new moons. Your brow is the ivory flag that will wave slightly, voicing your surrender and my victory.

Oh Beloved, our Kisses will ignite the Night! (Oh sica adámica). And leave the Window open, because I want to invite the Universe to my Wedding; I want the Air, the Sea, the Waters and the Trees, to enjoy the brief feverish Feast of your beauty and my strength.

* * *

Now my palate is a red yoke that hitches to the red flame of your tongue. . .The darkness is full of dawns.

* * *

Now your body, deliciously, like a star, trembles in my arms...

* * *

All darkness now has fallen asleep.

LA LLAMA

Bajo la larga urna del cielo—ante los mástiles del invierno que se alzan sobre las aguas sin ruido—y las luces verdes del puerto que en amplia inmóvil procesión, anilladas de rojo en la penumbra lo ciñen, —una llama torva ondula en el aire pardo y pesado a ras de la tierra —en el derrumbamiento de las cosas visibles,—en la angustiosa espera de la tormenta cercana. . .

La llama roja salta y chisporrotea.—Yo paso junto a la llama; yo escucho lo que quiere proclamar su lengua de fuego,—yo doy palabras y voz a lo que susurra esa llama.

Yo, latente bajo todas las máscaras,—nunca apagada y eternamente acechando,—hermana de la abierta herida de luz en el desnudo flanco del aire—hermana de lares y piras—hermana de astros que arden en los jardines colgantes cuya serenidad enorme yo envidio,—desterrada de las selvas del sol hace abismos de siglos—encarno la grande fatiga, la sed de no ser de todo cuanto en esta tierra poluta vibra, y sufriendo vive.

Te siento y paso.—Sigo a lo largo de la tarde lenta—y medito el significado de tu roja palabra—y veo que en verdad eres símbolo—de nosotros que inevitablemente sufrimos—uncidos al gris yugo del día—o al enjoyado yugo de la noche—y ansiamos como tú la alta serenidad y el desdén claro de la felina noche. . .

Espoleados—deseando deslumbrarnos y perdernos en los pasionales festines—en la crucifixión de cuerpos tremantes—(y pienso—que tal vez no es otra cosa la vida—que el ascua de una hoguera muerta hace siglos—que el último eco de una voz fenecida—que arrojó el azar a esa tierra—algo lejano a este orden de cosas del espacio y del tiempo). —Y la llama se hunde en el gran crepúsculo enfermo—que en jirones desgarran los grises vientos.

Grecia ns 41, Sevilla, 29 Feb. 1920   Jorge Luis Borges

THE FLAME

Beneath the long urn of the sky—before the masts of winter
rising silently over waters—and the port's green lights,
ringed with red in the semi-darkness, that in their wide immobile
procession encircle it,—a grim flame undulates in the grey and heavy
air at earth level—in the collapse of visible things,—in the
anguishing wait of the approaching storm. . .

The red flame hops and crackles.—I pass next to the flame; I
listen to what its fiery tongue wants to proclaim,—I give words and
voice to what that flame murmurs.

*I, latent under all masks,—never extinguished and eternally
observing,—sister of the open wound of light in the naked side of air—
sister of hearths and pyres—sister of stars burning in hanging gardens
whose enormous serenity I envy,—exiled from the sun's jungles an abyss of
centuries ago—I embody the great fatigue, the thirst of not being all of what
vibrates on this polluted earth, and suffering, lives.*

I feel you and pass by.—I follow the length of the slow evening
—and ponder the meaning of your crimson word—and see that in
truth you are a symbol—of us who inevitably suffer—hitched to the
grey yoke of day—or the jeweled yoke of night—and like you we
yearn for the high serenity and the clear disdain of the feline night. . .

Spurred on—desiring to dazzle and lose us in passionate feasts—
in the crucifixion of trembling bodies—(and I think—that life may
be nothing else—than a bonfire's ember from centuries ago—than
the last echo of an extinguished voice—that chance hurled onto
this earth—something remote from the space and time ordering of
things).—And the flame sinks into the great infirm twilight—tearing
the gray winds to shreds.

PLATE #4 – Cover of *Cervantes*, Madrid, 1920

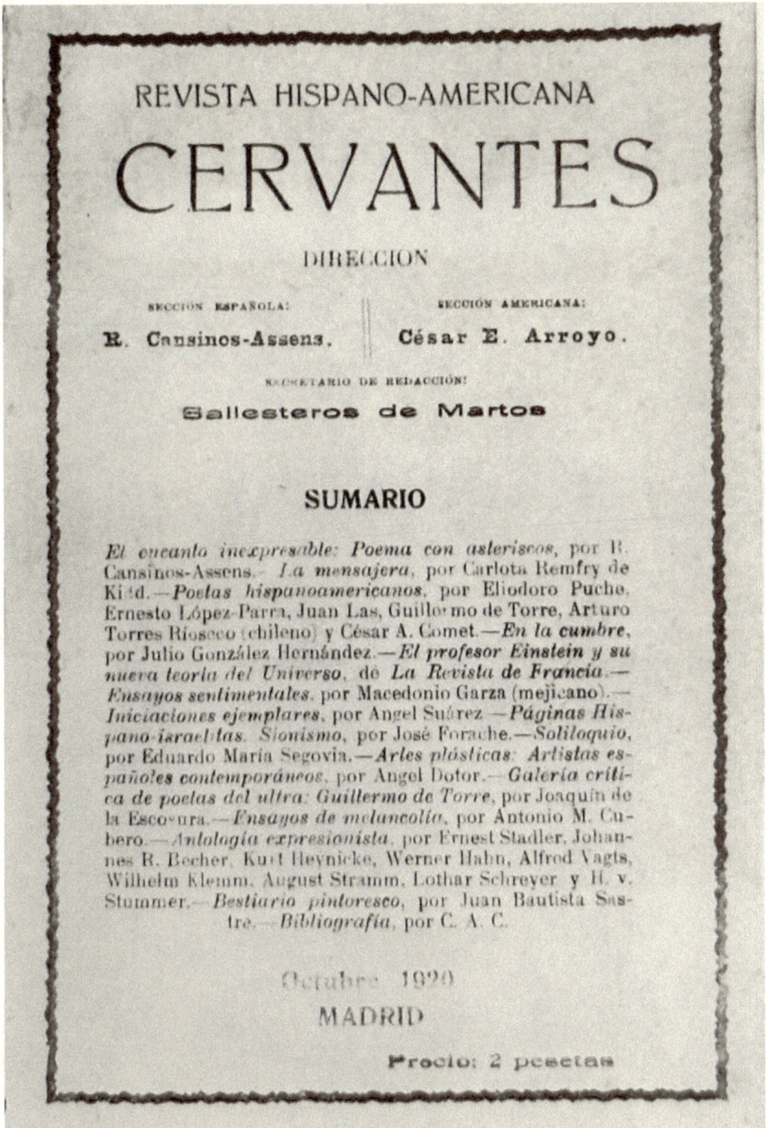

REVISTA HISPANO-AMERICANA

CERVANTES

DIRECCION

SECCIÓN ESPAÑOLA:
R. Cansinos-Assens.

SECCIÓN AMERICANA:
César E. Arroyo.

SECRETARIO DE REDACCIÓN:
Ballesteros de Martos

SUMARIO

El encanto inexpresable: Poema con asteriscos, por R. Cansinos-Assens.— *La mensajera*, por Carlota Remfry de Kidd.—*Poetas hispanoamericanos*, por Eliodoro Puche, Ernesto López-Parra, Juan Las, Guillermo de Torre, Arturo Torres Ríoseco (chileno) y César A. Comet.—*En la cumbre*, por Julio González Hernández.—*El profesor Einstein y su nueva teoría del Universo*, de *La Revista de Francia*.— *Ensayos sentimentales*, por Macedonio Garza (mejicano).— *Iniciaciones ejemplares*, por Angel Suárez —*Páginas Hispano-israelitas. Sionismo*, por José Forache.—*Soliloquio*, por Eduardo María Segovia.—*Artes plásticas: Artistas españoles contemporáneos*, por Angel Dotor.— *Galería crítica de poetas del ultra: Guillermo de Torre*, por Joaquín de la Esco-ura.—*Ensayos de melancolía*, por Antonio M. Cubero.—*Antología expresionista*, por Ernest Stadler, Johannes R. Becher, Kurt Heynicke, Werner Hahn, Alfred Vagts, Wilhelm Klemm, August Stramm, Lothar Schreyer y H. v. Stummer.— *Bestiario pintoresco*, por Juan Bautista Sastre.—*Bibliografía*, por C. A. C.

Octubre 1920

MADRID

Precio: 2 pesetas

PLATE #5 – Cover of *Cosmopolis* ns 29, Madrid, 1921

PLATE #6 – Cover of *Baleares* ns 121, Palma de Mallorca, 1920

PLATE #7 – Cover of *Baleares* ns 131, Palma de Mallorca, 1921

⁕

With the next poem "Trinchera," Borges clearly begins writing under the influence of the Spanish poet Rafael Cansinos-Assens' and his Ultraísmo movement. Note how Borges begins using the hyphen in his name, which coincides with the beginning of his apprenticeship under the admired author. As for his use of the word "unge," it is very likely that Borges's intentions here are obscured by either a typo *unge* from *ungir* and not *unce* from *uncir*, or an incorrect verbalization of *unción* (unction), which in the Catholic faith is in the context of "extremaunción," the anoitment or the administering of holy water or oil to those at the point of death. "Anoits" might be considered here in place of "yokes." Undoubtedly, this poem references the horror of what soldiers experienced during World War I, fighting with bayonets in the trenches.

TRINCHERA

Angustia
En lo altísimo una montaña camina
Hombres color de tierra naufragan en la grieta más baja
El fatalismo unce las almas de aquéllos
que bañaron su pequeña esperanza en las piletas de la noche
Las bayonetas sueñan con los entreveros nupciales
El mundo se ha perdido y los ojos de los muertos lo buscan
El silencio aúlla en los horizontes hundidos.

Grecia ns 43, Sevilla, 1 June 1920   Jorge-Luis Borges

TRENCH

Anguish
At the highest point a mountain moves
Earth-colored men drowning in the deepest fissure
Fatalism yokes the souls of those
who bathed their meagre hope in baptismal fonts of the night
Bayonets dream of nuptial intercourse
The world is lost and the eyes of the dead search for it
Silence howls in the sunken horizons.

HERMANOS

Crucificados en el tiempo
callábamos a lo largo de los ponientes gastados
que nos miraban con sus viejos ojos de ofidio,
y nuestros labios eran cicatrices.

                            Quién desgarró el conjuro.

Asombrada de azul
el alma destechó a los astros la casa
y nuestros corazones fueron guitarras de mil cuerdas
que se desangran hoy

                en la otra herida
de sombras y planetas.

Grecia ns 45, Sevilla, 1 July 1920   Jorge Luis Borges

BROTHERS

Crucified in time
we were silent throughout weary sunsets
looking at us with their old reptilian eyes,
and our lips were scars.

                          Who tore away the spell?

Awed by blue
the soul unroofed the star's abode
and our hearts were guitars of a thousand strings
bleeding today

                in the other wound
of shadows and planets.

⁂

Most *Madrileños* in my literary circle expressed certainty that, in his poem "Señal," Borges is referring to activities at houses of prostitution—toys analagous to prostitutes—where laisons occurred in the back rooms while card games and drinking took place, and musicians performed into the late hours of morning. See "Casa Elena" for another treatment of this same theme.

SEÑAL
A Maurice Claude.

Cuántas noches maduras
se desgajaron sobre nuestras frentes hermano
Fuimos abriendo como ramas las calles
Nuestras risas rodando se rompieron
frescos juguetes en los cristales del fondo
Tus manos beben el cercano silencio
Las melopeas
El piano late como un torrente enyugado
Tus manos arden en la luz de los sones
Alguien
     junto al farol decapitado
         ha de ceñirnos un collar de estepas

Grecia ns 46, Sevilla, 15 July 1920   Jorge Luis Borges

SIGNAL
To Maurice Claude.

How many late nights
have broken off on our foreheads brother
We went opening the streets like branches
Our rolling peels of laughter broke
fresh toys in the back windows
Your hands drink in the surrounding silence
Drunken sprees
The piano throbs like a yoked torrent
Your hands blaze in the light of the sounds
Someone
     next to the decapitated streetlamp
         must gird us with a collar of rockrose

⁂

Undoubtedly, with his next published poem, "Rusia," Borges is expressing his admiration for the Russian socialist revolution, as did many of his fellow poets in the ultraísta movement. Regrettably, due to liberties Guillermo de Torre took in his 1925 study *Literaturas Europeas de Vanguardia*, "Rusia" has been reproduced in several critical studies in verse form instead of its proper prose poem format as it first appeared. Today, one can only guess at his reasons for rearranging this prose poem into verse. As a result, subsequent critics: Gertel (1968), Barnatan (1972), and Meneses (1978), perhaps not having seen the poem as originally published in *Grecia* ns 48, Sept. 1920 have continued the structural error. Once again, notice the hyphen in Borges's name

RUSIA

La trinchera avanzada es en la estepa un barco al abordaje con gallardetes de hurras: mediodías estallan en los ojos. Bajo estandartes de silencio pasan las muchedumbres y el sol crucificado en los ponientes se pluraliza en la vocinglería de las torres del Kreml. El mar vendrá nadando a esos ejércitos que envolverán sus torsos en todas las praderas del continente. En el cuerno salvaje de un arco iris clamaremos su gesta bayonetas que portan en la punta las mañanas.

Grecia ns 48, Sevilla, 1 Sep. 1920   Jorge-Luis Borges

RUSSIA

The forward trench is on the steppe a ship being boarded with streamers of hurrahs: noon-days explode in the eyes. Under standards of silence the multitudes pass and the crucified sun setting in the western sky multiplies itself in the clamor from the Kremlin towers. The sea will come swimming at those armies whose torsos will be enveloped in all the meadows of the continent. On the savage horn of a rainbow we will cry out their heroic deeds bayonets that carry the mornings on their tips.

⁂

The poem "Insomnio" is not the poem of the same name that Borges published in his collection *El otro, el mismo* in 1964. Written and published in 1920, this "Insomnio" continues to show Borges's strong interest in the prose poem genre. The typography suggests prose poem intentions, and many lines like the opening line are clearly not an attempt at versification. As for the word "plano," which means flat or level, it is likely that Borges, with his knowledge of English, intends the word "plane" in the English to function as both "level," and "airplane," considering his use of "hanger" in the previous line. There is as well the possibility of a typo in prose paragraph 20 and "piano" should be "plano." Note how Borges continues to use the hyphen in his name.

INSOMNIO

Resulta legendariamente chica y lejana aquella etapa donde los relojes vertieron la media noche absoluta.

Estos seis muros estrechos llenos de eternidad estrecha me ahogan.

Y en el cráneo sigue vibrando esta lamentable llama de alcohol que no quiere apagarse.

Que no puede apagarse.

Reducción al absurdo del problema de la inmortalidad del espíritu.

Me he desangrado en demasiados ponientes.

La ventana sintetiza el gesto solitario del farol.

Apergaminado y plausible film cinemático.

La ventana imanta todas las ojeadas inquietas.

Cómo me ahorcan las cuerdas del horizonte.

¿Llueve? ¿Qué morfina inyectarán a las calles esas agujas?
No.

Son girones vagos de siglos que gotean isócronos del cielo raso.

Es la letanía lenta de la sangre.

Son los dientes de la obscuridad que roen las paredes.

Bajo los párpados ondean y se apagan nuevamente las tempestades rotas.

Los días son todos de papel azul bien cortaditos por la misma tijera sobre el agujero inexistente del Cosmos.

El recuerdo enciende una lámpara:

Otra vez arrastramos con nosotros esa calle que la ropa
tendida embanderó tan jubilosamente.
    Muy lejos se hundió el frondoso piano del tupi.
    El sol ventilador vertiginoso tumba los caserones.
    Al vernos navegar tan espirales se ríen a carcajadas las
puertas.
    Pedro-Luis me confía: —Yo soy un hombre bueno, Jorge.
    Tú eres un hombre bueno, Jorge. . .Ya se nos pasará tomando
una tacita de café
    Los ojos estallan cuando los golpean las aspas del sol.
    ¿Qué hangar cobijará definitivamente las emociones?
    Sin duda existe un plano ultra-espacial donde todas ellas son
formas de una fuerza utilizable y sujeta.
    Como el agua y la electricidad en este plano.
    Ira. Anarquismo. Hambre sexual.
    Artificio para hacernos vibrar mágicamente.
    Ninguna piedra rompe la noche.
    Ninguna mano aviva las cenizas del incendio de todos los
estandartes.

Grecia ns 49, Sevilla, 15 Sep. 1920   Jorge-Luis Borges.

INSOMNIA

Legendarily small and distant the era turns out where the clocks
pour out absolute midnight.
    These six narrow walls full of narrow eternity suffocate me.
    And in my skull this pitiful flame of alcohol continues vibrating
and won't be extinguished.
    Cannot be extinguished.
    The problem of the spirit's immortality reduced to the absurd.
    I have shed my blood in too many sunsets.
    The window synthesizes the solitary gesture of the lamp.
    Dried up and plausible cinematic film.
    The window magnetizes all the restless glances.
    How the cords of the horizon strangle me.
    It's raining? What morphine will those needles inject into the
streets?
    No.
    They are vague turns of centuries dripping in cadence from the
ceiling.

It's the slow litany of blood.
They are the teeth of darkness gnawing on the walls.
Under my eyelids the subdued storms ripple and subside anew.
The days are all of blue paper finely cut by the same scissors
over the nonexistent hole in the Cosmos.
Memory lights a lamp:
*Once again we drag with us that street that hanging clothes
flagged so jubilantly.*
The leafy piano of the Tupi has sunk far away.
The sun like a vertiginous fan knocks down large houses.
The doors guffaw to see us navigate in such spirals.
Pedro-Luis confides in me:—I am a good man, Jorge.
You are a good man, Jorge. . .It'll pass with a small cup of coffee
The eyes burst when beaten by the vanes of the sun.
What hanger will ultimately house the emotions?
No doubt an ultra-spacial plane exists where all of them are
forms of a usable and subjected force.
Like water and electricity on this plane.
Anger. Anarchism. Sexual hunger.
Artifice to make us magically vibrate.
Not one rock smashes the night.
Not one hand rekindles the ashes from all the burning standards.

⁂

In "Poema," Borges is obviously versifying as opposed to the previous poem in which prose poetry passages are clearly his intention. In Borges's verse poems, he will often play with typography, as he does in line 2 and 13. In the published version of "Poema," Baleares editors mistakenly printed another writers name as Borges's middle name. The poet Josep Llinás Simó had contributed a poem in the same issue in which "Poema" appeared. Also, "obaje" is a typo. The word should be "obraje" which in Latin American context means "mano de obra" or labor.

POEMA

La estrella
          que huyó de tu garganta madura
no es más que un eco del formidable poema.
Alguien lo ritma
en la orquesta monstruosa de tus nervios.
Alguien lo escribe
sobre la tela gris de tus días
y en el sopor de las alcobas pesadas
dolorosa, pueril absurdamente.
A penas dibujado el último rasgo
hace jirones de la obra
y su desnuda noche
                    en el ob[r]aje del silencio reposa.
Cajita negra para el violín que se ha roto.

Jorge Llinás [Luis] Borges.

Valldemosa 25 1920.

Balaeres ns 121, Palma de Mallorca, 15 Sep. 1920

POEM

The star
          that escaped from your mature throat
is nothing more than an echo of the formidable poem.
Someone is giving it rhythm

in the monstrous orchestra of your nerves.
Someone is writing it
on the gray fabric of your days
and in the lethargy of tedious bedrooms
painful, absurdly childish.
The last stroke barely drawn
he tears the work to shreds
and his naked night
                    in the labor of silence rests.
Little black case for the shattered violin.

Valldemosa 25 1920.

MAÑANA
A Antonio M. Cubero.

Las banderas cantaron sus colores
   y el viento es una vara de bambú entre las manos
El mundo crece como un árbol claro
            Ebrio como una hélice
   el sol toca la diana sobre las azoteas
   el sol con sus espuelas desgarra los espejos
Como un naipe mi sombra
   ha caído de bruces sobre carretera
Arriba   el cielo vuela
   y lo surcan los pájaros como noches errantes
La mañana viene a posarse fresca en mi espalda.

Ultra ns 1, Madrid, 27 Jan. 1921   Jorge Luis Borges

MORNING
To Antonio M. Cubero.

The flags sang their colors
   and the wind is a bamboo stick in hand
The world grows like a clear tree
            Drunk like a propeller
   the sun sounds reveille over the roofs
   the sun with its spurs rips the mirrors
Like a playing card my shadow
   has fallen face down on the highway
Above   the sky flies
   and the birds plow through it like errant nights
The fresh morning comes to perch on my back.

⁂

"Aldea" is a prose poem published in *Ultra* ns 2, February 1921, to which I have appended a bracketed roman numeral [I] so it is not confused with the poem "Aldea" Borges published in *Ultra* ns 21 in January 1922. The 1922 "Aldea" [II] is a shorter verse poem of nine lines and shares nothing in common with "Aldea" [I] except for the title. "Aldea" [II] is erroneously reproduced by numerous scholars in their critical works on young Borges, i.e., Gloria Videla (1963), Zunilda Gertel (1967), Marcos Ricardo Barnatan (1972), and Carlo Meneses (1978) causing confusion, because Borges will add a stanza to "Aldea" [II], rename it "Campos Ataracidos," and collect it in *Fervor*, as well as in later anthologies. "Aldea" [I] will never appear again after its magazine publication. Notice also Borges's similar prose poem line indentions as in his previous prose poems. Also, in the same *Ultra* issue, a prose poem by Arthur Rimbaud "Después del diluvio," ["Aprés le deluge" / "After the Deluge"] from his *Les Illuminations* (1873) sits side by side with Borges's "Aldea" [I], which displays the same individual prose paragraphs arrangement/typography of Rimbaud's poem. It is this same typography that Borges will use in his prose poems except for in "Rusia" and "Casa Elena."

ALDEA [I]

Las esquilas reunen la triseza dispersa de los crepúsculos.
El cielo está vacío.
Lápida de un silencio serio sobre el nihilismo ecuánime de la jornada.
Las fluviales lenguas frescas del viento lamen mis manos y mejillas.
En la barbería el reloj—sexagenario sistemático—sigue jugando al solitario con los minutos.
Ante la hipnosis rectilínea del caserío y curvilínea del camino y los montes, Sureda y yo somos las dos pirámides del pueblo. Culminantes sobre la democracia geométrica y encarrilada.
Apoyadas en la baranda nuestras manos tocan el piano de colores del paisaje.
En la caja del piano está enterrado Wagner. A veces se despierta y canta en la tumba. En la caja del craneo saltan entonces crimenes crucifixiones golpes de estado pronunciamientos piras fornicios y pluralizados suicidios.

Hasta que nos estruja un flaco silencio sin entorchados ni
estandartes.
    Los acordes histrionizan las acumuladas angustias.
    El aqueducto tiende su espinazo polvoriento de sol.
    El trasnochador dejó dos palanganas llenas de sueño.
    Los badajos ultiman otra jornada.
    Los párpados picotean la madeja de viento y polvo.
    El Sol que talaron los leñadores rueda a ras de los campos.
    Las noches náufragas han tapado el aljibe.
    Aguijoneando nuestro insomnio vuelan aureolas de
nerviosos insectos.
    Los árboles donde se diluye la fiebre del farol son árboles
de teatro.
    Durante la misa un perro menea la cola.
    Incensario cuyo optimismo biológico asciende—único—a
esa altitud azul donde reposa Dios y cantan los pajaritos.

Ultra ns 2, Madrid, 10 Feb. 1921   Jorge-Luis Borges

VILLAGE [I]

Sheep-bells gather the dispersed sadness of twilights.
The sky is empty.
    Tombstone of a grave silence over the peaceful nihilism of
a day's labor.
    Fresh fluvial tongues of the wind lick my hands and cheeks.
    The clock in the barber shop—systematic sexagenarian—keeps
playing solitaire with the minutes.
    Before the rectilinear hypnosis of houses and the curvature
of the road and hills, Sureda and I are two pyramids of the
village. Two peaks over the geometric and railed democracy.
    Leaning on the railing our hands play the piano of the
landscape's colors.
    In the piano case Wagner is buried. At times he wakens
and sings in his tomb. Then crimes crucifixions coups d'etat
rebellions pyres fornications and multiple suicides pop up
inside his skull case.
    Until a thin silence with neither torches nor standards
wrings us dry.
    The chords dramatize the accumulated anguish.
    The aqueduct extends its dusty spine from the sun.

The late-night carouser left two pots full of sleep.
Bell claps sound the close of another day.
Eyelids peck at the skein of wind and dust.
The sun cut down by woodsmen rolls level with the fields.
The shipwrecked nights have covered the cistern,
Aureolas of nervous insects fly stinging our insomnia.
The trees through which the street lamp's fever is dissolved
are theatrical trees.
During mass a dog wags its tail.
Incenser whose biological optimism ascends—only—to that
blue altitude where God rests and little birds sing.

✣

"Catedral" first appeared in *Baleares* in February 1921. Ten months later, Borges revised the poem and republished it in *Ultra* 19 on December 1921. I include the revised rendition as an example of how Borges, in the spirit of vanguardismo, experimented with typography. Also, note how Borges curiously doesn't use the hyphen in his name in the *Baleares* edition—perhaps just an oversight—but then goes back to the hyphen in subsequent poems, adding it to his name in the revised version.

CATEDRAL

Las olas de rodillas
    los músculos del viento
    las torres verticales como goitos [gritos]
        la catedral colgada de un lucero
la catedral que es una inmensa parva
    con espigas de rezos
    Lejos

                Lejos
los mástiles hilvanan horizontes
    y en las playas ingenuas
        las olas nuevas cantan los maítines
La catedral es un avión de piedra
    que puja por romper las mil amarras
        que lo encarcelan
la catedral sonora como un aplauso
    o como un beso.

Jorge Luis Borges
Baleares ns 131, Palma de Mallorca, 15 Feb. 1921

CATHEDRAL

Waves of kneeling
    the muscles of the wind
    vertical towers like shouts
        the cathedral hung from a bright star
the cathedral that is an immense heap of unthreshed corn

with ears of prayers
  Far-away
                                        Far-away
masts stitch the horizons
    and on the ingenuous beaches
        new waves sing the morning prayers
The cathedral is a stone airplane
    that strains to break the thousand mooring-ties
          that imprison it
the cathedral resounds like an applause
    or like a kiss.

CATEDRAL (revised)

Las olas de rodillas
  los músculos del viento
    las torrés escarpadas como gritos
        la catedral colgada de un lucero

la catedral que es una parva
con espigas de rezos

Lejos   Lejos

los mástiles hilvanan horizontes

    y en las playas ingenuas
    las olas nuevas cantan los maitines

La catedral es un avión de piedra
que puja por romper las mil amarras
que lo encarcelan
la catedral sonora como un aplauso
                    que ondea

Ultra ns 19, Madrid, 20 Dec. 1921   Jorge-Luis Borges

CATHEDRAL

Waves of kneeling
   the muscles of the wind
      scarped towers like shouts
         the cathedral hung from a bright star

the cathedral that is a heap of unthreshed corn
with ears of prayers

Far-away   Far-away

masts stitch the horizons

   and on the ingenuous beaches
   new waves sing the morning prayers

The cathedral is a stone airplane
that strains to break the thousand mooring-ties
that imprison it
the cathedral resounds like an undulating
                                        applause

(Grabado en madera por Norah Borges.)

PLATE # 8 – cover of *Ultra* ns 2, Madrid, 1921, by Norah Borges

El ultraísmo no tiene directores, representantes ni defendores, ni en España ni en el extranjero. El ultraísmo no tiene más que poetas, y a margen de su grupo, literatos que simpatizan más o menos con su labor.

Poemas automáticos

(Poémes automatiques)

PERPENDICULAR

Des arbres de tréteaux et des lumières brisées.

Árboles de escenarios y luces heridas
la encrucijada inmóvil reposa plata ni
los interiores encerrados al crepúsculo
desfilan por los patios a lo largo de los ex-
vadores
cuando la rosa eléctrica inciensa los espejos
la mujer en silencio pasa por la alfombra
vacía
escaleras profusas hacia todos los pisos
en lo más alto de la casa sobre la calle incli-
nada
los tejados se ponen en plan de filosofar
hay estrellas sutiles para todos los gatos
y buhardillas agachadas bajo los hilos del te-
léfono

JORNADA

*Avis serrure de sorete lettre recomman-
dée*

Aviso cerradura de seguridad certificado
ayuda de cámara propinas desayuno
salón de fumar grill room brasserie
pasillo centrífugo cuartos de baño
distribuidor general de las energías calculadas
carruaje radiograma bolsa de cambio
sleeping car oficina de correos *au revoir.*
Rafael LASSO DE LA VEGA

RAMONISMO

GARAGES

Por todos lados se hacen «garages», esas falsas habitaciones, esas precarias extensiones que ocupan vanamente el espacio. En gastar inútilmente sitio y diezmar la capacidad de habitaciones de que dispone la ciudad, el dejar que se tomacuyan en el cerebro, en cualquier momento de la ciudad como «gusano de la manzana». Son como estas huellas por el subfundido.

Me parece una cosa fría, vacía, con pobre aire de estilo el «garage». Donde una leve mancha negra de un aceite espeso, que no habrá baldeador que la logre limpiar. Ese solar tan ancioso de llo-
recer en forma de cordial casa llena de verdor, se eterniza como «garage».

Quizás, las estaciones futuras sean numerosos «garages» dispuestos a salir a toda fijo por los an-
terimos caminos que enlaces nacerán el mundo.

Los grandes «garages» serán especies de labe-
rintos superpuestos con escensores para subir los automóviles a colocarlos en sus alcobas. El «garage» está filmado si no seria una obra babilónica y anon-
ima. (Para esa hembria que parece que se ha es-
capado, que es la motocicleta, y adivirda a un co-
checito cubierto, también tendrá que haber hacia ciclos con habitaciones más chicas.)

Pero se reducirían los «garages» entonces a las cuadras y chanáncas en las afueras, sin mezclarse tan indisogniamente a las casas de la ciudad, como rabando el espacio cordial de la ciudad.

El espíritu del «garage» no es recomendable en

general, está lleno de hombres fuertes como gim-
nastas de circo que tienen grandes ambiciones y que aún siendo «chauffers», tienen una amalia con sombrero y pieles. Todos estudian la manera de robar más a sus dueños y se meten unos a otros como las criadas que van a la compra y se reúnen bajo los grandes «garages» de las mercados.

No sabemos apenas de esa vida y sólo vemos la sombra antipática que hay allí, sombra de cochera sin los nobles caballos y como, el perfume de ga-
lantería y de riqueza que sale de los «autos», se es-
capa a los coches, con pungencias para los cria-
dos.

Esa rosa, húmeda de cubos y cubos de agua ti-
rados contra el esmalte y por entre las ruedas, deslizándose el agua como se desliza en las ruedas de las norias, acaba de dar más ingratitud al «garage», en el que entran montones de tristes ca-
charros de gasolina, y donde los mecánicos, en cu-
clillas o debajo de los coches, con todos los sueños de su profesión tirados por el suelo, curan el coche.

Lo que yo veo es que se van a construir muchos y que se están construyendo demasiado. Lo que yo veo es que en el estudio del escultor Querol—
¡pobre artista mediocre!—resucitan los «plañidas» de los automóviles y al lado de mi casa es posible que levanten uno para lo que roncan de noche.
RAMÓN GÓMEZ DE LA SERNA

El ultraísmo es la rana que crió pelos.

Un poema de Rimbaud

INÉDITO EN CASTELLANO
(De «Les Illuminations», 1873)

Después del diluvio.

Tan pronto como la idea del diluvio se asuaga,
una liebre se detuvo en los esparcetas y las cam-
panillas movibles, y dijo su oración a través del arco-iris, al través de la tela de araña.

¡Oh, las piedras preciosas que se ocultaban,—
flores que ya miraban!

En la gran calle sucia, se levantaron los puestos de los vendedores, y se tiraban las barcas hacia el mar cuando arriba como en los grabados.

La sangre corrió, en casa de Barba-Azul, en los mataderos, en los circos, allí donde el sello de Dios empalideció las ventanas. La sangre y la leche corrieron.

Los castores edificaron. Los «mazagrans» hu-
mearon en los fumaderos.

En la enorme casa de vidrio aún brillantes, los niños apenados contemplan las maravillosas imágenes.

Cruje una puerta, y, y en el reducto del caserío, el niño vuelve sus brazos, hasta las veletas y las guías de los campanarios de todos los lugares, bajo el estrepitoso chaparrón.

Madame X estableció un piano en los Alpes.
La misa y las primeras comuniones se celebraron en los cien mil altares de la Catedral.

Las caravanas partieron. Y el Hotel Esplendi-
do fué construido en el caos de hielo y de noche del polo.

Desde entonces la luna escuchó a los chacales plesado por los furleríos de tomillo,—y las «gargas» en zuecos gruñendo en el verjel. Después, en la oquedad violeta, Puisin me dijo que era las pri-
maveras.

No respondemos de los poetas que poseyendo la habilidad de labrar en dos sentidos, acuden a nuestras páginas atraídos por el éxito del ultraísmo y su fuerza subyugadora. En nuestro afecto de ampliar esas páginas todo lo que, siendo nuevo, está bien. Si después deserten, peor para ellos.

Sueños, extinguen — espuma, rueda sobre el puente y pasa por encima de los bosques,— paños negros y órganos, relámpagos y truenos, subid y rodar,—aguas y tristezas, subid y relevar los di-
luvios.

Porque desde que se disiparon,—¡oh los piedras preciosas marchándose, y las flores, abiertas!—es esto un fastidio! Y la Reina, la hechicera que enciende o brasa, en el tiesto de tierra, no querrá contarnos jamás lo que ella sabe y nosotros no ig-
noramos.
JEAN-ARTHUR RIMBAUD
(R. Cansinos de la Vega, traduce)

El ultraísmo es el verso que se recita sin mover la lengua. La canción que se canta a un niño dormido sin desper-
tarlo.

ALDEA

Las esquilas reúnen la tristeza dispersa de los crepúsculos. El cielo está vario.
Lápida de un silencio serio sobre el nihilismo ecuánime de la jornada.
Las fluviales lenguas frescas del viento lamen mis manos y mejillas.
En la barbería el reloj—sexagenario sistemáti-
co—sigue jugando al solitario con los minutos.
Ante la lisposión rectilínea del caserío y curvilí-
nea del camino y los montes, Soreda y yo somos los dos pirámides del pueblo. Culminantes sobre la democracia geométrica y encarrilada.
Apoyadas en la baranda nuestras manos tocan el piano de colores del paisaje.
En la caja del piano está enterrado Wagner. A veces se despierta y canta en la tumba. En la caja del cráneo saltan entonces crímenes crecificiones golpes de estado pronunciamientos piras fornicica y pluralidades suicidios.
Hasta que nos extrae un fino silencio sin en-
lorchados ni estandartes.
Los acordes histrionizan las acumuladas angus-
tias.
El aqueducto tiende su espinazo polvoriento de sol.
El trasnochador de la pobregana lleva de sueño.
Los badajos últimos de la jornada.
Los párpados picotean la madeja de viento y polvo.
El Sol que labora los tenadores rueda a ras de los campos.
Las noches náufragos han topado el aljibe.
Aguardándose bestias insumisos vuelan aveni-
das de nerviosos insectos.
Los árboles donde se diluye la fiebre del farol son árboles de teatro.
Danzate la más sutil perro tronca la cola.
Incensario ciego optimismo biológico asciende humo a esa amistad azul donde reposa Dios y cantan los pájaros.
JorgeLuis BORGES

SOLEDAD

Frente a la pared de la montaña
lanzábamos las voces
con respuesta pagada.
Con el arco de nuestra garganta
disparábamos las flechas
que rebotaban en su coraza.
El viento
se llevó las palabras
como papeles viejos
Y todos los péndulos
seguían clavando en la pared del Silencio
el clavo sin fin del Tiempo.
GUILLERMO y FRANCISCO RELLO.

PLATE # 10 – Cover of *Tableros* ns 3, Madrid, 1922

⁂

"Gesta maximalista" refers to members of the left wing of the Russian Social Revolutionaries (opposed to Minimalist), or a Bolshevik. In his youth, Borges was greatly impressed by the Russian revolution as evidenced by the various poems written to honor the socialist experiment. Guillermo de Torre in his early study suggests—as does Borges himself in his "Autobiographical Notes"—that Borges destroyed a book of poems entitled "Red Psalms" shortly before returning to Argentina in 1921. The book, no doubt, was a collection of poems much like the above poem, as well as "Guardia roja," "Rusia," and "Trinchera," all of which pay homage to the communist struggle.

GESTA MAXIMALISTA

Desde los hombros curvos
   se arrojaron los rifles como viaductos
Las barricadas que cicatrizan las plazas
   vibran nervios desnudos
El cielo se ha crinado de gritos y disparos
Solsticios interiores han quemado los cráneos
Uncida por el largo aterrizaje
la catedral avión de multitudes quiere romper las amarras
y el ejército fresca arboladura
     de surtidores-bayonetas pasa
el candelabro de los mil y un falos
Pájaro rojo vuela un estandarte
      sobre la hirsuta muchedumbre extática

Ultra ns 3, Madrid, 20 Feb. 1921   Jorge-Luis Borges.

MAXIMALIST HEROISM

From their curved shoulders
   the rifles were flung like viaducts
The barricades scarring the plazas
   vibrate raw nerves
The sky is mane'd with shouts and gunshots
Interior solstices have burned skulls

Yoked by a long landing
the cathedral airplane of multitudes wants to
                              break its mooring-ties [t/o]
and the army with fresh masts
        of spouting-bayonets passes
candelabra of a thousand and one phalluses
Red bird flies a standard
        over the rugged and ecstatic crowd

PRISMAS

(Acordes - Mendicantes - Ciudad - Pueblo.)

Amanecen temblando las guitarras
mi alma   pájaro oscuro ante su cielo

Ya se murió la lámpara en la urna
más todavía
clama el silencio de las manos
como una herida abierta

Por la noche blindada
          vamos abriendo como ramas las calles
En los ciegos aljibes
se habían colmado de suicidio las manos
Las esquilas recogen la tristeza
dispersa de las tardes   La luna nueva
es una vocecita allá en el cielo

Ultra ns 4, Madrid, 1 Mar. 1921   Jorge-Luis Borges

PRISMS

(Chords - Beggars - City - People.)

Trembling guitars at daybreak
my soul   dark bird before its sky

Already the lamp in its glass urn has died
even still
cries silence from the hands
like an open wound

Through the armored night
          we go opening the streets like branches
In the blocked-up cisterns

hands had their fill of suicide
Sheep-bells gather the dispersed
sadness of the evening   The new moon
is a little voice out there in the sky

✳✳

"Guradia roja" is another of the poems in which Borges demonstrates his interest and empathy for what the Russian people are apparently accomplishing in the early 1920s with their revolution. He will revise and republish "Guardia roja" in *Tableros* ns 1, in November 1921. The typography will remain basically unchanged. However, in line four "planicie" becomes "estepa" reinforcing the fact that the setting is the Siberian plain in Russia; "Jesús-Cristo" becomes "el Nazarene" with little symbolic difference, while "torsos" is changed to "cuerpos," a more natural term for the human form.

GUARDIA ROJA

El viento es la bandera que se enreda en las lanzas
La estepa es una inútil copia del alma
De las colas de los caballos cuelga el villorrio incendiado.
La planicie rendida
no acaba de morirse
                                        Durante los combates
        el milagro terrible del dolor estiró los instantes
Ya grita el sol
Por el espacio trepan hordas de luces.
En la ciudad lejana
            donde los mediodías tañen los tensos viaductos
y de las cruces pende Jesús-Cristo
como un cartel sobre los mundos
se embozarán los hombres   en los torsos desnudos.

Ultra ns 5, Madrid, 17 Mar. 1921   Jorge-Luis Borges.

RED GUARD

The wind is the flag that entangles on the lances
The steppe is a useless copy of the soul
From the tails of horses hang the burned village.
The surrendered plain
will not finish dying

                                During the fighting
        the terrible miracle of pain extended the moments
Already the sun is screaming
Through space climb hordes of lights.
In the distant city
            where mid-days strum the taut viaducts
and Jesus Christ hangs from the crosses
like a poster above the worlds
the men will conceal themselves   in naked torsos.

TRANVÍAS

Con el fusil al hombro   los tranvias
patrullan las avenidas
Prora del imperial bajo el velámen
de cielos de balcones y fachadas

       verticales cual gritos

Carteles clamatorios ejecutan
su prestigioso salto mortal desde arriba
Dos estelas estiran el asfalto
y el trolley violinista

   va pulsando el pentágrama en la noche
   y los flancos desgranan
   paletas momentáneas y sonoras

Ultra ns 6, Madrid, 30 Mar. 1921   Jorge-Luis Borges

STREETCARS

With rifles on their shoulders   streetcars
patrol the avenues
Imperial prow underneath canvas sails
of balconied skies and facades

       vertical like shouts

Clamorous billboards execute
their prestigious mortal leap from above
Two wakes stretch along the asphalt
and the trolley violinist

   goes on playing the music staff through the night
   and the flanks shell out
   momentary and resounding palettes

NORTE

Los carteles borrachos
       saltan de las fachadas
y las proras enhiestas de las casas
van talando los años
Los edificios caen sobre mis ojos
Me lapidan los muros
Arrecian muchedumbres
      con un motín en los brutales puños
Yo he de romper en mi rodilla
el yugo de la noche que me unce

Ultra ns 7, Madrid, 10 Apr. 1921   Jorge Luis Borges

NORTH

Drunken billboards
       leap from the facades
and the years continue felling
the upright prows of the houses
Buildings fall on my eyes
The walls stone me
Crowds grow stronger
      with a riot in their brutal fists
Across my knee I must break
the yoke of night that binds me

⁂

The next poem, "Cingladura," published in April 1921, is not the same poem, "Singladura," Borges published in *Proa* ns 1 in 1924 and then included in *Luna de enfrente*, (see item 55 in Appendix). Once again, believing *Ultra* editors committed a typing error, Guillermo de Torre, in his 1925 study, begins mistitling this poem by changing the "C" to an "S." And, as with the versification of "Rusia," subsequent critics have appropriated the mistitling error: Videla (1961), Barnatan (1972), Meneses (1978), which has perpetuated the confounding of the two very distinct poems. A slight connection exists in that Borges inserts the last verse of "Cingladura," though changing "media" to "nueva," into the 1924 "Singladura." In *Ineditos Diccionario historica de la lengua Española*, "Cingladura" is defined as rowing a boat or canoe with one oar going from one side to the other, while "Singladura" is "a day's voyage at sea."

CINGLADURA

A Rivas Panedas.

He pulsado el violín de un horizonte
    brocal del mundo donde el Sol se macera
El viento esculpe oleaje
La neblina sosiega los ponientes
La noche rueda como un pájaro herido
En mis manos
       el mar
         viene a apagarse
el mar catedralicio
que iba empotrando agujas y vitrales
La media luna se ha enroscado a un mástil.

Ultra ns 8, Madrid, 20 Apr. 1921   Jorge-Luis Borges

SCULLING

To Rivas Panedas.

I have played the violin of a horizon
     rim of the world where the sun soaks
The wind sculpts the surf
The mist pacifies the setting sun
Night falls like a wounded bird
In my hands
        the sea
            comes to be extinguished
the cathedralic sea
that was embedding spires and stained glass
The half moon has wound itself around a mast.

✼

Traditionally "el aduar" [douar] is an encampment of Arabs whose tents are arranged in a circle, serving as an enclosure for horses. In Spain during the twenties the word is applied to a camp of gypsies.

DISTANCIA
A Elvira Sureda Montaner

Yo he quemado en mi lámpara   el sándalo
de tu haz de palabras
                    Otra mañana tiembla
              en sus manos
Tendidos de rodillas   los violines
rezan sus incensarios
Jadeantes lejanías
              se disputan
                    el aduar de un ocaso
La caravana lanza un ebrio lazo
                        horizonte de hierro
que derriba de bruces las ciudades
y en el prado relinchan los luceros

Ultra ns 9, Madrid, 30 April 1921   Jorge-Luis Borges

DISTANCE
To Elvira Sureda Montaner

In my lamp I have burned   the sandalwood
of your bundle of words
                        Another morning trembles
              in their hands
Spread out upon their knees   the violinists
pray their incensories
Panting distances
                    dispute
                        the sunset's douar
The caravan hurls a drunken rope
                        iron horizon
that knocks the cities face down
and in the meadow bright stars neigh

FIESTA

A Tomás Luque

Por la mañana suelta
se desperezan miles de banderas
La luz
        como una enredadera
                pende de las paredes
El viento late
Los edificios enhiestos son estandartes de piedra
Una canción sin música ni versos
de pie sobre mi pecho
ha sacudido el corazón del cielo

Ultra ns 15, Madrid, 30 June 1921   Jorge-Luis Borges

FIESTA

To Tomás Luque

In the lazy morning
        thousands of flags stretch out
The light
        like a climbing vine
                hangs from the walls
The wind throbs
The erect buildings are banners of stone
A song without music nor words
standing on my chest
has shaken the heart of the sky

mano, en el fondo de esas casas abandonadá
grandes rejas...

NORTE

Los carteles borrachos
         saltan de las fachadas
y las proras enhiestas de las casas
van talando los años
Los edificios caen sobre mis ojos
Me lapidan los muros
Arrecian muchedumbres
      con un motín en los brutales puños
Yo he de romper en mi rodilla
el yugo de la noche que me unce
             Jorge-Luis BORGES.

1422-M.

red de miradas concéntricas

El purismo al cubismo: «dicen que
no nos queremos porque no nos ven
hablar...»
      MARJAN PASZKIEWICZ
Saint-Raphaël.

FIESTA

         A Tomás Luque

    Por la mañana suelta
      se desperezan miles de banderas
La luz
    como una enredadera
        pende de las paredes
El viento late
Los edificios enhiestos son estandartes
             (de piedra
Una canción sin música ni versos
de pie sobre mi pecho
ha sacudido el corazón del cielo
         Jorge-Luis BORGES

CREPÚSCULO

Lluvia fina
      las últimas notas
      del canto lejano

PLATE #11 – Cover of *Ultra* ns 7. Madrid, 1921, and "Norte"; cover of
Ultra ns. 15, Madrid, 1921, and "Fiesta"

⁂

"Arrabal" has the distinction of being one of only four poems written and published during Borges's ultraísta phase (1920-1922) that was collected in *Fervor,* with minor revisions, and then continued to be selected by the poet for inclusion in his mature poetry anthologies. The poem initially appeared in a Madrid magazine, *Cosmopolis,* in Aug. 1921. Borges included the poem in *Poemas 1922-1943* but with the following alterations: "estuve" becomes "quedé," "juiciosas cual ovejas en manada" is cut, "Buenos Aires" inside the parenthesis is changed to "1921," and the last five lines are replaced with:

> y sentí *Buenos Aires:*
> esta ciudad que you creí mi pasado
> es mi porenir, mi presente;
> los años que he vivido en Europa son ilusorios,
> yo he estado siempre (y estaré) en Buenos Aires.

> [and I felt *Buenos Aires:*
> this city which I believed was my past
> is my future, my present;
> the years I've lived in Europe are illusory,
> I have always been (and shall be) in Buenos Aires.]

"Arrabal" continues to be revised in each anthology from *Poemas 1922-43* through *Obra poetica 1923-76.*

ARRABAL
A Guillermo de Torre, por contraste.

El arrabal es el reflejo
de la fatiga del viandante.

Mis pasos claudicaron
cuando iban a pisar el horizonte
y caí entre las casas
miedosas y humilladas
juiciosas como ovejas en manadas
encarceladas en manzanas
diferentes e iguales

como si fuesen todas ellas
recuerdos superpuestos barajados
de una sola manzana.
El pastito precario
desesperadamente esperanzado
salpicaba las piedras de la calle
y mis miradas constataron
gesticulante y vano
el cartel del poniente
en su fracaso cotidiano.
Y sentí *Buenos Aires*
y literaturicé en el fondo del alma
la viacrucis inmóvil
de la calle sufrida
y el caserío sosegado.

(Buenos Aires)
Cosmópolis ns 32, Madrid, Aug. 1921   Jorge-Luis Borges.

SUBURB
To Guillermo de Torre, for contrast.

The suburb is the reflection
of the traveler's fatigue.

My steps faltered
as they were about to step on the horizon
and I fell among the humbled
and fearful houses
judicious as sheep in flocks
imprisoned in blocks
different and the same
as if they were all
shuffled and superimposed memories
of one single block.
The precarious patch of grass
hopelessly hopeful
speckled stones from the street
and my glances noted
the gesticulating and vain

billboard of sunset
in its daily failure.
And I felt *Buenos Aires*
and deep in my soul I literaturized
the immobile way of the cross
from this suffering street
and the pacified block of houses

(Buenos Aires)

✻

Borges's prose poem, "Casa Elena," was first published in *Ultra* ns 17. The editors of the magazine allowed him five-and-a-quarter inch lines across the page, perhaps not considering it a prose poem. Most magazines publish both verse and prose poems with no more than four-and-a-quarter inch lines across the page. I consider the work another of Borges's experiments in prose poetry. As such, I have narrowed the margins to the normal width for poetry—to which most poems are limited in standard six by nine inch books. As prose poetry, the narrowed margins do not change the poem.

CASA ELENA
(Hacia una Estética del Lupanar en España)

Las paredes petrificadas en un gesto de máxima severidad nos lapidan. Los carteles borrachos saltan de los balcones. Pero junto a un rectángulo iluminado que susurra

C A
F E

hay un zaguán y una escalera vehemente, y una puerta que cede con esa sumisión de los libros que se abren en la página manoseada y requeteagotada por el estudio.
Luego = el burdel.

* * *

Un cuartujo donde algún que otro sombrero decapitado se desangra en las perchas. Unas cuantas muchachas. Un tropical enroscamiento de risas. Ciñendo un velador donde se pluraliza la mentira de un carnaval de naipes, se despereza nuestro aburrimiento. Las mujeres—el muestrario esperanzado y ecuánime del burdel de provincias—se ofrecen con la porfía intermitente de un albarán demasiado alto.
Domina una atmósfera de espontaneidad y de puericia. Un ambiente de cuarto de juguetes y de patio con surtidor. Enteramente primitivo, anti-cristiano, anti-pagano, anti-maximalista y anti-patético.

* * *

Aquí fracasan todas las religiones. La concepción judáica fracasa, ya que al árbol del Génesis lo han talado a golpes de falo y Adán y Eva se ven aquí reducidos a su actuacion más lamentable de mercancía y comprador. La concepción hedónica fracasa, ya que al placer lo han mutilado, robándole las tiaras prestigiosas de la visión romántica y subrayando su tonalidad de fatalismo duro.

Todo es amaestrado, manso, oficial. Primitivo al mismo tiempo que encarrilado, tal un caballo que hace pruebas o una vidalita donde rimen *dolor y amor*. . .Y nosotros aguardamos al margen de la media noche como al margen de un río.

El día, como un perro cansado, se tiende a nuestros pies y le acariciamos el lomo. Y la Estatuaria—esa cosa gesticulante y mayúscula—la comprendemos, al deliciarnos con las combas fáciles de una moza, esencial y esculpida como una frase de Quevedo. Y gue acepta—sin mayor alarde de asombro—la oxidada moneda falsa de nuestros verbalismos.

* * *

Después = la trabazón carnal. Con estas tres palabras me basta. Y que el placer, siendo algo que no está en el recuerdo, es igualmente inabarcable para todas las fórmulas.

De la madeja sensorial, la memoria sólo almacena los datos auditivos y visuales. Los otros—placer, dolor, estados térmicos—únicamente persisten vertidos al lenguaje de la visualidad y de la audición. E íntimamente, ¿qué pueden importarnos las interjecciones y la plasticidad cambiante de las etapas del ayuntamiento, si éstas cosas tienen sólo un valor de paralelismo con el placer, que es lo único esencial y que nadie logrará jamás encerrar en una urdimbre de arte?

* * *

Salimos. El bloque de aire cuadrangular que oprimía nuestras espaldas se hunde. El andamiaje de guirnaldas de brazos y voces acarameladas también se aleja. El cielo se ha llenado de astronomía. Una estrella jadeante tiembla sobre los techos del mercado. Nuestros ojos pulsan muchas estrellas. Las calles, como rieles expertos, nos empujan no se sabe a qué parte.

Contra el silencio de acero de la ciudad nuestros pasos
rebotan, como si fuésemos las advanzadas de un ejército que
viniera a conquistar la ciudad desmantelada y desnuda. Una hora
floja cae tropezando de un reloj. El viento escamotea las luces o
las ahorca. En los arrabales del mundo el amanecer monstruoso y
endeble ronda como una falsedad.

Ultra ns 17, Madrid, 30 Oct. 1921   Jorge-Luis Borges

CASA ELENA
(Towards a Brothel Esthetic in Spain)

The petrified walls in a gesture of utmost severity stone us.
The drunken billboards spring from the balconies. But next to an
illuminated rectangle that whispers

C A
F E

there is a foyer and a vehement stairway, and a door that yields with
the same submission of books that open to a much handled
page tattered from study.
Then = the bordello.

* * *

A miserable little room where a headless hat or two bleeds
on the hat rack. A few girls. A tropical peel of laughter. Gathered
around a pedestal table where a carnival of playing cards multiplies
the lie, our boredom stretches out its lethargy. The women—the
hopeful and equanimous display of the provincial bordello—offer
themselves with the flashing persistence of a "to-let" sign placed
much too high.

An air of spontaneity and puerility prevails. A fountain'd
patio and a toy-room atmosphere. Completely primitive, anti-
christian, anti-pagan, anti-elitist and anti-pathetic.

* * *

Here all religions fail. The Judaic concept fails, since the tree of Genesis has been chopped down by phallic blows and here, Adam and Eve find themselves reduced to their most pitiful act of merchandise and buyer. The hedonist concept fails, since they have mutilated pleasure, stealing prestigious "tiaras" from the romantic vision, and emphasizing the tone of harsh fatalism.

Everything is school'd, tame, official. Primitive as well as systematic, like a horse put through its paces or a melancholic folk song where "dolor" and "amor" rhyme. . .And we wait at the edge of midnight like on the bank of a river.

The day, like a tired dog, lays at our feet and we stroke its back. And the Statuary—that beckoning and monumental thing—we comprehend it, as we delight in the easy curves of a young girl, essential and sculpted like a phrase by Quevedo. And who accepts—without much show of surprise—the rusty fake coin of our words.

* * *

Then = the carnal bond. With these three words, enough said. Since pleasure, being something not within memory, likewise cannot be grasped by means of all the formulas.

Of the sensory skein, memory only stores auditory and visual data. The others—pleasure, pain, thermal states—only remain when translated into visual and auditory language. And personally, what do we care of the interjections and the changing plasticity of the stages of sexual intercourse, if these things merely have a value parallel to pleasure, which is the only important thing, and no one will ever succeed in containing it in a scheme of art?

* * *

We leave. The square block of air that pressed against our backs sinks away. The scaffolding of garlands of arms and caramel voices fades as well into the distance. The sky has become filled with astronomy. A panting star trembles above the roofs of the marketplace. Our eyes feel the pulse of many stars. The streets, like experienced rails, drive us on to who knows where.

Against the steel silence of the city our steps resound, as if we were the advanced guard of an army coming to conquer the naked and abandoned city. A lazy hour falls stumbling from a clock. The wind makes the lights vanish or strangles them. In the outskirts of the world the monstrous and feeble daybreak prowls like a lie.

ÚLTIMO ROJO SOL

Las casas a media asta
casi a ras de la calle
y un poniente monstruoso
que tiene abiertas todas sus alas

(dolorida y desnuda
una guitarra brusca se desangra)

El poniente de pie como un Arcángel
tiraniza la calle

Recién cuando el ocaso
es ya una cosa legendaria
se imponen los acordes al paisaje

Ultra ns 20, Madrid, 15 Dec. 1921   Jorge-Luis Borges

FINAL RED SUN

The houses at half-mast
almost level with the street
and a monstrous sunset
with all its wings open

(wounded and naked
a brusque guitar bleeds)

The sunset standing like an Archangel
tyrannizes the street

Just when the sunset
is already something legendary
the chords impose themselves on the landscape.

MONTAÑA

De espaldas a la tierra   yo recojo la sombra vendimiaria
que se derrama desnudo oleaje en las órbitas
abajo se hunden las ciudades
          empedradas de puños y de injurias
          la noche es vertical
Amanecen temblando las guitarras
mi alma   pájaro oscuro ante su cielo
Frescas eternidades resbalaron
por las montañas
que prolongan un gesto fatalista
la luna nueva fue una vocecita en la tarde.

Tableros ns 2, Madrid, 15 Dec. 1921   Jorge-Luis Borges

MOUNTAIN

My back to the earth   I gather shade like harvesting grapes
naked waves overflowing into orbits
below the cities sink
          paved with fists and insults
          the night is vertical
The guitars at daybreak rise trembling
my soul   dark bird before its sky
Fresh eternities slid
through the mountains
that prolong a fatal gesture
the new moon was a little voice in the evening.

⁂

For this "Aldea," Borges borrows the same title he used for his 1921 prose poem, "Aldea" [I], published nine months earlier. I have appended a roman numeral [II] to this 1922 "Aldea" to help draw a distinction between the two very different poems. In its brevity and playful typography, "Aldea" [II] resembles Borges's ultraistic verse poems while "Aldea" [I] is a lengthy prose poem. "Aldea" [I] will never be republished after its initial appearance in *Ultra* ns 2, February 1921.

ALDEA [II]

El poniente de pie como un Arcángel
tiranizó el sendero
La soledad repleta como un sueño
       se ha remansado al derredor del pueblo
Las esquilas recogen la tristeza
dispersa de las tardes   La luna nueva
es una vocecita bajo el cielo
        Según va anocheciendo
      vuelve a ser campo el pueblo

Ultra ns 21, Madrid, 1 Jan. 1922   Jorge-Luis Borges

VILLAGE [II]

The sunset standing like an Archangel
tyrannized the path
Solitude packed full like a dream
      has slowly flowed around the village.
Sheep-bells gather the dispersed
sadness of the evenings   The new moon
is a little voice under the sky
        As night gradually falls
      the village becomes a field again

⁂

"Aldea" [II] will be given a second stanza and collected in *Fervor* as "Campos Atardecidos" with slight typographical changes and one word change: "bajo" to "desde" ["under" to "from"]. In this incarnation, "Campos Atardecidos" becomes one of only four ultraistic poems written between 1920-1922 and collected in *Fervor*, then subsequently included in all his future anthologies of poetry, with numerous revisions, of course. In *Poemas 43*, the last four verses of the second stanza are rewritten and reduced to three verses. Minor word changes occur in *Poemas 58*, and again in *Obra Poética 69*. But in *Obra poética 76*, three more verses are cut from the second stanza: "al caminar mis pasos desmienten / la fatiga del tiempo / desparramada sobre el campo lacio," and makes word changes: (first stanza) "el sendero" to "el camino," "repleta" to "poblada," las esquilas" to "los cencerros;" (second stanza) "temblando" to "los trémulos" which is now placed before "colores," "se acurrucan" to "se guarecen," "la alcoba" to "el dormitorio," and "ajusticiará" to "cerrará." Curiously, the first stanza that was once "Aldea" [II], other than three word changes, remains the same from its first appearance in *Ultra* (1922) as "Aldea" [II] to its last appearance as "Campos Atardecidos" in Borges's final anthology, *Obra Poética 85*. Below is how the poem appears in the original 1923 edition of *Fervor*.

CAMPOS ATARDECIDOS

El poniente de pie como un Arcángel. . ..(see "Aldea [II]")

*
*　*

El poniente que no se cicatriza
aún le duele á la tarde.
Los colores temblando se acurrucan
en las entrañas de las cosas.
Al caminar mis pasos desmienten
la fatiga del tiempo
　　　　　desparramada sobre el campo lacio.
En la alcoba vacía
la noche ajusticiará los espejos.

FIELDS AT TWILIGHT

The sunset standing like an Archangel. . . .

*

*   *

The setting sun unhealed
still hurts the evening.
The trembling colors nestle
into the inner core of things.
As I walk my steps belie
the fatigue of time
        spread over the languid field.
In the empty bedroom
the night will execute the mirrors.

⁂

In the prose poem, "Escaparate," Borges indicates he is observing a porcelain vase or plate being displayed in a shop window which depicts the scene described in the poem—perhaps after Keats' *Ode on a Grecian Urn*. When one considers how little Borges treats the theme of love in his work, the poem seems to prefigure his life-long inclination towards isolation and solitude—which he once commented was the inevitable existence of a writer.

ESCAPARATE

PORCELANA

Semejante a ese guerrero chino que encima de las olas espumosas y malvas saluda la mansión donde los gestos de su hijito florecen.

Semejante al guerrero chino que se dirige, gracias al dragón monstruoso y pueril, hacia la costa adorable.

Y su esposa le tiende el cuerpito radioso y vivo del niño.

Pero siempre el espacio dorado los separa, siempre el héroe venera los suyos sin lograr abrazarlos.

Así yo ignoraré mis amores.

Así yo deberé desconocerte.

Tableros ns 3, Madrid, 15 Jan. 1922   Jorge Luis-Borges

SHOP WINDOW

PORCELANA

Like that Chinese warrior that on the mauve and foaming waves salutes the mansion where the gestures of his little son flourish.

Like the Chinese warrior that heads, thanks to the monstrous and puerile dragon, towards the venerable coast.

And his wife extends to him the small and radiant living body of the child.

But always the golden space keeps them apart, the hero always honors his own unable to embrace them.

Like this I shall never know my loves.

Like this I must disown you.

PLATE #12 – Cover of *Ultra* ns 17, Madrid, 1921

CASA ELENA

(Hacia una Estética del Lupanar en España)

Las paredes petrificadas en un gesto de máxima severidad nos lapidan. Los carteles borrachos saltan de los balcones. Pero junto a un rectángulo iluminado que susurra

C	A
F	E

hay un zaguán y una escalera vehemente, y una puerta que cede con esa sumisión de los libros que se abren en la página manoseada y requeteagotada por el estudio.

Luego = el burdel.

* * *

Un cuartujo donde algún que otro sombrero decapitado se desangra en las perchas. Unas cuantas muchachas. Un tropical enroscamiento de risas. Ciñendo un velador donde se pluraliza la mentira de un carnaval de naipes, se despereza nuestro aburrimiento. Las mujeres —el muestrario esperanzado y ecuánime del burdel de provincias— se ofrecen con la porfía intermitente de un albarán demasiado alto.

Domina una atmósfera de espontaneidad y de puericia. Un ambiente de cuarto de juguetes y de patio con surtidor. Enteramente primitivo, anti-cristiano, anti-pagano, anti-maximalista y anti-patético.

* * *

Aquí fracasan todas las religiones. La concepción judaica fracasa, ya que al árbol del Génesis lo han talado a golpes de falo y Adán y Eva se ven aquí reducidos a su actuación más lamentable de mercancía y comprador. La concepción hedónica fracasa, ya que al placer lo han mutilado, robándole las tiaras prestigiosas de la visión romántica y subrayando su tonalidad de fatalismo duro.

Todo es amaestrado, manso, oficial. Primitivo al mismo tiempo que encarrilado, tal un caballo que hace pruebas o una vidalita donde rimen *dolor* y *amor*... Y nosotros aguardamos al margen de la media noche como al margen de un río.

El día, como un perro cansado, se tiende a nuestros pies y le acariciamos el lomo. Y la Estatuaria —esa cosa gesticulante y mayúscula— la comprendemos, al deliciarnos con las combas fáciles de una moza, esencial y esculpida como una frase de Quevedo. Y que acepta —sin mayor alarde de asombro— la oxidada moneda falsa de nuestros verbalismos.

* * *

Después = la trabazón carnal. Con estas tres palabras me basta. Ya que el placer, siendo algo que no está en el recuerdo, es igualmente inabarcable para todas las fórmulas.

De la madeja sensorial, la memoria sólo almacena los datos auditivos y visuales. Los otros —placer, dolor, estados térmicos— únicamente persisten vertidos al lenguaje de la visualidad y de la audición. E íntimamente, ¿qué pueden importarnos las interjecciones y la plasticidad cambiante de las etapas del ayuntamiento, si estas cosas tienen sólo un valor de paralelismo con el placer, que es lo único esencial y que nadie logrará jamás encerrar en una urdimbre de arte?

* * *

Salimos. El bloque de aire cuadrangular que oprimía nuestras espaldas se hunde. El andamiaje de guirnaldas de brazos y voces acarameladas también se aleja. El cielo se ha llenado de astronomía. Una estrella jadeante tiembla sobre los techos del mercado. Nuestros ojos pulsan muchas estrellas. Las calles, como rieles expertos, nos empujan no se sabe a qué parte.

Contra el silencio de acero de la ciudad nuestros pasos rebotan, como si fuésemos las avanzadas de un ejército que viniera a conquistar la ciudad desmantelada y desnuda. Una hora floja cae tropezando de un reloj. El viento escamotea las luces o las ahorca. En los arrabales del mundo el amanecer monstruoso y endeble ronda como una falsedad.

Jorge-Luis BORGES

PLATE #13 – "Casa Elena" in *Ultra* ns 17

PLATE #14 – Cover of *Cosmópolis* ns 32, Madrid, 1921

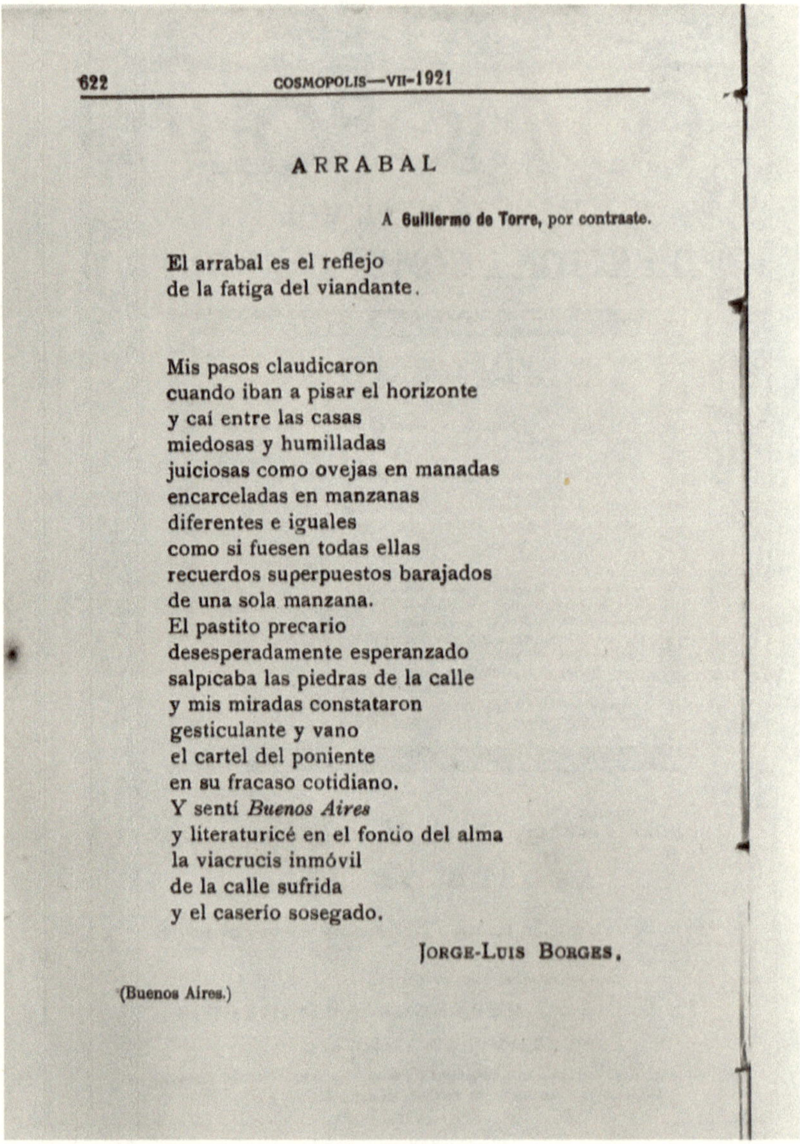

ARRABAL

A Guillermo de Torre, por contraste.

El arrabal es el reflejo
de la fatiga del viandante.

Mis pasos claudicaron
cuando iban a pisar el horizonte
y caí entre las casas
miedosas y humilladas
juiciosas como ovejas en manadas
encarceladas en manzanas
diferentes e iguales
como si fuesen todas ellas
recuerdos superpuestos barajados
de una sola manzana.
El pastito precario
desesperadamente esperanzado
salpicaba las piedras de la calle
y mis miradas constataron
gesticulante y vano
el cartel del poniente
en su fracaso cotidiano.
Y sentí *Buenos Aires*
y literaturicé en el fondo del alma
la viacrucis inmóvil
de la calle sufrida
y el caserío sosegado.

JORGE-LUIS BORGES.

(Buenos Aires.)

PLATE #15 – "Arrabal" in *Cosmópolis* ns 32

⁂

"Prismas: Sala vacia" has the distinction of being another one of the four ultraísta poems that Borges continues to publish throughout his career. It was first published in *Ultra* ns 22 in 1922, then collected in *Fervor* essentially unrevised, except for the elimination of "Prismas" from the title. Also, "vejez encerrada" becomes "vejez enclaustrada," and periods are added after "siempre," "borrosos," "infancia," and "antepasados." The dedication to Humberto Rivas is also eliminated. The poem receives one more word change in *Poemas 58*: "aplaude" to "festeja." "Sala vacia" has the added distinction of being the *only* ultraist poem translated into English for *Jorge Luis Borges: Selected Poems, 1923-1967*, and edited under the supervision of Borges himself. As the editor Norman Thomas di Giovanni states, "This is the first systematic presentation in English of the poems of a writer who made his initial fame in his own country nearly fifty years ago with his poetry, but whose present-day universal acclaim happens to rest on the small body of his prose." The version as it appeared in *Obra Poética 1923-1967* was the version employed for *Selected Poems* except for two additional changes: "borrosos" is placed before "anniversarios," and the elimination of "a puñetazos" after "mientras la luz." But even while *Selected Poems* was making its debut, Borges was giving the poem more extensive revisions for publication in *Obra poética 1923-1969*. The poem as seen today includes these revisions: "de vejez enclaustrada en un espejo" to "de tiempo detenido en un espejo"; "Con ademan desdibujado" to "Desde hace largo tiempo"; "su casi-voz angustiosa" to "sus angustiadas voces nos buscan"; the elimination of the two verses following "angustiosa"; "y apenas si estará ahora" becomes "y ahora apenas están"; the elimination of five verses after "infancia"; "mientras la luz" to "La luz del día de hoy"; "abre un boquete en los cristales" to "exalta los cristales de la ventana"; followed by the addition of the verse "desde la calle de clamor y de vértigo"; "ahorca" becomes "apaga" and with "la voz lacia" forms one verse. Again, I include the history of revisions to demonstrate and emphasize Borges consistent revising of his early work—in this case, almost out of recognition—to the point that the work should be considered another poem.

PRISMAS: SALA VACIA
A Humberto Rivas

Los muebles de caoba perpetúan
entre la indecisión del brocado
su tertulia de siempre
Los daguerrotipos
mienten su falsa cercanía
de vejez encerrada en un espejo
y ante nuestro examen se escurren
como fechas inútiles
de aniversarios borrosos
Con ademán desdibujado
su casi-voz angustiosa
corre detrás de nuestras almas
con más de medio siglo de atraso
y apenas si estará ahora
en las mañanas iniciales de nuestra infancia
La actualidad constante
convincente y sanguínea
aplaude en el trajín de la calle
su plenitud irrecusable
de apoteosis presente
mientras la luz a puñetazos
abre un boquete en los cristales
y humilla las seniles butacas
y arrincona y ahorca
la voz lacia
de los antepasados.

Ultra ns 22, Madrid, 15 Jan. 1922   Jorge-Luis Borges

PRISMS: EMPTY DRAWING ROOM
To Humberto Rivas

The mahogany furniture perpetuates
amid the uncertain brocade
its never ending conversation
The daguerreotypes
belie their false proximity
of old age enclosed in a mirror
and as we look they slip away
like useless dates
of blurred anniversaries
With hazy features
their anguished almost-voice
runs after our souls
more than a half century late
and now it is scarcely there
in the initial mornings of our childhood
The constant here and now
definitive and full-blooded
applauds in the bustle of the street
its unchallengeable plenitude
of present apotheosis
while the light with jabs
breaks through a narrow gap in the windows
and humbles the senile armchairs
and corners and strangles
the withered voice
of ancestors

SIESTA

Muchedumbres de sol
    bloquean la casa
y el tiempo acobardado se remansa
detrás de las persianas
    verdes como cañaverales
Margenándolo todo
    hallamos nuestro cuerpo
como una misma acotación inútil
hasta que las campanas rebosantes
    vierten la tarde
y se arrodilla el humillado cielo
y nos vestimos de previstos paisajes

Ultra ns 24, Madrid,15 Mar. 1922   Jorge-Luis Borges

SIESTA

Multitudes of sun
    blockade the house
and cowardly time flows slowly
behind green venetian blinds
    like reeds of cane
Marginalizing it all
  we find our body
like a same useless annotation
until the overflowing bells
    spill the afternoon
and the humbled sky kneels
and we dress in predictable landscapes

SÁBADO

Benjuí de tu presencia
que iré quemando luego en el recuerdo
y miradas felices
de bordear tu vivir
Afuera hay un ocaso joya oscura
engastada en el tiempo
que redime las calles humilladas
y una honda ciudad ciega
de hombres que no te vieron
La tarde calla o canta
Alguien descrucifica los acordes
clavados en el piano
Siempre la multitud de tu belleza
en claro esparcimiento sobre mi alma

Nosotros ns 160, Buenos Aires, Sep. 1922
                                        Jorge Luis Borges.

SATURDAY

Your presence of Benjamin incense
that I'll be burning later in my memory
and contented glances
from surrounding your being
Outside there is a sunset dark jewel
set in time
that redeems the humble streets
and a profoundly blind city
of men that didn't see you
The evening grows silent or sings
Someone uncrucifies the chords
nailed into the piano
Always the multitude of your beauty
in clear dispersion over my soul

⁂

To create the poem "Sabados," Borges adds four stanzas to "Sabado," except "Afuera hay" becomes "Hay afuera"; "joya" is changed to the more arabic term for jewel "alhaja"; "acordes" in line 11 becomes "anhelos" (desires); and "belleza" becomes the more colloquial "hermosura." Standard punctuation is introduced as well. Sabados" is then collected in *Fervor* and is one of the four ultraist poems Borges continues to collect in his anthologies. In *Poemas 1922-1943*, "Sabados" has the following revisions: the second stanza is cut; the third stanza remains the same while the first two verses of the fourth are cut and "Empujando" becomes "Agravando"; in addition, the dedication is reduced to: "Para C.G." Curiously, Borges leaves the first stanza, the original "Sabado" of 1922, intact, except for the elimination of the last verse. "Sabados" remains unchanged in *Poemas 1923-1958*. But in *Obra Poética 1923-1969*, the poem again receives major revisions: the first four verses and the seventh verse of the first stanza (the original "Sabado") are cut and "Hay afuera" reverts back to "Afuera hay"; the sixth and seventh verse of the second stanza are cut, and the third stanza (originally the fourth) is completely rewritten:

> Agravando la reja está la noche.
> En la sala severa
> se buscan como ciegos nuestras dos soledades.
> Sobrevive a la tarde
> la blancura gloriosa de tu carne.
> En nuestro amor hay una pena
> que se parece al alma.

Thus, the original "Sabado" as it appeared in *Nosotros* in September 1921 barely exists. I feel Borges's poem "Sabados," though it had its genesis in ultraísmo, should be considered a "mature" poem that he continued to rewrite throughout his career.

SABADOS (the original 1923 *Fervor* version)
Para mi novia, Concepción Guerrero.

Benjuí de tu presencia. . . .(see "Sabado" with noted revisions)

*
* *

No hay más que una sola tarde
la única tarde de siempre.

Aquí está su remanso. Las palabras
no logran arraigarse en su paraje
y se escurren como agua.
El corazón refleja
tus labios que una noche serán besos
y mis ojos abiertos como heridas
habrán de sostener otros lugares.
Te traigo vanamente
mi corazón final para la fiesta.

*
* *

A despecho de tu desamor
tu hermosura
                prodiga su milagro por el tiempo.
Está en tí la ventura
como la primavera en la hoja nueva.
Quedamente a tu vera
se desangra el silencio.
Ya casi no soy nadie,
soy tan solo un anhelo
que se pierde en la tarde.
En tí está la delicia
como está la crueldad en las espadas.

*
* *

Suave como una rosa fué tu silencio,
mas hoy lo rayan los presentimientos.
Empujando la reja
está la noche dura que desalma la quinta.
Nuestras dos soledades en la sala severa
se buscan como ciegos.
Acallando palabras momentáneas
hablan la angustia y tu pudor y mi anhelo.
Sobrevive a la tarde
la blancura gloriosa de tu carne.
En nuestro amor no hay algazara,
hay una pena parecida al alma.

*
* *

Tú
    que ayer solo eras toda la hermosura
    eres también todo el amor, ahora.

SATURDAYS

For my girlfriend, Concepción Guerrero.

Your presence of Benjamin incense . . . .

*
* *

There is only one evening
always the only evening.
Here is it's tranquil pool. Words
don't take root in her waters
but like water they trickle out.
My heart reflects on
your lips that one night will be kisses
and my open eyes like wounds
shall have to endure other places.
Vainly I bring you
my final heart for your fiesta.

*
* *

Despite your disregard
your loveliness
            lavishes its miracle through time.
In you exists good fortune
like Spring within a new born leaf.
Quietly at your side
the silence bleeds.
Now I'm almost nobody,
I'm merely a longing
that is lost in the evening.
In you is delight
like cruelty is in swords.

*
* *

Soft as a rose was your silence,
but today it is marked by forebodings.
Pushing on the grated window
the merciless night "de-souls" the villa.
Our two solitudes in the stark drawing room
seek each other like the blind.
Anguish, your modesty and my longing speak out
hushing momentary words.
The glorious whiteness of your flesh
survives the evening.
In our love there's no Arabic war cry,
there is a sorrow that resembles the soul.

*

* *

You
· that yesterday was merely all loveliness
are now as well, all love.

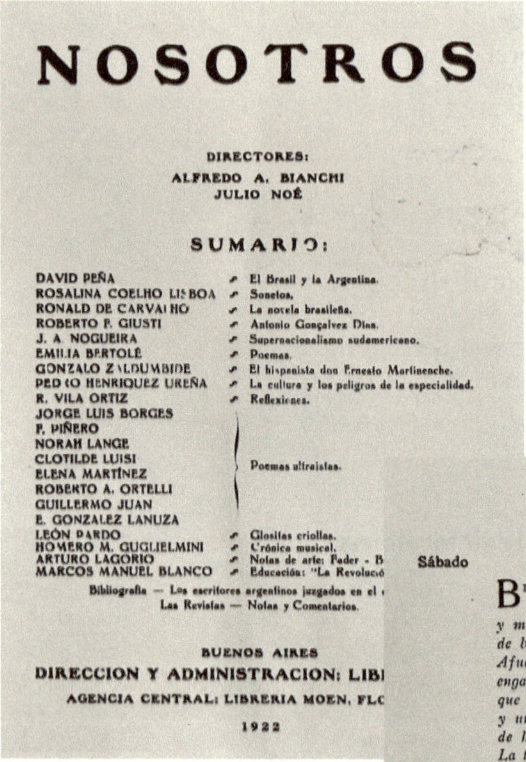

NOSOTROS

DIRECTORES:
ALFREDO A. BIANCHI
JULIO NOÉ

SUMARIO:

BUENOS AIRES
DIRECCION Y ADMINISTRACION: LIBI
AGENCIA CENTRAL: LIBRERIA MOEN, FLC
1922

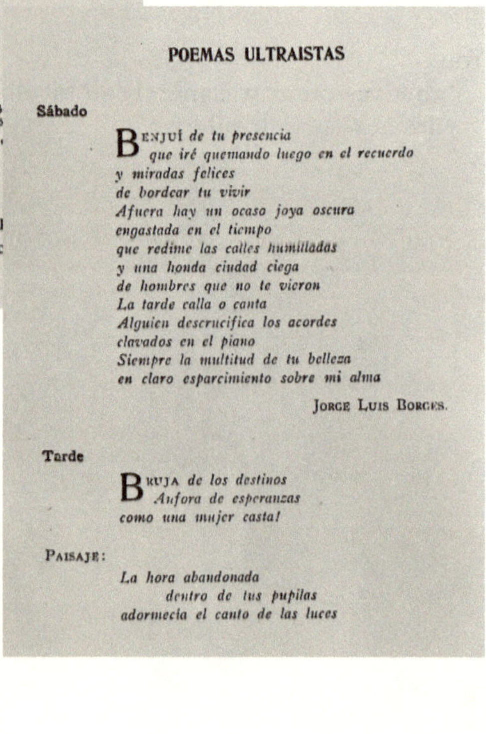

POEMAS ULTRAISTAS

Sábado

Benjuí de tu presencia
    que iré quemando luego en el recuerdo
y miradas felices
de bordear tu vivir
Afuera hay un ocaso joya oscura
engastada en el tiempo
que redime las calles humilladas
y una honda ciudad ciega
de hombres que no te vieron
La tarde calla o canta
Alguien descrucifica los acordes
clavados en el piano
Siempre la multitud de tu belleza
en claro esparcimiento sobre mi alma

JORGE LUIS BORGES.

Tarde

Bruja de los destinos
    Anfora de esperanzas
como una mujer casta!

PAISAJE:

La hora abandonada
    dentro de tus pupilas
adormecía el canto de las luces

PLATE #16 – Cover of *Nosotros* ns 160, Buenos Aires, 1922, and
"Sabado"

PLATE #17 – Cover of *Alfar* ns 36, La Coruña, January 1924

MAGNOLIAS

MADERA DE FRANCISCO MIGUEL

ALEJAMIENTO

Más allá de las casas del suburbio
sórdidas como puños llenos de flaca ira
por el campo espaciado
sobre el Tajo donde dos ríos
adunan sus pueblos de agua
cantando,
tu recuerdo ya doloroso
dió demasiadas veces su resplandor a mi sombra,
su resplandor de quemazón que me abrasa.

JORGE LUIS BORGES.

Negado por las cosas y negándolas,
caminé yo con tu recuerdo por esos campos
que sólo eran la certitud de tu ausencia.
Hoy me vino tu carta
embanderando con su claror mi jornada.
Tu carta me devuelve las campiñas
y la enhiesta arboleda que enriquece
con su soberbia de hojas el cielo atardecido:
Tierras que nunca vistu!

Ginebra, 1943.

25

PLATE #18 – "Alejamiento" in *Alfar* ns 36

⁂

Borges wrote "Alejamiento," in late 1923 in Geneva and published the poem in January 1924 in *Alfar* ns 36 during his second residency in Spain. At that time, he had already begun to distance himself from Ultraismo. Still, certain ultraistic tendencies remain, such as the odd simile in line two. "Alejamiento" is never collected or published again. Curiously, it is one of Borges's few love poems, which may have something to do with why he chose to ignore the poem after its inicial publication.

ALEJAMIENTO

Más allá de las casas del suburbio
sórdidas como puños llenos de flaca ira
por el campo espaciado
sobre el Tajo donde dos ríos
adunan sus pueblos de agua
cantando,
tu recuerdo ya doloroso
dió demasiadas veces su resplandor a mi sombra,
su resplandor de quemazón que me abrasa.

Negado por las cosas y negándolas,
caminé yo con tu recuerdo por esos campos
que sólo eran la certitud de tu ausencia.
Hoy me vino tu carta
embanderando con su claror mi jornada.
Tu carta me devuelve las campiñas
y la enhiesta arboleda que enriquece
con su soberbia de hojas el cielo atardecido:
Tierras que nunca viste!

Jorge Luis Borges.   Ginebra, 1923
Alfar ns 36, La Coruña, Jan. 1924

ESTRANGEMENT

Beyond the houses of the suburb
sordid like fists full of feeble rage
by the open field
over the Tajo where two rivers
unite their populace of water
singing,
your memory so painful now
too many times gave its brilliance to my shade,
its glow of intense heat that burns me.

Denied by things and denying them,
I walked with your memory through those fields
that were only the certainty of your absence.
Today your letter arrived
adorning my day with its brightness.
Your letter returned to me the countryside
and the upright woods that enriches the evening sky
with its haughty magnificence of leaves:
                    lands you never saw!
                                        Geneva, 1923

⁂

The two sonnets, "Villa Urquiza" and "Las palmas" appear together in *Alfar* ns 59 in 1926 under the general title *Dos Sonetos*. But this "Villa Urquiza" is not the poem of the same title that Borges publishes in *Fervor* and collects in *Poemas 43*, then, subsequently, eliminates from his future anthologies starting with *Poemas 58*. I include these sonnets, though they are published more than a year outside of the logical span of what might be called Borges's "early writing," because a date on the poems indicate that they were written in 1923. Moreover, I am certain the poems have never again been published since their inicial publication. An additional interest for including these poems is that they are a curiosity to me. It seems odd that Borges would attempt to take on the challenge of writing in such a strict form and rhyme scheme—when he never did before. I suspect that they may be early evidence of his growing lack of confidence in his poetic skills, which he expressed in his interview with Jean Millerert. Perhaps he is seeking validation as a poet by taking on the challenge of a classical form after several years writing only "free verse" poetry and prose poetry without rhyme. In addition to this, the publication of *Fervor* in 1923, funded by his father, seems not to have brought him the success he sought—the same success other Latin American poets are enjoying at that time. Indeed, in the October 1923 issue of *Alfar*, in which his sister's wood carving is displayed, César Vallejo's seminal poem "Trilce" appears from his collection *Trilce*—inarguably the most significant, ground-breaking work by a Latin American poet of the twentieth century. Certainly Borges did not fail to see the growing importance of other poets at this time. As for *Dos Sonetos*, to my knowledge, Borges never attempts a fixed-form poem again—in fact, his poetry becomes increasingly more prosaic between 1924 until he stops writing poetry all together in 1929, resuming his poetic practice around 1959.

DOS SONETOS:
VILLA URQUIZA

Un huraño tranvía rezonga rendimiento
En la borrosa linde que los campos vislumbra
Y una corazonada de lluvia apesadumbra
Este domingo pobre de arrabal macilento.

Una que otra chicuela sonríe su contento
De posibles piropos en la acera y encumbra
Un prestigio fiestero la placita que alumbra
Con limpidez de luces el turbio dejamiento.

De golpe un organito profundiza la tarde
Publicando en arranque de sonido viviente
Lo que en las hondonadas del corazón nos arde:

Urgencia de ternura, esperanza vehemente,
Carne en pos de la carne con silencio cobarde:
Burdo secreto a voces que unifica la tarde.

LAS PALMAS

En la ruidosa punta de veinte singladuras
Supo alistar con arte sorprendente la noche
Ese alivio de mares, ese manso reproche
A las olas derechas y a las tormentas duras.

Después en mi conciencia dejaron grabaduras
Entre zangoloteos bruscos de carricoche
El mercado y la torre, serenísimo broche
Juntando calles quietas y celestes alturas.

Algunos caserones pintarrajeados de ocre,
Unas cuantas plazuelas, orondas como altares,
El palmar cuya cima la suave noche encierra,

Alcores que altivecen la población mediocre. . .
En ese sitio el alma, quebrantada de mares,
Recobró la caricia familiar de la tierra.

1923.

Jorge Luis Borges.
Alfar ns 59, La Coruña, July 1926

THE TOWN OF URQUIZA

A surly streetcar grumbles exhaustedly
In the hazy edge faintly delineated by fields
And a feeling of rain hangs above
This poor pale suburban Sunday.

Here and there a young girl smiles pleasingly
At possible compliments on the sidewalk and the small Plaza
Takes on an air of gay prestige, that with the clarity
Of its lights illuminates the turbid neglect.

Suddenly a hurdy-gurdy deepens the evening
Announcing in bursts of living sound
What burns in the hollows of our hearts:

An urgent need for tenderness, a vehement hope,
Flesh in search of flesh with cowardly silence:
Voicing the clumsy secret that unifies the evening.

THE PALMS

At the noisy end of a twenty day sea voyage
The night with astonishing art found a way to enlist
That relief from the seas, that gentle reproach
To the huge waves and the harsh storms.

Later they remained etched into my conscience
Amidst the brusque rattlings of an old jalopy,
The market and the tower, like a very serene brooch
Joining the quiet streets and celestial heights.

Some large rambling houses daubed ochre,
A few small plazas, adorned like altars,
The palm grove whose crest the gentle night enfolds,

Hills that dignify the mediocre town. . .
In that place my soul, broken by the sea,
Regained the familiar caress of land.

PLATE # 19 – *Fervor de Buenos Aires*, 1st edition, 1923, cover

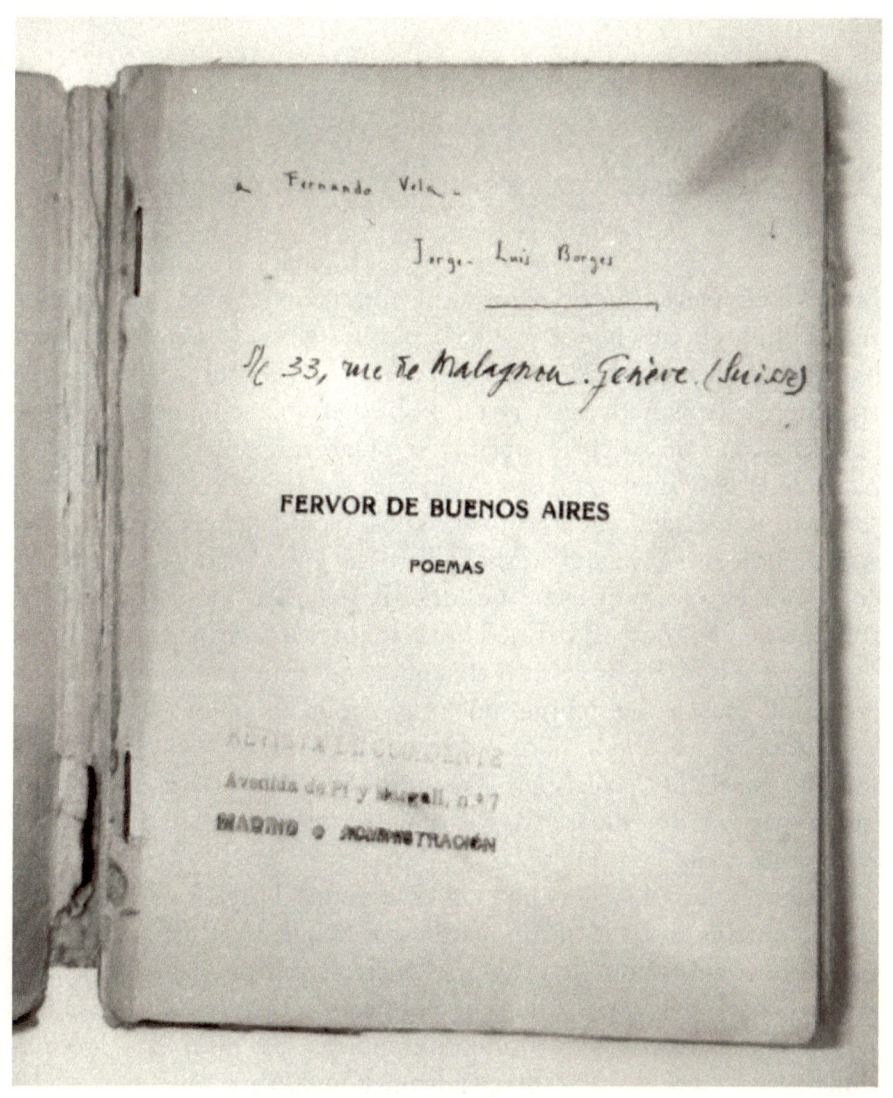

PLATE # 20– *Fervor de Buenos Aires*, 1ˢᵗ edition, 1923, title page.

Selected Essays, Reviews, and Manifestos, 1919 to 1922

From documented autobiographical comments, Borges never considered himself *only a poet*. His first published work was not a poem but rather an essay he'd written in French: "Chronique des lettres espagnoles: Trois nouveaux livres," published in the Geneva newspaper *La Feuille*, on August 20, 1919. Ana Gargatagli of the Universitat Autónoma de Barcelona has written that the paper *La Feuille* in 1918 "backed Switzerland's neutrality and took a stand against the war, [and was] a platform for anarchist thought in the French language." Apparently, Borges wrote the essay while reading Baroja "intensely, [and] at a time when he [Borges] defined himself as an anarchist, a freethinker and a pacifist" (4). His critical thoughts and opinions on other writers I find most enlightening, not only about his fellow writers, but what they reveal about Borges himself. Indeed, his review of James Joyce's *Ulysses: "El Ulises de Joyce,"* published in *Proa* ns 6, Buenos Aires in Jan 1925, per my research, is the first one written in Spanish on this important book.

Few scholars, I believe, would find young Borges's early literary essays, reviews and Ultraísmo manifestos deficient or misguided. I've included in this book eleven works written and published in magazines through Dec. 1921. After the publication of *Fervor* in the fall of 1923, Borges's critical essay production increased as his poetry production began to diminish. From 1923 through 1926, a great majority of the essays (the titles of which I've included in the Appendix) were collected in his first two essay collections *Inquisiciones* (1925) and *El Tamaño de mi Esperanza* (1926). In keeping with the subject and theme of this book, I reprint only those essays published before 1923 and which Borges did not collect, even though the essays in these two essay collections are no longer available to the reader. That I have copies of them as they first appeared in magazines set up a conflict in me—especially after taking the time and energy to translate them. But my decision not to include them in this study seems the correct decision. Perhaps one day, his two early collection of essays will be reprinted for public consumption. If not, a future book from me may be forthcoming—if given the permission—presenting and critically discussing the essays I've kept out of this study, which is a considerable number.

Those essays, reviews and manifestos that are reproduced in this chapter are presented exactly as they appeared when first published in the magazines. These disregarded essays, I feel, reveal a sharp, creative, and erudite intellect at work at a very young age, and, after years hidden away on the shelves of bibliotecas and private collections, I make them available.

AL MARGEN DE LA MODERNA LIRICA

Para el hombre, y más aún para el adolescente, sobre cuyas espaldas descansa todo lo que posee el orbe de arrogante y de audaz, un nuevo poema, una novela nueva, puede ser una Atlántida, una íntima y estupenda aventura.

Mas la potencia de admirar que hay en nosotros es limitada y, agotados los primeros hallazgos, la ley de lasitud nos impone una concepción rígida del arte, hecha de normas inflexibles entre las cuales queremos aprisionar todas las emociones y toda la belleza que han sentido o sentirán jamás los otros hombres. Para la crítica existente, estas normas son hoy la limpidez y la armonía. En todos los países donde han surgido las modernas tendencias, en Bohemia, en Francia, en Alemania y en España, la crítica las ha sacrificado sobre la vieja cruz de claridad y de euritmia. No han advertido en la labor ultraísta más que los barroquismos de la forma, sin inquietarse del espíritu, del nuevo ángulo de visión que la subraya.

Este ángulo de visión es diametralmente diferente del suyo. Por eso, toda advertencia cauta, toda burla, todo mohín de desdén basados en los viejos idearios, no muestran más que una total incomprensión del verdadero espíritu del ultra.

Intentaré una exégesis. Es posible que muchos ultraístas hállense desacordes conmigo, por tratarse de un arte que traduce impresiones esencialmente individuales, que abandona la grey y busca al individuo.

Las palabras que siguen quieren únicamente ser la expresión de una actitud ante el ultra. No aspiran a un valor objectivo.

El cristianismo y aun el paganismo se basaron sobre una concepción de la vida esencialmente estática. Por eso, mientras las almas fueron cristianas o paganas, el arte pudo buscar la euritmia, la arquitectura, lenta y segura. Hoy triunfa la concepción dinámica del kosmos que proclamara Spencer y miramos la vida, no ya como algo terminado, sino como un proteico devenir, como una rauda

carnavalesca teoría hecha de sufrimientos y de goces. Como un
febril frondoso rojo aquelarre ante el blanco terror de las estrellas...
El ultraísmo es la expresión recién redimida del transformismo en
literatura. Esa floración brusca de metáforas que en muchas obras
creacionistas abruma a los profanos, se justifica así plenamente y
representa el esfuerzo del poeta para expresar la milenaria juventud
de la vida que, como él, se devora, surge y renace en cada segundo.

Verdad que hemos llegado tarde también. . .Miles de otros
artistas han pulsado las cuerdas del vivir. Entre el mundo externo y
nosotros, entre nuestras emociones más íntimas y nuestro propio yo,
los fenecidos siglos han elevado espesos bardales. Se nos ha querido
imponer la obsesión de un eterno y mustio universo, de ramaje
agobiado bajo las grises telarañas y larvas de pretéritos símbolos. Y
nosotros queremos descubrir la vida. Queremos ver con ojos nuevos.
Por eso olvidamos la fastuosa fantasmagoría mitológica, que en toda
hembra lúbrica quiere visualizar una faunesa y ante las formidables
selvas del mar, inevitablemente nos sugiere, con lívida sonrisa
encubridora, la visión lamentable de Afrodita surgiendo de un
Mediterráneo de añil ante un coro de obligados tritones. . .

La miel de la añoranza no nos deleita y quisiéramos ver todas
las cosas en una primicial floración. Y al errar por esta única noche
deslumbrada, cuyos dioses magníficos son los augustos reverberos de
luces áureas, semejantes a genios salomónicos, prisioneros en copas
de cristal, quisiéramos sentir que todo en ella es nuevo y que esa luna
que surge tras un azul edificio no es la circular eterna palestra sobre
la cual los muertos han hecho tantos ejercicios de retórica, sino uno
luna nueva, virginal y auroralmente nueva.

Aun lo trivial como esas vívidas naranjas, auroras que en
fervorosas, lujuriosas piras, incendian los claustrales mercados, es
también único, como única es la estremante (sic) noche deslumbrada,
atónita de azul, como una gran montaña con surtidores de astros y
selvas claras de constelaciones. . .

* * *

El ultraísmo no es quizás otra cosa que la espléndida síntesis
de la literatura antigua, que la última piedra redondeando su
milenaria fábrica. Esa premisa tan fecunda que considera las palabras

no como puentes para las ideas, sino como fines en sí, halla en él su apoteosis.

Tal vez esta verdad no sea absoluta pero por un instante al menos es sorprendente ver en las tendencias novísimas, algo así como el divino crepúsculo, como la última roja floración, como el canto del cisne de la retórica. . .

Grecia ns 39, Sevilla, 31 Jan. 1920   Jorge Luis Borges

AT THE MARGIN OF MODERN LYRIC

For man and even more for the adolescent, on whose shoulders rests all the arrogance and audacity the world possesses, a new poem, a new novel, can be an Atlantis, an intimate and wonderful adventure.

But the potential in us to admire is limited and, once the first discoveries are exhausted, the law of lassitude imposes on us a rigid conception of art, made of rigid norms with which we'd like to imprison all the emotions and all the beauty other men have felt or will ever feel. For today's critics, these norms are order and harmony. In every country where the modern trends have emerged, in Bohemia, France, Germany and in Spain, the critics have nailed them to the old cross of clarity and eurhythmy. They've noticed in the ultraist work nothing but the baroque elements in the form, without bothering with the spirit of the ultra, the new scope of vision underscoring it.

This scope of vision is diametrically different from his. That's why all cautious warning, all taunting, all grimace of disdain based on the old ideology, merely show a total misunderstanding of the true spirit of the ultra.

I'll attempt an exegesis. It's possible that many ultraists find themselves in disagreement with me, for it concerns an art that translates impressions which are essentially individual, that abandons the flock and seeks the individual.

The following words are only intended to be the expressed attitude of one with respect to ultra. They don't aspire to be objective.

Christianity and even paganism were based on a conception of life as essentially static. Therefore, as long as souls were Christian or pagan, art could search for eurhythmy, structure, slowly and surely. Today, what prevails is the dynamic conception of the cosmos that Spencer proclaimed and we see life, not as something finished, but as a protean flux, a swift "carnivalesque" theory made of pain and joy. Like a feverish, luxuriant, red Sabbat orgy before the white terror of the stars. . .Ultraism is the expression recently redeemed from "transformism" in literature. That sudden flowering of metaphors that, in many creationist works, overwhelms the uninitiated reader, fully justifies itself and represents the poet's efforts towards expressing the youthful millennium of life, that, like him, devours itself, surges and is reborn each second.

True, we too have arrived late. . .Thousands of other artists have plucked the strings of life. Between the external world and ourselves, between our most intimate emotions and our own ego, the perished centuries have raised thick barbed-topped walls. They've tried to impose on us the obsession of an eternal and wilted universe, with its branches burdened by gray spider-webs and the larvae of past symbols. And we want to discover life. We want to see with new eyes. For that we forget the pompous mythological phantasmagoria which converts every lubricous female into a "faun-ette" and which bid us see, standing before formidable jungles of the sea, the pitiful vision of Aphrodite, with his slight concealing smile, emerging from an indigo Mediterranean before a chorus of mandatory tritons. . .

The sweetness of nostalgia does not delight us and we would like to see all things in a primeval flowering. And roaming through this unique dazzled night, whose magnificent gods are the august reflectors of golden light, similar to Solomonic geniuses imprisoned in crystal cups, we would like to feel that everything in it is new and the moon that emerges from behind a blue building is not the eternal circular literary stage on which the dead have performed so many rhetorical exercises, but rather a new moon, virginal and day-break new.

Even what is trivial, like those vivid oranges, dawns that in fervent, lecherous pyres, inflame the cloistral market-place, is likewise unique, like the startling dazzling night is unique, aghast of blue, like a great mountain with fountains of stars and bright jungles of constellations. . .

* * *

Ultraism is perhaps nothing else but the magnificent synthesis of ancient literature, nothing but the last stone that completes the factory a thousand years in the making. That premise so prolific that it considers the words not as bridges for the ideas, but as ends in themselves, finds in Ultraism it's culmination.

This truth perhaps is not absolute, but at least for an instant it is surprising to see in the newest trends, something like the divine twilight, like the ultimate red flowering, like the swan song of rhetoric. . .

LIRICA EXPRESIONISTA: SINTESIS

La palabra *expresionismo*—tan cenital o tan brumosa como cualquier otra palabra—la difundió en 1914 Paul Fechter para signar el movimiento literario dramático pictórico y escultórico que, irradiando de Alemania y de Austria (dos de los principales precursores del expresionismo lírico, Rainer Maria Rilke y Jorge Trakl, fueron austriacos. . .), se pluraliza hoy entierras escandinavas y en Zurich.

Si quisiéramos definirlo—y no ignoro lo carcelarias que suelen ser estas definiciones—diríamos que es la tentativa de crear para esta época un arte matinalmente intuicionista, de superar la realidad ambiente y elevar sobre su madeja sensorial y emotiva una ultra-realidad espiritual. Diríamos que el expresionismo (con los demás impulsos paralelos que accionan bajo distintas latitudes) no es otra cosa en última exégesis que el arte *subrayado*. . .

Su fuente la constituye esa visión ciclópea y atlética del pluriverso que rimara, Walt Whitman (partiendo a su vez de Fechte y de Hegel). Las ramificaciones occidentalistas de esta visión hallaron principalmente reflejo en las hímnicas estrofas de Stadler y fueron posibles en Alemania hasta el 1914, cuando gritó la guerra. Ante aquel derrumbamiento de un mundo, el occidentalismo con sus corolarios optimistas, púgiles y sensuales se vino abajo, o debió al menos transformarse hondamente. Los jóvenes poetas de Alemania se encontraron frente a una crisis decisiva de su mentalidad. Ser occidentalista significaba aplaudir la sociedad industrializada, culpable de la guerra; significaba la claudicación del espíritu ante los barrotes temporales y espaciales que eran su cárcel. La realidad tangible sólo ofrecía una demencia dolorosa y absurda. Urgia superarla, vencerla, visualizarla de manera nueva. . .Y fruteció el expresionismo.

A despecho de algunas componendas y pragamatismos más
o menos hipócritas, el cambio se operó. El expresionismo tomó ese
carácter dostoicvskiano, utópico, místico y maximalista a la vez que
aún tiene. Asi vemos a la revista *Die Aktion*—que con *Der Sturm* es
una de las lámparas del renacimiento literario tudesco—ejercer una
influencia paralelamente anarquizante sobre los dos opuestos sectores
de la estética y la cuestión social. . .

Detrás del frente

Nos morimos en la soledad
Los ojos cansados beben en la calma el desierto
a lo largo del camino se detiene en las cruces
Vientos traen los gritos de la batalla
en el oriente antorchas
pétreas son nuestras manos
y nuestras almas llevan un milagro
Mujeres y hogar se hunden
Crepúsculo

Esperanza

Primavera mansa me cuelga del corazón
Florece
y hace dormir púdicamente las horas
el valle lanza sombras tranquilas
Luego
mana fatiga de las jóvenes ramas
y yemas que frutecidas mueren son bálsamo
El alma asiente
y rie como un viejo

Kurt HEYNICKE

(De *Der Sturm*)

Los sentidos

De palacio en palacio
se transforma la reluciente sangre de los colores
Por las grutas de las líneas
todas las máscaras humanas relampaguean
Los sonidos se divinizan hasta un susurro
desde donde lenguas innumerables nos hablan
Ruge vibrando en la tormenta la sangre
y resuena en la soledad que murmura
Los negros jardines de los olores se abren
amplificándose hasta copas inasequibles
que luego se derraman en nuevas copas
minadas por una fuerza espiral
El aroma de los bosques se disuelve en los labios
Derretirse de la comida que hace hinchar nuestras venas
Carne de los frutos y fruta de la carne
y vinos que pesados en la sangre maduran
El calor nos mece   Felicidad del tacto
Sol cavidad agua convexidad
Sabemos los caminos del amor el festín fabuloso
Inagotable se nos antoja   Y sin embargo está contado todo

Wilhelm KLEMM

(de *Die Aktion*.)
Nota y Trad. de Jorge-Luis BORGES.
Grecia ns 47, Sevilla, 1 Aug. 1920

EXPRESSIONIST LYRIC: SYNTHESIS

The word *expressionism*—as zenithal or hazy as any other word—was spread in 1914 by Paul Fechter to mark the literary, dramatic pictorial, and sculptural movement that, radiating from Germany and Austria (two of the principal precursors of lyric expressionism, Rainer Maria Rilke and Jorge Traki, were Austrian. . .) generalizes itself today in Scandinavia and Zurich.

If we wanted to define it—and I am very well aware of how confining these definitions usually are—we would say that it is the attempt to create for this era a dawning intuitionist art, to surpass the physical reality and to raise above it's sensory and emotive skein, a spiritual ultra-reality. We would say that expressionism (along with other parallel impulses that act under different latitudes) is nothing more, in the final analysis, than art with a capital A *underlined*.

What constitutes its source is that "cyclopean" and athletic vision of the multi-verse that Walt Whitman would give rhythm to (starting in turn form Fechte and Hegel).

The occidentalist ramifications of this vision found for the most part reflection in the hymn-like strophes of Stadler that were possible in Germany until 1914, the year the war came screaming in. Faced with a crumbling world, occidentalism with its corollaries of optimism, pugilism and sensuality, collapsed, or at least it must have radically transformed itself. The young poets of Germany found themselves facing a decisive crisis in the way they thought. To be an occidentalist meant applauding the industrialized society which was to blame for the war; it meant the spirit's resignation to the iron bars of time and space which imprisons it. Yet, tangible reality offered only a painful and absurd madness. It was urgent to overcome it and conquer it, visualize it in a new way. . .And Expressionism bore fruit.

In spite of some compromises and pragmatisms more or less hypocritical, the change was brought about. Expressionism took on simultaneously that Dostoievskian, utopic, mystic and maximalist character that it still possesses today. Thus, we see the magazine *Die Aktion*—that with *Der Sturm* is one of the lanterns of German literary "renaissance"—exercising an influence at once anarchic over the two opposed sectors of the aesthetic and the social issue. . .

Behind the Front

We die in solitude
In the stillness tired eyes drink the desert
along the way the road stops at the crosses
Winds bring the screams of battle
in the east stony

torches are our hands
and our souls bear a miracle
Wives and home submerge
Twilight

Hope

Gentle spring hangs from my heart
It blossoms
and chastely lulls the hours to sleep
the valley hurls tranquil shades

Then
fatigue oozes from my young limbs
and buds that die bearing fruit become balsam
The soul approves
and laughs like an old man

Kurt HEYNICKE

(de *Der Sturm*)

The Senses

From palace to palace
the gleaming blood of colors is transformed
Throughout the cavities of lines
all human masks flash like lighting
The sounds are deified even a whisper
from where countless tongues speak to us
The blood roars vibrating in the storm
and re-echoes in the murmuring solitude
Black gardens of fragrances open themselves
even unattainable goblets of drink amplify
that then spill over into new goblets
undermined by a spiral force
The aroma of the forests dissolves on the lips

Burning with desire for food that swells our veins
Flesh of the fruit and fruit of the flesh
and wines that heavy in the blood mature
The heat rocks us   Happiness from the touch
Sun cavity water convexity
We know the ways of love the fabulous feast
We deem them inexhaustible And never the less
              everything has already been said [t/o]

                  Wilhelm KLEMM

(de *Die Aktion*)

Commentary and Translations [Spanish] by Jorge-Luis BORGES.[1]

---

[1] With regards to the essays on German Expressionism, all English translations of poetry in the body of the text are mine. They are translated from Borges's Spanish translation from the original German.

LIRICA EXPRESIONISTA: WILHELM KLEMM
Efigie prefacial.

Durante la lucha dubitativa del Marne, un hombre que ceñía el uniforme gris de los ejércitos imperiales creó un poema, donde resalian las siguientes líneas:

"La hierba brilla como un metal verde. La batería eleva su voz de león. Una y dos veces. Mi corazón es amplio cual Alemania y Francia reunidas. . ."

Este suceso—no inscrito por los historiógrafos y plasmable en fáciles exaltaciones de oratoria maximalista o cristiana—nos revela el cimental whitmanismo que subrayaba entonces a Klemm. Ahora—ya evadido de la madeja carcelaria guerrera y aplaudida su obra poemática por la crítica de más agudos anteojos—esta actitud no impera totalmente en sus versos. Wilhelm Klemm es hoy el poeta que diversifica los ángulos de visión, que refracta los datos sensoriales y prismatiza carnavalescamente esa realidad que la ideología naturalista venera y que apenas ocupa un punto momentáneo y finito en la plana cuadriculada donde se atraviesan tiempo y espacio. Su mirada perfora el mundo real, y en su hiperestesia creatriz opone al traumatismo de los sufrimientos la visión goyesca y barroca de otro kosmos absurdo, de trayectoria fija por los rieles de un férreo fatalismo y delirantemente pleno de aquel método que traza las complejas espirales de la locura. (Ya Guillermo Shakespeare lo dijo.)

Aunque no es de aquellos poetas que siembran sus escritos de notaciones cromáticas hasta hacernos dudar de su memoria y de la exactitud de tantos oportunos matices, hay un personalísimo colorismo en sus versos. De la paleta verbal le gusta elegir el adjetivo "negro," que une siempre a substantivos frescos y limpios, escamoteándole así su carácter enlutado y adusto y dándole un valor luminoso, semejante al de un cristal ahumado.

"Los negros jardines de los olores se abren. . .Un negro arco
iris atraviesa diagonalmente el cielo. . ."

La ascensión

El se apretó el cinturón hasta que le ciñó estrechamente.
Su armazón desnuda de huesos crujió. En el costado la herida.
Tosió baba sangrienta. Flameó sobre su martirizado cabello.
Una corona de espinas de luz. Y los perros siempre curiosos
Los discípulos husmeaban en torno. Golpeó como un gong
                                                    su pecho.   [t/o]
Gesticuló con los brazos, hasta que sus agujereadas aletas
Por segunda vez largamente dispararon gotas de sangre,
Y entonces vino el milagro. El cielo raso del cielo
Se abrió color limón. Un vendaval aulló en las altas trompetas.
El, sin embargo, ascendió. Metro tras metro en el hueco
Espacio. Las getas palidecieron en profundísimo asombro.
De abajo sólo veían las plantas de sus pies sudorosos.

Extracto

La noche vierte sus viscosas lágrimas negras,
Sobre lechos fabulosos arde nuestra lascivia:
Con una vela en el orificio posterior, un mono ilumina
Desnudos innumerables y alumbramientos terribles.
Cada perro barbudo sufre su monodrama.
La muerte se presenta como ayudante de barbería,
La luna discute de la inmortalidad con una rata,
Ante nosotros pasan copias indescifrablemente chicas.
Progresos ilusorios nos embaucan.
Atravesamos todos los pisos del mundo:
Cuando arribamos al infierno nos repartieron cigarros.
Los canes ladraron himnos religiosos en coro.
Fundadores de religiones saltaron de los pescantes.
A sus pies yacían enormes palomas.

Sobre una inundación de barro y cadáveres
Chisporrotea el poniente amargo de la bancarrota.

Wilhelm KLEMM
(del libro *Traumschutt*, 1920.)
Nota y traducción de Jorge-Luis BORGES.
Grecia ns 50, 1 Nov. 1920

EXPRESSIONIST LYRIC: WILHELM KLEMM
Prefatory Effigy.

During the doubtful struggle of the Marne, a man wearing the gray uniform of the Imperial armies created a poem, in which the following lines stand out:

"The grass shines like green metal. The battery raises its lion's voice. Once and twice. My heart is as vast as Germany and France put together. . ."

This moment—not recorded by historiographers nor captured in easy exaltations of maximalist or Christian oratory—reveals the foundational Whitmanism that underlined Klemm at that time. Now—having escaped the incarcerating skein of war and his poetic work applauded by critics with the sharpest lenses—this attitude no longer completely dominate his verses. Wilhelm Klemm is today the poet who diversifies his scope of vision, who refracts sensorial data and "prismatizes" in a carnivalesque manner that reality that naturalist ideology reveres and that scarcely occupies a momentary and finite point on a graphed plane through which time and space intersect. His glance pierces the real world, and in his creative "hyperaesthesia," he presents as an antithesis to all the trauma of those who are suffering, the "Goyesque" and Baroque vision of another absurd cosmos, a vision with a fixed railed path of an iron fatalism, deliriously full of that method that traces the complex spirals of madness. (William Shakespeare already said it.)

Although he is not like one of those poets who always impregnate their writings with chromatic notations until they make us doubt their memories and the exactness of so many apropos shades, in his verses there is a very personal coloring. From his verbal palette he likes to select the adjective "black," which he often mixes with fresh, clean nouns, thus depriving the color of its mournful and harsh character and giving it a luminous value, similar to the effect of tinted glass:

"Black gardens of fragrances open themselves. . .A black rainbow diagonally crosses the sky."

The Ascension

He tightened his belt cinching it tightly.
His naked frame of bones creaked. The wound in his side.
Coughed bloody spittle. Flaming over his martyred hair.
A crown of thorns of light. And the dogs ever curious
Disciples each in turn sniffed him out. He struck his chest
                                                    like a gong. [t/o]
He gestured with his arms, until his punctured fins
For the second time spurted drops of blood at great length,
And then the miracle happened. Heaven's ceiling cracked open
the color of lemon. A strong wind howled like high trumpets.
He, nevertheless, ascended. Meter by meter into the hollow
Space. Faces turned pale in profound amazement.
From below they saw only the soles of his sweaty feet.

Extract

The night sheds its sticky black tears,
On fabulous beds burns our lechery:
With a candle in his posterior orifice, a monkey illuminates
Countless nudes and terrible illuminations.
Each bearded dog suffers his monkey-drama.
Death shows up as a barber's apprentice,
The moon discusses immortality with a rat,
Undecipherably small copies pass before us.

Illusory progress deceive us.
We passed through all the layers of the world:
On arrival in hell we were handed cigars.
The dogs barked religious hymns in chorus.
From the coachmen's seat jumped founders of religions.
At their feet lay enormous doves.
On a flood of mud and cadavers
Sputters the bankrupt embittered west.

Wilhelm Klemm
(From the book *Traumschutt*, 1920.
Commentary and translation by Jorge-Luis Borges.

PLATE # 22 – Cover of *Inicial* ns 5, Buenos Aires, May 1923

VERTICAL:
Reseña de Guillermo de Torre's Manifesto Ultraísta

Ya—presintiendo el obsoletismo del libro como
instrumento expresional—Ludwig Rubiner proclamó que el
manifiesto constituiría el órgano más acto de nuestros intercambios
intelectuales. Ante todo, su forma: esa gran foja abierta como un
lecho, con sus alardes de bandera, y sin la humildad falso del libro
que con sus ocho aristas penetra como un ariete en nuestros estantes.
Claro que el manifiesto es algo que grita, pero que grita con esa
ingenuidad gesticulante y espontánea con que discuten en el cénaculo
los compañeros. . .

Guillermo de Torre, que se empina hoy verticalmente sobre
el tablado de su manifiesto, transvasará mañana sus ideaciones a la
pantalla cinemática o se alzará, bocinero de sus propios poemas,
sobre los zancos de una plataforma. Desde hoy su Manifiesto—cálido,
primordial, convencido—posee ante la democracia borrosa del medio
ambiente todo el prestigio audaz de una desorbitada faloforia en un
pueblo jesuítico.

El estiércol dorado de los caminos es amarillo como el sol que
lo estruja.

Este es el truco de los optimistas.

El sol transfijo en lo vertiginoso es amarillo como el estiércol
que estruja.

Este es el truco de los pesimistas.

Erigir una de estas analogías en dogma, agotar todas las
variaciones factibles, disfrazar el arlequín primicial con todos los
trapos, plasmar el rostro en una serie de muecas y exhibir una
mentalidad disecada al gusto del público, crearse una actitud, en una
palabra: he aquí la volición de casi todos los escritores.

Contra esta voluntad de imponer a las fracciones anímicas
un denominador común, Torre se alza. El se proclama creacionista,
cubista, expresionista, futurista, dadaista. . .Y volando a la vez en
tantas pajareras, no se encierra en ninguna y bajo el entusiasmo de

su gesta verbal se adivina una gran invectiva subcutánea contra las escuelas, en lo que tienen de carcelario y de uniformizado, en lo que contradicen al instante. Y en su actitud hímnicamente egoísta, literaturiza la jubilosa estela stirneriana—la de aquel hombre que habló de la significación formidable de un grito de alegría sin pensamiento—y arquitecta nuestras orientaciones rebasadoras de las glorias baratas.

Reflector ns 1, Madrid, Dec. 1920   Jorge-Luis Borges.

VERTICAL:
Review of Guillermo de Torre's Ultraist Manifesto

Ludwig Rubiner—foreseeing the obsolescence of the book as an instrument of expression—already proclaimed that the manifesto would be the organ most suitable for our intellectual exchanges. Above all, its form: that great open folio like a river bed boasting colorful flags, and without the false humility of the book that with its eight edges penetrates our bookshelves like a battering ram. Clearly the manifesto is something that screams out, but it shouts with that gesticulate and spontaneous candor used by companions at a dinner party. . .

Guillermo de Torre, who today rises and stands vertically on the platform of his manifesto, tomorrow will pour his ideas into the movie screen or he will rise on stilts, trumpeting his own poems, from a platform. As of today, his Manifesto—hot, fundamental, convinced—possesses before the blurred democracy of the milieu all the bold prestige of a "dis-orbited" phallic symbol in a Jesuit town.

The golden manure on the road is yellow like the sun that dries it.

That is the optimist's trick.

The sun, transfixed in its vertiginous orbit, is yellow as the manure dried by the sun.

That is the pessimist's trick.

To raise one of these analogies as dogma, to drain it of all feasible variations, to mask the fundamental harlequin with his patch-rag costume, to capture his face in a series of grimaces and exhibit a stuffed mentality befitting public taste, to create an attitude, in one word: this is the wish of almost all writers.

Against this will of imposing a common denominator to the psychic fractions, Torre rises up. He proclaims himself creationist, cubist, expressionist, futurist, dadaist. . .And while fluttering about in so many bird cages, he doesn't allow himself to be locked into any of them, and beneath the enthusiasm of his verbal feat, one surmises a great subcutaneous invective against schools, which in themselves bear the stigma of uniforms and prisons, in as much as they contradict the immediate moment. And in his "hymnically" egoistic attitude, he "literaturizes" the jubilant path of Stirner—the one belonging to that man who spoke about the formidable significance of a joyous shout without thought—and constructs our course so that we pass beyond cheap glories.

MANIFIESTO DEL ULTRA
Firmado por Jorge Luis Borges, Jocobo Sureda,
Fortunio Bonanova, and Juan Alomar

[Prólogo del redactor]:

Guiándonos siempre el deseo de dar a conocer todo cuanto
significa avance hacia el ideal, y habiendose iniciado en Mallorca
el movimiento ultraísta que está llamando la atención en todas las
naciones del mundo, no hemos vacilado un momento en acoger en
nuestras páginas las palpitaciones de ese nuevo grupo de valiosos
jóvenes que en esta isla cultivan con gran acierto esa nueva corriente
literaria y pictórica. Para que nuestros lectores puedan hacerse
cargo de lo que es el Ultra y lo que significa en la moderna escuela,
publicamos a continuación el brillante manifiesto que los jóvenes
ultraístas de Mallorca dirigen al público:

Manifiesto del Ultra

Existen dos estéticas: la estética pasiva de los espejos y la
estética activa de los prismas. Guiado por la primera, el arte se
transforma en una copia de la objetividad del medio ambiente o
de la historia psíquica del individuo. Guiado por la segunda, el arte
se redime, hace del mundo su instrumento, y forja—más allá de las
cárceles espaciales y temporales—su visión personal.

Esta es la estética del Ultra. Su volición es crear: es imponer
facetas insospechadas al universo. Pide a cada poeta una visión
desnuda de las cosas, limpia de estigmas ancestrales; una visión
fragante, como si ante sus ojos fuese surgiendo auroralmente el
mundo. Y, para conquistar esta visión, es menester arrojar todo lo
pretérito por la borda. Todo: la recta arquitectura de los clásicos,
la exaltación romántica, los microscopios del naturalismo, los
azules crepúsculos que fueron las banderas líricas de los poetas
del novecientos. Toda esa vasta jaula absurda donde los ritualistas

quieren aprisionar al pájaro maravilloso de la belleza. Todo, hasta arquitectar cada uno de nosotros su creación subjetiva.

Por lo arriba expuesto habrá visto el lector que la orientación ultráica no es, no puede ser nunca patrimonio—como se ha querido suponer—de un sector afanoso de arbitrariedades que encubran malamente su estulticia. Los ultraístas han existido siempre: son los que, adelantándose a su era, han aportado al mundo aspectos y expresiones nuevas. A ellos debemos la existencia de la evolución, que es la *vitalidad de las cosas*. Sin ellos seguiríamos girando en torno a una luz única, como las falenas. El Greco, con respecto a sus demás coetáneos, resultó tambien altruista [ultraísta], y así tantos otros. Nuestro credo audaz y *consciente es no tener credo*. Es decir, desechamos las recetas y corsés absurdamente acatados por los espíritus exotéricos. *La creación por la creción*, puede ser nuestro lema. La poesía ultráica tiene tanta cadencia y musicalidad como la secular. Posee igual ternura. Tiene tanta visualidad, y tiene más imaginación. Pero lo que sí modifica es la modalidad estructural. En ese punto radica una de sus más esenciales innovaciones. La sensibilidad, la sentimentalidad son eternamente las mismas. No pretendemos rectificar el alma, ni siquiera la naturaleza. Lo que renovamos son los medios de expresión.

Nuestra ideología iconoclasta, la que dispone a los filisteos en nuestro contra, es precisamente la que nos enaltece. *Todo gran afirmación necesita una gran negación*, como dijo, o se olvidó de decir, el compañero Nietzsche. . .Nuestros poemas tienen la contextura escueta y decisiva de los marconigramas.

Para esta obra de superación adicionamos nuestro esfuerzo al que realizan las revistas ultráicas *Grecia, Cervantes, Reflector* y *Ultra*.

Jocobo Sureda.—Fortunio Bonanova.—
Juan Alomar.—Jorge Luis Borges.
Baleares ns 131, Palma de Mallorca, 15 Feb. 1921

ULTRA MANIFESTO
Co-signed by Jorge Luis Borges, Jocobo Sureda, Fortunio Bonanova, and Juan Alomar

[Editor's foreword]:

Guiding us always is the desire to reveal all that signifies an advance towards the ideal, and since the ultraist movement began in Mallorca, and is attracting the attention of all the nations in the world, we haven't hesitated a moment in welcoming into our pages the pulsations of this influential group of worthy young men who on this island, and with great skill, have cultivated this new literary and pictorial trend. So that our readers can take notice of what Ultra is, its significance among modern schools, we publish below the brilliant manifesto which the young Mallorcan ultraists address to the public:

Ultra Manifesto

Two aesthetics exist: the passive aesthetic of mirrors and the active aesthetics of prisms. Guided by the first, art becomes a copy of either the objectivity of the milieu, or the psychic history of the individual. Guided by the second, art is redeemed, the world becomes its instrument, and it forges—beyond the prisons of space and time—a personal vision.

This is the ultraist's aesthetic. His wish is to create: to impose unsuspected facets to the universe. It demands of each poet a naked vision of things, devoid of ancestral stigmas; a fragrant vision, as if the world rising up were dawning before his eyes. And, in order for this vision to be triumphant, it is imperative that all things of the past be tossed overboard. Everything: the straight architecture of the classics, the romantic exaltation, the microscopic view of naturalism, the blue twilights that were the lyric banners of the nineties poets. The entire vast and absurd cage in which the ritualists wish to imprison the wonderful bird of beauty. Everything, until each one of us has constructed his own subjective creation.

From the aforementioned, the reader can see that the ultraist orientation is not, nor can it ever be patrimony—as some would like to suppose—of a sector whose enthusiasm for all things outrageous hardly conceals their foolishness. Ultraists have always existed: they are the ones that, ahead of their time, have given the world new aspects and expressions. To them we owe the existence of evolution, which is the *vitality of all things*. Without them we would continue spinning around a single light, like moths. El Greco, with respect to his contemporaries, turned out also to be an ultraist, and likewise many others. Our bold and *conscious credo is not to have a credo* . That is to say, we reject the recipes and corsets that the esoteric spirit absurdly respects. *Creation for creation's sake,* could be our motto. Ultraist poetry has as much cadence and musicality as age-old poetry. It possesses equal tenderness. It has as much visuality, and has more imagination. But what it does modify is the structural modality. On this point stands one of its most essential innovations. Its sensibility, its sentimentality are eternally the same. We don't pretend to rectify the soul, not even nature. What we are out to renew are the means of expression.

Our iconoclastic ideology, the one that turns the Philistines against us, is precisely the one that elevates us. *Every great affirmation needs a great negation,* as our comrade Nietzsche said, or forgot to say . . .Our poems have the succinct and decisive contextual quality of wireless telegrams.

So that this labor overcome and be triumphant, we add our efforts to those already being put forth by other ultraist magazines *Grecia, Cervantes, Reflector*, and *Ultra.*

ANATOMÍA DE MI "VLTRA"

La estética es al andamiaje de los argumentos edificados a *posteriori* para legitimar los juicios que hace nuestra intuición sobre las manifestaciones de arte. Esto, en lo referente al crítico. En lo que atañe a los artistas, el caso cambia. Puede asumir todas las formas entre aquellos dos polos antagónicos de la mentalidad, que son el polo impresionista y el polo expresionista. En el primero, el individuo se abandona al ambiente; en el segundo, el ambiente es el instrumento del individuo. (De paso, es curioso constatar que los escritores autobiográficos, los que más alarde hacen de su individualidad recia, son en el fondo los más sujetos a las realidades tangibles. Verbigracia, Baroja.) Sólo hay, pues, dos estéticas: la estética pasiva de los espejos y la estética activa de los prismas. Ambas pueden existir juntas. Así, en la renovación actual literaria—esenci—mente expresionista—el futurismo, con su exaltación de la objetividad cinética de nuestro siglo, representa la tendencia pasiva, mansa, de sumisión al medio. . .

Ya cimentadas estas bases, enunciaré las intenciones de mis esfuerzos líricos.

Yo busco en ellos la *sensación en sí,* y no la descripción de las premisas espaciales o temporales que la rodean. Siempre ha sido costumbre de los poetas ejecutar una reversión del proceso emotivo que se había operado en su conciencia; es decir, volver de la emoción a la sensación, y de ésta a los agentes que la causaron. Yo—y nótese bien que hablo de intentos y no de realizaciones colmadas—anhelo un arte que traduzca la emocion desnuda, depurada de los adicionales datos que la preceden. Un arte que rehuyese lo dérmico, lo metafisico y los últimos planos egocéntricos o mordaces.

Para esto—como para toda poesía—hay dos imprescindibles medios: el ritmo y la metáfora. El elemento acústico y el elemento luminoso.

El ritmo: no encarcelado en los pentágramas de la métrica, sino ondulante, suelto, redimido, bruscamente truncado.

La metáfora: esa curva verbal que traza casi siempre entre dos puntos—espirituales—el camino más breve.

Ultra ns 11, Madrid, 20 May 1921   Jorge-Luis Borges

ANATOMY OF MY "VLTRA"

Aesthetic is a scaffold of arguments built *after the fact* in order to validate the judgements made by our intuition concerning artistic manifestations. The previous point is in reference to critics. As for the artist, the case is otherwise. He can assume all the forms between the two opposing poles of the mind, which are the impressionistic pole and the expressionistic pole. In the former, the individual sur-renders himself to the environment; in the the latter, the environ-ment is the instrument of the individual. (Incidently, its curious to note that the autobiographical writers, the ones that boast of their strong individuality are intrinsically those most subject to tangible reality. For example, Baroja.) Thus, there are only two aesthetics: the passive aesthetic of mirrors and the active aesthetic of prisms. Both can exist together. Therefore, in the current literary renova-tion—essentially expressionistic—futurism, with its exaltation of the "film-like" objectivity of our century, represents the meek, passive tendency, in submission to the common classes. . .

With these foundations already laid, I will enunciate the intentions of my lyrical efforts.

In them I am seeking *sensation itself,* and not the description of the space or time premises that surround it. It has always been the habit of poets to carry out a reversal of the emotional process that had taken effect in his conscience; that is to say, to come back from emotion to sensation, and from there to the agents that caused the emotion. I—and note well that I am speaking of intentions and not of fulfilled realizations—long for an art that translates naked emotion, purified of the additional data that precedes it. An art that avoids flesh and blood reality, the metaphysical, and the ultimate lev-els of caustic egocentricity.

For this—as for all poetry—there are two indispensable means: rhythm and metaphor. The acoustic element and the luminous element.

The rhythm: not an imprisoning meter on the music staff, but a rhythm that is undulant, free, redeemed, abruptly truncated.

The metaphor: that verbal curve that almost always traces the shortest path between two points—spirtual points.

HORIZONTES:
Reseña de la antología *Die Aktions-Lyrik*—1914-1916—Berlin

Este libro lo eslabonan unos cincuenta poemas,
conscientemente duros y dolorosos, forjados por Wilhelm Klemm,
Ludwig Baümer, Alfred Vagts, Julius Talbot Keller y otros poetas,
en la nadería y el fatalismo de las trincheras, en Polonia, en Rusia
y en Francia. Como una estatua jónica, o, más sencillamente, como
cualquier moneda, presenta dos aspectos: el uno, documental,
histórico, de apuntación inmediata de los instantes de la guerra; el
otro, de muestrario del expresionismo lírico en sus albores.

El primero no debe detenernos. Eso de concederle más
importancia a los escritos que reflejan la realidad visible y palpable
que a los que son espejos de la emotiva y pasional, es un prejuicio
ayuno de todo justificativo. Deriva de los enciclopedistas y de las
teorizaciones de Zola, y se basa en el absurdo de suponer que un
árbol o un tranvía son más reales que yo que los comprendo. En el
fondo, lo visto, lo sufrido, lo imaginado y lo soñado son igualmente
reales, es decir, existen. La objetividad no es en última exégesis
más que una suerte de denominador común de muchas sensaciones
subjetivas. . .Cuando Pedro Garfias afirma: *El mar es una estrella de
mil puntas*, y Rodríguez Navas, en cambio, lo define como *el conjunto
de aguas que rodean la Tierra*, ambos tienen razón, si bien el primero
busca una finalidad estética y el segundo una fórmula, basándose
en la cual pueden sacarse determinadas consecuencias físicas o
geográficas. Y que no vengan a decirme que aquello de subrayar
la verdad sensualista de las cosas más que las otras verdades es un
prejuicio eterno. Los griegos visualizaban, verbigracia, la Historia
como una bella narración o como una herramienta de moral, sin
preocuparse mayormente de la verdad—supuesta—objetiva. Y tal vez
hacían bien.

Con lo cual queda dicho que si en el libro que glosamos sólo
hallásemos cosas como que un ruiseñor cantó en la iglesia derruída

y otros datos asi, lo pasaríamos por alto. Pero también hallamos emoción. Una emoción viviente que tiembla muchas veces en el fondo como una lámpara sepulta y que se expresa en frases truncadas y en un heróico barroquismo verbal.

Escuchad como prueba estas estrofas:

Chillan las balas,
pájaros astrales
de una fauna metálica sin sangre

(J.T. Keller.)

Y éstas:
Las ametralladoras charlan todavia un rato
Y se van entretejiendo en las horas larguísimas.
Pero a las seis de la mañana bebe el inglés su café.
Entonces podremos enterrar nuestros muertos.
(Wilhelm Klemm.)

Las copas de los árboles penden como globos cautivos.
(Oscar Kanchl.)

Los heridos en las ventanas
como plantas marchitas.

(Walter Ferl +.)

Sobre nosotros chorrean los schrappnells y
cantan los insectos de las balas.
A un muerto lo arrojan por el parapeto
como lastre de un barco,
y una tropa de hombres temerarios corren
como jugadores de football.
De pronto no se sabe por qué está sin segar
el trigo y las patatas se pudren,
y por qué hay formas pardas que hacia
nosotros avanzan

enormes en la tarde
y alzan las manos en alto como mendigos extâticos.

(Hermann Plagge.)

Claro que "1914-1916" tiene, como todas las antologías, un carácter de cosa desigual y fragmentaria. Pero también campea en sus páginas un gran calor de corazón, cualidad notable y extraña si lo contrastamos con la fecha de su génesis. Fecha en la cual hasta los virtuosos de la sonrisa marginal como France y los profesionales del lustrabotismo democrático como Almafuerte se olvidaron de su actitud y celebraron con un entusiasmo a la vez inexperto y periodístico las excelencias de la guerra.

Ultra ns 16, Madrid, 20 Oct. 1921   Jorge-Luis BORGES

HORIZONS:
Review of the anthology *Die Aktions-Lyrics*—1914-1916—Berlin

This book is linked by some fifty poems, consciously harsh and painful, forged by Wilhelm Klemm, Ludwig Baümer, Alfred Vagts, Julius Talbot Keller and other poets, inside the nothingness and the fatalism of the trenches of Poland, Russia and France. Like an ionic statue, or, more simply, like any coin, it presents two aspects: one documentary, historical, of immediate wartime notations; and the other, as a sampler of lyric Expressionism in its dawning hours.

The first must not detain us. The tendency of giving more importance to writers who reflect visible and palpable reality over those who are mirrors of the emotional and the passionate is a prejudice lacking all justification. It comes from the encyclopedists and the theorizing of Zola, and is based on the absurd supposition that a tree or a streetcar are more real than I who comprehends them. Essentially, the visible, the suffered, the imagined and the dreamed are equally real, that is, they exist. Objectivity in the final analysis is no more than a sort of common denominator of many subjective sensations. . .When Pedro Garfias states: *The sea is a star of a thousand* points, and Rodriguez Navas, on the other hand, defines it as *the collection of water surrounding the Earth*, both are right, even though the first is seeking an esthetic objective, and the second, a formula, based on which certain physical or geographic corollaries can be drawn. And don't come to tell me that the tendency to emphasize the sensorial truth of things more then the other truths is an eternal prejudice. The Greeks, for example, used to visualize History as a beautiful narration or as a moral tool, without concerning themselves too much with—supposedly—objective truth. And perhaps they were right.

And so it stands on record that if in the book we are examining we were to find only things such as a nightingale sang in the church ruins and other such details we would ignore it. But we find emotion as well. A vital, living emotion that often trembles in its central core like an entombed lamp, expressing itself in truncated phrases and in a heroic verbal "baroqueism".

As proof listen to these stanzas:
The bullets screach,
astral birds
of a metallic bloodless fauna

(J.T. Keller)

and these:
The machine guns still chatter awhile longer
And gradually interweave into the long long hours.
But at six in the morning the English drink their coffee.
Then we can bury our dead.

(Wilhelm Klemm)

The treetops hang like captive balloons.

(Oscar Kanchl)

The wounded in the windows
like withered plants.

(Walter Ferl +·)

The shrapnel showers over us and
    the insect bullets sing.
A dead man is tossed over the parapet
    like a ballast of a ship,
and a troop of daring men run
    like football players.
Suddenly no one knows why the wheat is
    unreaped and potatoes rot,
and why there are brown forms advancing
    towards us
huge in the early evening
and they raise their hands high like
    entranced beggars.

                               (Hermann Plagge)

Of course "1914-1916" has, like all anthologies, an unequal and fragmentary quality. But within its pages a heartfelt warmth also exists, a strange and noble quality if we contrast it with the date of its birth. It is a date in which even the virtuous men of the non-committal smile like France [Anatole] and the professionals of the democratic boot-shiners like Almafuerte forgot their attitude and celebrated with an enthusiasm at once inexperienced and journalistic, the excellence of war.

PROSISTAS NUEVOS: CRITICA DEL PAISAJE

El paisaje del campo es la retórica. Es decir, las reacciones del individuo ante la madeja visual y acústica que lo integra han sido ya delimitadas. Hasta hoy—1921—ninguna reacción nueva se ha sumado a la totalidad de reacciones ya conocidas; actitud lacrimosa, actitud panteísta, actitud estoica y antitética entre el—supuesto—lujo ciudadano y el escueto franciscanismo de la visión rural. (Apuntemos de paso cómo el mismo fray Luis de León, tan verdadero, tan arrebujado en la vida campestre, escamotea muchas veces el paisaje que lo ciñe y le concede únicamente un valor de contrapeso espiritual, de sordina o cilicio contra los incentivos de la vida ambiciosa. Y cómo el oro, el jaspe, los techos artesonados y demás prestigiosas zarandajas que anatematiza, le sirven para decorar sus poemas. . .)

Ir a admirar adrede el paisaje es paralelizarnos con los salvajes de la cultura, con esos indios blancos que desfilan en piaras militarizadas por los museos y se quedan con los ojos arrodillados ante cualquier lienzo garantido por una firma sólida, y no saben muy bien si están ebrios de admiración o si esa misma voluntad de entusiasmo les ha inhibido la facultad de admirarse.

Desconfiemos de su indecencia emocional.

Desconfiemos de las reacciones organizadas, de las emociones previstas y de las actitudes de recluta en que se plasman los espíritus amaestrados. El Arte—comprendido, como ellos lo comprenden, con A mayúscula—es una falsedad, es una cosa que en lugar de enriquecer la vida la estruja y empobrece.

El paisaje—como todas las cosas en sí—no es absolutamente nada. La palabra *paisaje* es la condecoración verbal que otorgamos a la visualidad que nos rodea, cuando ésta nos ha untado con cualquier barniz conocido de la literatura. Desgraciadamente no hay gran acervo de barnices. El ruiseñor que se derrama entero en el quietismo de la selva nos sugiere, con una regularidad geometral, los instantes del *Intermedio Lírico*, y el tren que opera la bisección de la planicie

mansa, espolea inevitablemente en nosotros los recuerdos de dos
visiones literarias ya trasnochadas: la del naturalismo (nexo causal
inaflojable, enfermedades hereditarias, puestas o salidas de sol en los
momentos oportunos. . .) y la de los albores del futurismo (belleza
del esfuerzo, Whitman mal traducido al italiano, instalación de
luz eléctrica en la retórica. . .) Y no me refiero al agotamiento del
tren y del ruiseñor como elementos literarios. Pluma en ristre, les
impondremos la traducción que más nos convenga, y descubriremos
en el ruiseñor ironía, desesperanza o cualquier otra cosa, y diremos
que su cantar le saca punta al silencio, o que se enreda en las estrellas,
o que sacude el liso corazón del plenilunio. . .

Eso hablando en urdidor de verbalismos. Pero hablando en
espectador *aprofesional* del paisaje, las viejas sugestiones clásicas y
románticas aun me doblegan, y lo veo persistente, enorme, tedioso
y como atorado de ritmos sentimentales, de estatuaria esponjosa, de
proyectos y de posturas de alma gastadas.

El paisaje de campo es la mentira.

Por eso he vuelto la espalda a sus alcores, a sus tablados y a los
colorines gesticulantes de sus ponientes.

Hasta que alguna vez—obliterados ya los versos que Juan
Ramón Jiménez dibujó en mi pizarra espiritual—pueda volver y
descubrir, sin desviación ni finalidad artística alguna, la mejorana y el
tomillo.

Lo bello es lo espontáneo lo que carece de últimos planos
declamatorios o egocéntricos. (La idea estilizada en frases bien
peinaditas y eslabonadas sobre una firma en letras de mold, siempre
será inferior a la idea repartida humanamente, sencillamente, sin
mirar de reojo a la fama y ofrecida a los demás como quien ofrece un
pitillo.)

Un verso puede ser muy bello, pero nunca un libro de versos.

Lo marginal es lo más bello.

Por ejemplo: Cualquier casita del arrabal, seria, pueril y
sosegada. El café donde estoy (cuyos detalles sólo nebulosamente
conozco). El paisaje urbano que los verbalismos no mancharon aún.
La cantinela intermitente de un organillo que se derrama por los
cangilones de los ruidos más duros.

BUENOS AIRES

Ni de mañana ni al atardecer ni en la noche vemos realmente
la ciudad. La mañana es una prepotencia de azul, un asombro de
abiertas claraboyas agujereando el cielo decisivo y completo, un
cristalear y un despilfarro escandaloso de sol amontonándose en las
plazas y hasta metiéndose en los espejos y en los aljibes. La tarde
es el momento dramámatico de la jornada: es como un retorcerse
y un salirse de quicio de las cosas, y nos desmadeja, nos carcome y
nos manosea. Después, y ya convalecientes de la tarde, la noche es
el milagro trunco: la culminación de los embanderados faroles y el
tiempo en que la objetividad palpable se hace menos insolente y
menos maciza. La madrugada, en cambio, siempre es una cosa infame
y rastrera, pues encubre la gran conjuración tramada para poner en
pie todo aquello que fracasó diez horas antes, y va alineando calles,
decapitando luces y repintando colores por los idénticos lugares de
la tarde anterior, hasta que nosotros—ya con la ciudad al cuello y el
día abismal unciendo nuestros hombros—temenos que rendirnos a la
desatinada plenitud de su triunfo y resignarnos a que nos remachen
un día más en la frente.

No; las etapas que acabo de enunciar son demasiado literarias
para que en ellas pueda el paisaje gozar de vida propia. Yo estoy
seguro que el amanecer en Benares tiene el mismo sentido emocional
que el amanecer en Madrid. . .(¡Oh lenta luna rezagada encima del
Viaducto y actuación mentirosamente optimista de los pajaritos que
chillan tras las verjas de los jardines húmedos!)

Para apresar integramente el alma—imaginaria—del paisaje,
hay que elegir una de aquellas horas huérfanas que viven como
asustadas por los demás y en las cuales nadie se fija. Por ejemplo:
las dos y pico, p.m. El cielo asume entonces cualquier color. Ningún
director de orquesta nos impone su pauta. La cenestesia fluye por
los ojos pueriles y la ciudad se adentra en nosotros. Así nos hemos
empapado de Buenos Aires.

Aunque a veces nos humille algún rascacielos, la visión total de Buenos Aires no es whitmaniana. Las lineas horizontales vencen las verticales. Las perspectivas—de casitas de un piso alienadas y confrontándose a lo largo de las lequas de asfalto y piedra—son demasiado fáciles para no parecer inverosímiles. En cada encrucijada se adivinan cuatro correctos horizontes. Horizontes que intentan distraídamente escalar mis ojos de miope. Horizontes con esa lejanía exasperante que tienen las mangas de los gabanes, a veces. . .Y además: automóviles y vehementes anuncios de cigarrillos, y, como un eficaz terrón de azúcar que endulzase él solo la ciudad desdibujada y lacia, el último tango—siempre hay un último tango—enhebra todos los oídos y en su flojo compás disloca las actitudes.

He mentado las casas. Y es que las casas constituyen lo más conmovedor que existe en Buenos Aires. Tan lamentablemente iguales, tan incomunicadas en su apretujón estrechísimo, tan únicas de puerta, tan petulantes de balaustradas y de umbralitos de mármol, se afirman, a la vez, tímidas y orgullosas. Siempre campea un patio en el medio, un pobre patio que nunca tiene surtidor y casi nunca tiene parra o aljibe; pero que está lleno de ancestralidad y de primitiva eficacia, ya que se encuentra cimentado en las dos cosas más primordiales que existen: en la tierra y el cielo.

Estas casas de que hablo son la traducción, en cal y ladrillo, del ánimo de sus moradores, y expresan: Fatalismo. No el fatalismo individualista y anárquico que se gasta en España, sino el fatalismo vergonzante del criollo que intenta hoy ser occidentalista y no puede. ¡Pobres criollos! En los subterráneos del alma nos brinca la españolidad, y empero quieren convertirnos en yanquis, en yanquis falsificados, y engatusarnos con el aguachirle de la democracia y el voto. . .

Pero me olvido de las plazas. Y en Buenos Aires las plazas—nobles piletas abarrotadas de frescor, congresos de árboles patricios, escenarios para las citas románticas—son el remanso único donde por un instante las calles renuncian a su geometralidad persistente, y rompen filas y se dispersan corriendo como después de una pueblada.

Si las casas de Buenos Aires son una afirmación pusilánime, las plazas son un ejecutoria de momentánea nobleza concedida a todos los paseantes que cobijan.

Casas de Buenos Aires con azoteas de baldosa o de cinc, huérfanas de torres excepcionales o de briosos aleros, comparables a pájaros mansos con las alas cortadas. Pero ¿qué importa? En una de ellas murió Evaristo Carriego, el hombre que dijo:

> El ciego
> evoca memorias de cosas
> de cuando sus ojos tenían mañanas. . .

Y en otra de ellas ha de nacer nuestro Mesias.

(Buenos Aires, 1921.)   Jorge Lus Biorges (sic)
Cosmópolis ns 36, Madrid, Dec. 1921

NEW PROSISTS: CRITIQUE OF THE LANDSCAPE

The countryside's landscape is rhetoric. That is to say, individual reactions before the visual and acoustic skein that comprise it have already been defined. Until today—1921—not one new reaction has been added to the sum total of known reactions: lachrymose attitude, pantheist attitude, stoic attitude and the antithetical attitude between the—so-called—city dweller's luxurious vision and the plain, unadorned Franciscanism of the rural vision. (Let us point out in passing how Friar Luis de Leon himself, so genuine, so wrapped up in rural life, often conjures the landscape that surrounds him and grants it value only as a spiritual counterbalance, of muted bells or coarse hair-cloth garments versus the incentives of ambitious life. And how the gold, the jasper, the coffered ceilings and other prestigious trifles he anathematizes, serve to decorate his poems. . .)

To deliberately go and admire the landscape is to equate us with the savages of culture, with those white Indians that parade through museums in militarized herds and remain with genuflected eyes before any canvas guaranteed by a solid signature, and are unsure whether they are drunk with admiration or if that same will of enthusiasm has inhibited their ability to admire.

Let us distrust their emotional indecency.

Let us distrust organized reactions, anticipated emotions and the attitudes of army recruits in whom trained spirits are molded. Art—understood, as they understand it, with a capital A—is a lie, it is something that instead of enriching life, withers and impoverishes it.

The landscape—like all things per se—is not absolutely nothing. The word *landscape* is the verbal decoration we grant to the visuality that surrounds us, when it has covered us with any known literary varnish. Unfortunately there is no great wealth of varnishes. The nightingale who spills himself completely into the quietude of the forest suggests to us, with a geometric regularity, the moments of *Lyric Intermission*, and the train that executes the bisection of the tranquil plain, inevitably spurs in us the memories of two literary visions already hackneyed and stale: the one of naturalism (unrelenting causal link, hereditary diseases, the rising or setting of the sun at opportune moments. . .) and the dawning of futurism (the beauty of effort, Whitman badly translated into Italian, installation of electric light into rhetoric. . .) And I'm not referring to the exhaustion of both the train and the nightingale as literary elements. Pen in hand, we will now impose the translation that suits us most, and we'll discover irony, hopelessness or whatever else in the nightingale, and we will say that its song sharpens silence, or that it gets entangled in the stars, or that its song shakes the smooth heart of the full moon.

The previous, speaking as a weaver of mere verbiage. But speaking of the landscape as an *unprofessional* spectator, the old classical and romantic suggestions still humble me, and I see it persistent, huge, tedious and jammed with sentimental rhythms, fluffy statuary, projects and attitudes of spent souls.

The countryside landscape is the lie.

That is why I've turned my back on its hills, its plateaus and the vivid gesticulating colors of its sunsets.

Until sometime—obliterated now are the verses that Juan Ramon Jiménez drew upon my spiritual slate—I can return and discover, without deviation nor some artistic motive, the sweet marjoram and thyme.

What is beautiful is that which is spontaneous, that which lacks final declamatory or egocentric drafts. (The idea stylized in neatly groomed phrases and linked to a signature in printed letters, will always be inferior to the idea shared humanly, simply, without one eye on fame, and offered to the rest as one offers a cigarette.)

A verse can be very beautiful, but never a book of poetry.

What is marginal is the most beautiful.

For example: Any small house in the outskirts of town, serious puerile and quiet. The café where I am (whose details I only nebulously know). The urban landscape that words have not yet soiled. The intermittent ballad of a hurdy-gurdy that spills out through the harshest noises coming from the streets' wagon ruts.

BUENOS AIRES

Neither in the morning, evening nor at night do we really see the city. The morning is a prepotency of blue, an astonishment of open skylights perforating the decisive and complete sky, a shimmering and a scandalous squandering of sun piling itself upon the plazas and even putting itself into mirrors and water wells. Dusk is the dramatic moment of the day's journey: it's like things writhing and a wild coming out of things, and it unravels us, it gnaws on us and fondles us. Later, and already convalescing from dusk, nighttime is the truncated miracle: the culmination of lamp posts adorned with flags and the time when palpable objectivity becomes less insolent and less solid. Dawn, on the other hand, is always an infamous and creeping thing, as it conceals the great conspiracy plotted to put aright all that failed ten hours earlier, and goes about aligning streets, decapitating lights and repainting colors throughout the identical sites of the previous evening, until we—already with the city at our throats and the abysmal day yoking our shoulders—must surrender to the reckless plenitude of its triumph and be resigned to have another day riveted to our forehead.

No; the stages I've just named are too literary to enable the landscape to enjoy in them its own life. I'm sure that dawn in Benares has the same emotional feeling as dawn in Madrid. . .(Oh! Lazy moon left behind atop the Viaduct and the deceitfully optimistic performance of little birds screeching behind the gratings of the humid gardens.)

To wholly capture the soul—imaginary—of the landscape, one must choose one of those orphan hours that live as if frightened by the others and to which no one pays attention. For example: a little past two P.M. The sky then assumes whichever color. No orchestra conductor imposes upon us his tempo. The synesthesia of life flows through childish eyes and the city deepens in us. Thus we are steeped in Buenos Aires.

Although at times we are humbled by a sky scraper, the total view of Buenos Aires is not Whitmanian. The horizontal lines overpower the vertical ones. The perspectives—of small, one-story, isolated houses confronting each other along miles of asphalt and stones—are too elementary to seem verisimilar. At each crossroad one can surmise four correct horizons. Horizons which surreptitiously attempt climbing into my myopic eyes. Horizons with that exasperating distance that overcoat sleeves have sometimes. . . And in addition: cars and brazen cigarette adds, and like an effective lump of sugar that sweetens by itself the dissolving, withering city, the last tango—there always is a last tango—strings together all the ears and with its lazy tempo disjoints attitudes.

I've mentioned the houses. And it is the houses that constitute the most moving aspect of Buenos Aires. So lamentably alike, so solitary in their extremely narrow confinement, such unique doors, so pretentious with their balustrades and marble thresholds, they assert themselves, at once, timid and proud. A patio in the middle always commands the center, a poor patio that never has a fountain and almost never has ivy or a well; but its always full of ancestry and of primitive efficiency, since it finds itself founded on the two most essential things that exist: earth and sky.

These houses I am talking about are the translation, in lime and brick, of the soul of its inhabitant, and express: Fatalism. Not the worn out, individualistic and anarchic fatalism of Spain, but the shameful fatalism of the "criollo" that today tries to be occidentalist and cannot. Poor criollos! In the underground passages of our soul our Spanishness leaps up within us, nevertheless they want to convert us into Yankees, counterfeit Yankees, and wheedle us with watered down democracy and the vote. . .

But I'm forgetting about the plazas. And in Buenos Aires the plazas—noble fountains packed with coolness, congregations of patrician trees, scenarios for romantic dates—are the only haven where for an instant the streets renounce their persistent geometric alignment, and break ranks and disperse, running as after a riot.

If the houses of Buenos Aires are a pusillanimous affirmation, the plazas are a momentary title of nobility granted to all the strollers they shelter.

Houses of Buenos Aires with flat roofs of tile or zinc, devoid of exceptional towers or spirited eaves, comparable to pet birds with clipped wings. But what does it matter? In one of them Evarist Carriego died, the man who said:

> The blind man
> evokes memories of things
> from when his eyes had tomorrows. . .

And in another of them our Messiah must be born.

(Buenos Aires, 1921.)

APUNTACIONES CRITICAS: LA METÁFORA[2]

No existe una esencial desemejanza entre la metáfora y lo que los profesionales de la ciencia nombran la explicación de un fenómeno. Ambas son una vinculación tramada entre dos cosas distintas, a una de las cuales se la trasiega en la otra. Ambas son iqualmente verdaderas o falsas.

Explicar, por ejemplo, el dolor en términos de histología, de sacudimiento del sistema nervioso, de caries..., equivale a escamotear lo explicado. Claro que esta nomenclatura puede ofrecer una utilidad practicista, semejante al alivio intelectual que proporciona en una operación algebraica el hecho de rotular las cantidades x, y o z. Pero es absurdo creer que estas claves puedan cambiar o esclarecer en modo alguno las cosas que rotulan. La luz—la sensación lumínica, verbigracia—es algo definitivamente demarcable de las vibraciones en que la traduce la óptica. Estas vibraciones no constituyen la realidad de la luz. ¿Cómo creer, además, que una cosa pueda ser la realidad de otra, o que haya sensaciones trastrocables—definitivamente—en otras sensaciones?

Asi, cuando un geómetra afirma que la luna es una cantidad extensa en las tres dimensiones, su expresión no es menos metafórica que la de Nietzsche cuando prefiere definirla como un gato que anda por los tejados. En ambos casos se tiende un nexo desde la luna (sintesis de percepciones visuales) hacia otra cosa: en el primero, hacia una serie de relaciones espaciales; en el segundo, hacia un conjunto de sensaciones evocadoras de sigilo, untuosidad y jesuitismo...Ahora bien; ninguno de estos mitos, ni el mito geometral que identifica la luna con un sólida, ni el mito fisico que identifica este sólido con un acervo de átomos fragmentables a su vez en electricidad, ni el mito lírico, se presentan como simples reemplazos del trozo de realidad que demudan. Antes son—como todas las explicaciones y todas los nexos causales—subrayaduras de

---

[2] This is not the essay "La Metáfora" published in *Historia Eternidad* in 1936.

aspectos parcialísimos del sujeto que tratan hechos nuevos que se añaden al mundo. Considerada así la metáfora asume el carácter religioso y demiúrgico que tuvo en sus principios, y el creacionismo—al menos en teoria—se justifica plenamente. Definamos, pues, la metáfora como una identificación voluntaria de dos o más conceptos distintos, con la finalidad de emociones, y estudiemos algunas de sus formas.

Las distinciones gramaticales entre comparación y tropo, distinciones determinadas por el empleo o la ausencia de la palabra *como*, no deben detenernos.

Empecemos considerando una notable idiosincrasia de nuestras facultades.

Nuestra memoria es, principalmente, visual y secundareamente auditiva. De la serie de estados que eslabonan lo que denominamos conciencia, sólo perduran los que son traducibles en términos de visualidad o de audición. Asi, mientras un pormenor ocular sin importancia intrinseca alguna—el dibujo de las baldosas de un patio o el desfile de libros en una estanteria, por ejemplo—puede entretejerse a nuestra vida interior y persistir indefinidamente, la feroz estrujadura del dolor fisico se borra apenas ha pasado y sólo es recordable en abstracciones de agresividad, angustia, etc., o en símbolos concretos de punzada, de dolor macizo o de dolor puntiagudo. . .Ni lo muscular ni lo olfatorio ni lo gustable, hallan cabida en el recuerdo, y el pasado se reduce, pues, a un montón de visiones barajadas y a una pluralidad de voces. Entre éstas tienen más persistencia las primeras, y si queremos retrotraernos a los momentos iniciales de nuestra infancia, constataremos que únicamente recuperamos unos cuantos recuerdos de índole visual. . .

Nombrar un substantivo cualquiera equivale a sugerir su contexto visual, y hasta en palabras de subrayadisima intención auditoria como *violin-tambor-vihuela*, la idea de su aspecto precede siempre a la de su sonido y se opera casi instantáneamente.

De ahí que la metáfora que se limita a aprovechar un paralelismo de formas existente entre dos visibilidades sea la más sencilla y la más fácil. A priori esperaríamos hallar numerosos ejemplos de este tipo de imagen en los poemas primitivos, pero no es asi, y el examen de una obra como la versión inglesa del *Shi-King* de Confucio, donde se encuentran compiladas las más arcaicas canciones del Imperio Central de 600 ó 700 años antes de nuestra era, nos convence de lo contrario. En la poesia castellana, recién Góngora, sistematiza la explotación de las coincidencias formales en líneas como el verso crisográfico:

En campos de zafir pacen estrellas

o cuando afirma: *Los arados peinan los agros*. Martingala que alcanzó luego su más plenaria reducción al absurdo en el axiomático Lunario Sentimental de nuestro Tagore, Lugones, y de la cual también se burló Heine cuando dijo que la noche era una capa renegrida de armiño con pintitas doradas. Justificándose después con la admisión de que, sin duda, el peletero a quien se le ocurrió el desatino de teñir de negro el armiño era un demente.

Quizá de menos fijación efectiva, pero mucho más audaces, son las metáforas conseguidas mediante la traducción de percepciones acústicas en percepciones oculares, y vice-versa. Los ejemplos son múltiples.

Ya alrededor de 1620, Quevedo habló de negras voces y apostrofó al jilguero: voz pintada. En 1734, realizando una idea parecida, el padre Castel inventó un clavicordio de los colores, destinado a hacer visible el sonido y a interpretarlo en términos cromáticos. ¡Notable caso del entrometimiento en la especialidad de una ideación que, en sus albores, fué casi un juego de palabras! Carlyle, describiendo una ovación, comparó las voces de los hombres con una gran montaña roja, y rindiéndose a la necesidad de redondear su frase, añadió que las voces femeniles ondeaban entorno como una niebla azulenca. Saint-Pol-Roux, guiado por la similitud entre las palabras cog y coquelicot, y sugestionado sin duda por el color de la cresta, dijo que el canto del gallo era una amapola sonora. René Ghil, amplificando ciertas celebérrimas declaraciones de Rimbaud sobre el color de las vocales, intentó crear una estética cimentada en la visualización de los sonidos. Escuchad las siguientes procesionales cláusulas de su *Traité du Verbe:*

Constatant les souverainetés les Harpes sont blanches; et blaus sont les
Violons mollis souvent d'une phosphorescence pour surmener les paroxysmes;
en la plénitude des Ovations les cuivres sont rouges; les Flûtes, jaunes, qui
modulent l'ingénu s'étonnant de la lueur des lèvres; et, sourdeur de la Terre
et des Chairs, synthèse simplement des seuls simples, les Orgues toutes noires
plangorent. . .

Esto fué escrito el 86. Once años antes, ya el profesor austriaco Bruhl había estudiado la ligazón de sonidos y de colores. El 83, Francis Galton investigó también el fenómeno, y una encuesta bastante extensa, realizada por él, reveló cierta influencia hereditaria en las maneras de visualizar los sonidos. En cambio, tratándose de individuos no vinculados, se halló que las diferencias eran enormes. Así, Rimbaud, veía las vocales de siguiente manera: *A negra, E blanca, I roja, O azul, U verde.* Una persona citada por Galton las veía: *A azul, E blanca, I negra, O blanquecina, U parda.* Otra, a su vez: *A blanca, E bermeja, I amarilla, O negra y transparente, U violácea. . .*[3] La verdad es, como apuntan Nordau y Suárez de Mendoza, que la audición colorativa es consecuencia de asociaciones casuales y carece de universalidad. . .

De índole más estrictamente literaria son las metáforas que trasladan las sensaciones oculares al terreno auditivo. No derivan, como las anteriores, de idiosincrasias psíquicas, y antes son el resultado de una libre volición del poeta que de una asociación brumosa. (No empleo la frase *asociación subconciente*, por la razón de que no creo en la subconciencia, que conceptúo como una hipótesis provisoria—e indubitablemente efímera—de la psicología.)

Nobilísimo ejemplo del orden de metáfora que nombro es el trazado en los dos versos primeros del *Sendero Innumerable* que compuso Ramón Pérez de Ayala:

Y por la noche un libro y una boca de miel.

De miel, y que las rosas de corazón riente
canten todo a lo largo de las sendas del huerto.

---

3 Borges's note in body of text: "Galton.—Inquiries into Human Faculty and its Development.—Everyman's Library, pág. 109-110."

Y la boca y las rosas yazgan sobre tu frente
cuando hayas terminado tu labor y estés muerto.

Paralelamente Walt Whitman en su ciclo lírico *Cálamus*
celebra un árbol, que sin un compañero ni un amante junto a él pasó
todos sus días diciendo hojas felices. . .(Los ultraístas hemos forjado
muchas imágenes de técnica semejante. Escuchad a Jacobo Sureda:
Era la rebelión de una mañana—y cantaba la luz como un clarín. Y estos
versos por Adriano del Valle: *Al alba la bahía parecía—un do re mi fa
sol que se extinguía.* Y este de mi poema Pueblo: *La luna nueva es una
vocecita en la tarde.*)

Allende las metáforas que se limitan a barajar los datos
sensoriales y a equivocar su trabazón causal existen muchas otras de
mecanismo más complejo, pero no menos discernible. Por ejemplo:
las imágenes creadas mediante la materialización de conceptos que
pertenecen al Tiempo. Recordemos, para ilustrar esta categoría, las
palabras de Kamaralzaman el las *Mil y una noches*, al ensalzar su novia:
*Cuando su cabellera está dispuesta en tres obscuras trenzas, me parece mirar
tres noches juntas.* Y las del brioso Johannes R. Becher, al consumar su
himnario *Derrumbamiento y Triunfo* (Berlín-Hyperionverlag-1914): *Una
última noche, angosta como un lecho, leñosa, rectangular y homed. . .*

De excepcioanl (sic) eficacia son también las imágenes
obtenidas transmutando las percepciones estáticas en percepciones
dinámicas: tropo que es en el fondo una inversión del anterior, ya que
en aquél el tiempo se cristaliza en el espacio, y en éste el espacio se
desborda en el tiempo. Ejemplificaremos tal caso con una acelerada
imagen de Guillermo de Torre: *Los arcoiris*

saltan hípicamente el desierto

y otra de Maurice Claude: *Los rieles aserran interminables asfaltos.*

¿Y la adjetivación antitética? El hecho de que existe basta
para probar el carácter provisional y tanteador que asume nuestro
lenguaje frente a la realidad. Si sus momentos fueran enteramente
encasillables en símbolos orales, a cada estado correspondería
un rótulo, y únicamente uno. Fórmulas como *altanera humildad,*

universalmente solo, y aquella línea decisiva de Shakespeare, sobre *la obscuridad que ven los ciegos*[4] serían incapaces de suscitar en nosotros idea de comprensión alguna. En álgebra, el signo más y el signo menos se excluyen; en literatura, los contrarios se hermanan e imponen a la conciencia una sensación mixta; pero no menos verdadera que las demás. (Según las teorizaciones de Abel[5] sobre el comienzo del lenguaje, el mismo sonido originariamente abarcaba los términos contrarios de un concepto, ambos de los cuales se presentaban simultáneamente al espíritu, de acuerdo con la ley de asociación. En una etapa ulterior estos sonidos fueron perdiendo su valor ambilátero y resbalaron hacia uno u otro de sus dos polos antagónicos, hasta reducirse a una acepción privativa.

Creo que en árabe aun perduran muchos vocablos que traducen a la vez dos cosas opuestas. Sin ir tan lejos, recordaré el sentido anfibológico de la voz española *huésped* y el modismo *un pedazo de hombre*, empleado para designar todo un hombre, un espécimen de humanidad vigoroso. En inglés asimismo nos encontramos con los verbos *to cleave* [hender o adherir] y *to ravel* [desenredar o enmarañar].)

Pero es inútil proseguir esta labor clasificatoria comparable a dibujar sobre papel cuadriculado. He analizado ya bastantes metáforas para hacer posible, y hasta casi segura, la suposición de que en su gran mayoría cada una de ellas es referible a una fórmula general, de la cual pueden inferirse, a su vez, pluralizados ejemplos, tan bellos como el primitivo, y que no serán, en modo alguno, plagios. ¿Y las metáforas excepcionales, las que se hallan al margen de la intelectualización?. . ., me diréis. Esas constituyen el corazón, el verdadero milagro de la milenaria gesta verbal, y son poquísimas. En ellas se nos escurre el nudo enlazador de ambos términos, y, sin embargo, ejercen mayor fuerza efectiva que las imágenes verificables sensorialmente o ilustradoras de una receta. Arquetipo de esas metáforas únicas puede ser el encerrado en la siguiente estrofa que vedesca, inmortalizadora de la muerte de don Pedro Girón, virre y capitán general de las Dos Sicilias:

---

4 Borges's note in body of text: "'Looking on darkness which the blind do see' (Sonnets-27)."

5 Borges's note in body of text: "Cit. Max Nordau—'Degeneración' (3-V)."

Su tumba son de Flandes las campañas
Y su epitafio la sangrienta luna.

Y ésta de Pedro Garfias:

El mar es una estrella.
La estrella es de mil puntas.

En frases como las anteriores, la realidad objetiva—esa objevidad (sic) supuesta que Berkeley negó y Kant envió al destierro polar de un nóumeno inservible, reacio a cualquier adjetivación y ubicuamente ajeno—se contorsiona hasta plasmarse en una nueva realidad. Realidad tan asentada y brillante, que desplaza la inicial impresión que la engendró, y completamente distinta de la que miente un poema confesional, autobiográfico, el cual sólo vive cuando lo referimos a una etapa—a veces momentánea—en la existencia de su autor, y cuando esta etapa puede paralelarse con otra de nuestra propia vida.

Crítica es la anterior que enderezo en contra del aguachirlismo rimado que practican aquí en mi tierra la Argentina, los lamentables "sencillistas," y en pro del creacionismo y de la tendencia jubilosamente barroca que encarna Ramón Gómez de la Serna.

En apuntaciones sucesivas pienso ahondar ambos temas, y mostrar cómo últimamente en ciertas proezas líricas de Gerardo Diego y otros ultraístas, vemos realizadas íntegramente (sic) las intenciones huidobrianas contenidas, a su vez, en los postulados del cubismo literario, y cómo la prosapia de la obra de Ramón es ilustre y engarza su raíz trisecular en las visiones de Quevedo.

Jorge-Luis Borges.

Buenos Aires, 27, 8, 1921

Cosmópolis ns 35, Madrid, Nov. 1921

CRITICAL NOTES: THE METAPHOR

An essential difference does not exist between the metaphor and what the professionals of the science call the explanation of a phenomenon. Both are a woven tie between two distinct things, one of which pours into the other. Both are equally true or false.

To explain, for example, in histological terms, the pain of a tremor in the nervous system, of cavities. . ., is like playing "sleight of hand" with what is to be explained. Of course this nomenclature can be of practical use, similar to the intellectual relief attained by an algebraic operation, labeling the quantities *x, y, or z*. But it's absurd to think that these signs can change or clarify in any way the things they label. Light—the luminous sensation, for example—is something definitely delimited by the vibrations into which it is translated by Optics. These vibrations do not constitute the reality of light. How can we believe, besides, that one thing can be the reality of another, or that there may be sensations which are—definitely—transposable into other sensations?

And so, when a geometrician affirms that the moon is an extensive quantity in three dimensions, his expression is no less metaphoric than the one by Nietzsche when he prefers to define it as a cat walking on the roof. In both cases a link is extended from the moon (synthesis of visual perceptions) towards another thing: in the first one, towards a series of space relations; and in the second, towards a group of sensations that evoke stealth-ness, unctuosity, and jesuitism. . .Now; none of these myths nor the geometric myth that identifies the moon with a solid, nor the physics myth which identifies this solid with a pile of fragmentary atoms, which in turn he identifies as electricity, nor the lyric myth, present themselves as simple replacements of the piece of reality that they. Above all they are—like all explanations and all casual links—so underlinings of minute aspects of the subject dealing with new facts added to the world. Considered in this manner, the metaphor assumes the religious semi-urgent character it had in its beginnings, and Creationism—at least in theory—is fully justified. Let's define, then, the metaphor as a voluntary identification of two or more distinct concepts, with an emotional reaction as the objective, and let us study some of its forms.

The grammatical distinctions between comparison and figure of speech, distinctions determined by the use or absence of the words *like* or *as*, should not stop us.

Let's begin considering a notable idiosyncrasy of our faculties.

Primarily, our memory is visual and secondarily auditory. Of the series of states that link what we denominate as consciousness, only the ones that are translatable endure in terms of visuality or audition. In this way, while an ocular detail without any intrinsic importance whatsoever—the design of tiles on a patio or the parade of books in a book shelf, for example—can be interwoven into our inner life and last forever, the fierce wrenching of physical pain is erased, after having barely gone away, and is only remembered in abstractions of aggressivity, anguish, etc., or with concrete significations such as shooting pain, strong pain or sharp pointed pain. . .Neither the muscular nor the olfactory nor the savoring faculties, find room in our memory and the past is reduced, then, to a pile of shuffled visions and a plurality of voices. Among these, the first have more persistence, and if we wish to return to the beginning moments of our infancy, we prove that we only recover a few memories of a visual nature. . .

To name any noun whatsoever is equal to suggesting its visual context, and even in words of very marked auditory connotations like *violin-drum-guitar*, the idea of its appearance always precedes that of its sound and it takes effect almost instantly.

Hence, the metaphor is limited to taking advantage of a parallelism of existing forms within two visibilities, be it the most simple one or the easiest. A priori we would have hoped to find numerous examples of this type of image in primitive poems, but it isn't so, and the study of a work such as the English version of Confucius's *Shi-King*, where one finds compiled the most archaic songs of the central empire from 600 or 700 years before our era, convinces us to the contrary. Beginning with Góngora, Castillian poetry systematizes the exploitation of formal coincidences in lines such as this "chrysograhic" verse:

In fields of sapphire stars graze

or when he affirms: *plows comb the fields.* A verbal trick which later on reached its full reduction to the absurd in the axiomatic Lunario Sentimental by our Tagore, Lugones, and about which Heine also mocked when he said, that the night was a darkened ermine cloak with gilded specks. Justifying himself later on with the admission that, no doubt, the furrier who got the idea of tinting the ermine black was mad.

Perhaps the metaphors with the least staying power are those obtained through the translation of acoustic perceptions into optic perceptions, and vice versa. The examples are plentiful.

Already around 1620, Quevedo spoke of *black voices* and apostrophized the linnet: *painted voice.* In 1734, working on a similar idea, father Castel invented a clavichord of colors, intended to make sound visible, and interpret it in chromatic terms. A remarkable case of intrusion into the specialty of an idea that, in its beginnings, was almost a play on words, Carlyle, describing an ovation compared men's voices with a huge red mountain, and submitting to the need to round off his phrase, added that the feminine voices in turn undulated like a bluish fog. Saint-Pol-Roux, guided by the similarity between the words *coq* [rooster] and *coquelicot* [red, black spotted poppy], and influenced undoubtedly by the color of the cockscomb, said that the crow of the rooster was a sonorous poppy. René Ghil, expanding on certain renowned declarations by Rimbaud concerning the color of vowels, attempted to create an esthetic, founded on the visualization of sounds. Listen to the following parade of clauses from his *Traité du Verbe: The sovereignties verify that Harps are white; and for the sake of over-working the paroxysms, the soft Violins are often a phosphorescent blue; in the fullness of Ovations the brass instruments are red; the Flutes, yellow, which modulates the ingénu who is astonished by the*

*light from her lips; and, the deafness of Earth and flesh, simply a synthesis
of mere simpletons, the pure black Organs plunge. . .*

This was written in '86. Eleven years before, the Austrian
professor Bruhl had already studied the connection of colors and
sounds. In '83, Francis Galton also investigated the phenomenon, and
a quite extensive inquiry, carried out by himself, revealed a certain
hereditary influence in the way sounds are visualized. Speaking of
individual writers with no common bond, on the other hand, one
finds enormous differences of opinion. And so, Rimbaud, looked
at vowels in the following manner: *A black, E white, I red, O blue, U
green.* Someone quoted by Galton perceived them in the following
manner: *A blue, E white, I black, O whitish, U gray.* Another in turn:
A white, E red, I yellow, O black and transparent, U violet. . .[6] The
truth is, as pointed out by Nordau y Suárez de Mendoza, that the
auditory coloration is a consequence of casual associations lacking
universality...

Of a more strict literary nature are the metaphors that
transfer the ocular sensations to the auditive domain. They don't
derive, as the earlier ones, from psychic idiosyncrasies, and are more
the result of the poet's free will than of a hazy association. (I don't
use the phrase *subconscious association*, because I don't believe in
subconsciousness, which I consider as a provisional hypothesis—and
undoubtedly ephemeral—of psychology.)

The most noble example of the metaphoric order which
I have mentioned is the one outlined in the first two verses from
Sendero Innumerable composed by Ramón Pérez de Ayala:

And at night a book and a mouth of honey.

Of honey, and I want the roses of a cheerful heart
to sing throughout the path of the garden.
And I want the mouth and the roses to lie on your brow
when you have finished your work and are dead.

---

[6] Borges's note in body of text: "See note number 2."

In parallel, Walt Whitman in his lyric cycle *Cálamus* celebrates an Oak tree, that, with neither a companion nor lover close by, spent all its days next to him uttering joyous leaves. . .(We ultraists have forged many images with similar technique. Listen to Jacobo Sureda: *It was the rebellion of a morning—and the light was singing like a bugle.* And these verses by Adriano del Valle: *at dawn the bay appeared—a do re mi fa sun dying away.* And this from my poem *Pueblo: The new moon is a tiny voice in the evening.*)

Beyond the metaphors that limit themselves to shuffling sensorial data and to misconstruing casual connections there exists many others of a more complex, but no less discernible mechanism. For example: the images created through the materialization of concepts belonging to Time. In order to illustrate this category, let us remember the words of Kamaralzaman in *Thousand and One Nights*, as he exalts his bride: *when her long hair is arranged in three dark braids, I seem to see three nights together.* And those of the spirited Johannes R. Becher, as he completed his hymnal Derrumbamiento y Triunfo (Berlin-Hyperionverlag-1914): *one last night, narrow like a bed, woody, rectangular and damp. . .*

As well, images of exceptional effectiveness are obtained by transmuting static perceptions into dynamic perceptions: figure of speech that in essence is an inversion of the first, since in the former, time is crystalized in space, and in the latter space overflows into time. We shall exemplify such a case with an accelerated image of Guillermo de Torre: *Rainbows*

leap the desert, like horses

and another by Maurice Claude: *rails sawing the endless asphalt.*

And the antithetical adjectivizing? The fact that it exists is enough to prove the provisional and reckoning character our language assumes in the face of reality. If its moments were entirely classifiable in verbal signs, each state would have a corresponding sign, and only one. Formulas such as *haughty humility, universally alone,* and that decisive Shakespearean line, about *the darkness seen by the blind*[7] would be incapable of generating in us any understanding.

---

7 Borges's note in body of text: "'Looking on darkness which the blind do see' (Sonnets-27)."

In algebra, the plus sign and the minus sign cancel themselves; in literature, opposites fraternize and impose on consciousness a mixed sensation; but no less true then the rest. (According to Abel's theorizings[8] about the beginning of language, the same sound originally covered opposite terms of a concept, both of which presented themselves simultaneously to the spirit, according to the law of association. In a later stage these sounds started losing their duality and slipped towards one or the other of its two antithetical poles, until finally they were reduced to an exclusive meaning.

I think that in Arabic many words still exist that represent two opposite things at the same time. Without going so far, I'll bring to mind the amphibological sense of the Spanish term *huésped* [guest] and the idiom *un pedazo de hombre* [a piece of man], used to designate a complete man, a vigorous human specimen. In English likewise we find ourselves with the verbs *to cleave* [hender o adherir] and *to ravel* [desenredar o enmarañar].)

But it's useless to continue this classification chore, one comparable to drawing on graph paper. I have already analyzed enough metaphors to establish the possibility, almost the certainty, of the supposition that, for the most part, each one of them are referible to a general formula, from which at the same time, many pluralized examples as beautiful as the original one can be inferred, and which in no way would be plagarisms. And what about the exceptional metaphors, the ones found at the margin of "intellectualization"? . . ., you will ask. Those constitute the heart, the true miracle of the millenary verbal feat, and they are very few. In them the knot joining both terms comes undone, and nevertheless, they exercise a more effective force than the images which are verified sensorially or depictions from recipes. Archetype of these unique metaphors could be enclosed in the following stanza by Quevedo, immortalizing the death of Don Pedro Girón, viceroy and general captain of the Two "Sicilys":

> *The bells of Flanders are his tomb*
> *and the bloody moon his epitaph.*

---

[8] Borges's note in body of text: "Citing Max Nordau-'Degeneración' (3-V)."

And this one by Pedro Garfias:

> *The sea is a star.*
> *The star is of a thousand points.*

In phrases like the previous ones, objective reality—that alleged objectivity that Berkeley denied and Kant sent away to a polar exile as useless noumenon, reluctant to any adjectiving and strange placement—twists itself around until it gels into a new reality. A reality, so set and brilliant, that it replaces the initial impression that conceived it, and so completely different from the one fabricated in the confessional, autobiographical poem, which only comes alive when we connect it to the period—sometimes momentary—in its author's life, and when this period can parallel another one from our own lives.

The previous is a critique that I direct against the rhymed balderdash that the pitiful "simplistics" practice here in my country Argentina, and in favor of Creationism and the jubilantly baroque trend that Roman Gomez de la Serna embodies.

In future critiques, I plan to go deeper into both topics, and ultimately show how in certain lyric feats of Gerardo Diego and other ultraists, we see integrally realized Huidobro's intentions, and in turn, in the premises of literary cubism, and how the lineage of Ramon's work is illustrious and how its tri-secular root connects with Quevedo's visions.

Buenos Aires, 27, 8, 1921

Año II   N.º XI

Revista de Occidente

Director:
José Ortega y Gasset

Sumario

J. ORTEGA Y GASSET: *Kant. (Conclusión.)* • P. SALINAS:
Delirios del chopo y el ciprés • PEDRO GIRARD:
Yuna, Felipe y el almirante • Nuevos hechos,
nuevas ideas: G. WORRINGER: *El espí-*
ritu del arte gótico • A. ESPI-
NA: *Bi o el edificio en humo*

NOTAS: Adolfo Salazar: Polichinela y maese Pedro
J. Ortega y Gasset: Sobre la sinceridad triunfante
E. Díez-Canedo: Fernández Moreno • Ángel Sánchez
Rivero: Waldo Frank, *Salvos* • ASTERISCOS

Precio: 3,50   Madrid   Mayo 1924

PLATE #23 – Cover of *Revista de Occidente* ns 11, Madrid, 1924

PLATE #24 – Cover of *Proa* ns 2, Buenos Aires, 1924

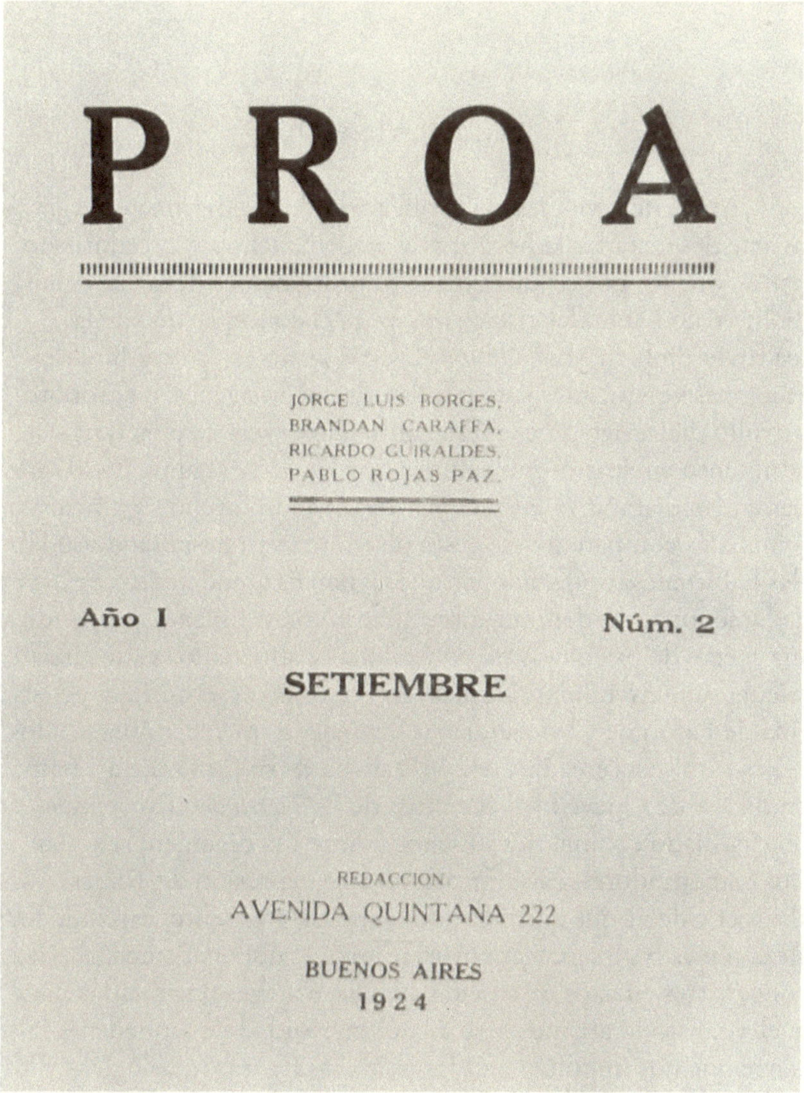

PROA

JORGE LUIS BORGES,
BRANDAN CARAFFA,
RICARDO GÜIRALDES,
PABLO ROJAS PAZ.

Año I   Núm. 2

SETIEMBRE

REDACCION:
AVENIDA QUINTANA 222

BUENOS AIRES
1924

PLATE #25 – Editor's page of *Proa* ns 2

ULTRAÍSMO

Antes de comenzar la explicación de la novísima estética, conviene desentrañar la hechura del rubenianismo y anecdotismo vigentes, que los poetas ultraístas nos proponemos llevar de calles y abolir. Y no hablo del clasicismo, pues el concepto que de la lírica tuvieron la mayoría de los clásicos—esto es, la urdidura de narraciones versificadas y embanderadas de imágenes, o el sonoro desarrollo dialéctico de cualquier intención ascética o jactancioso rendimiento amatorio—no campea hoy en parte alguna. En lo que al rubenianismo atañe, puedo señalar desde ya un hecho significativo. Los iniciales compañeros de gesta de Rubén van despojando su labor de las habituales topificaciones que signan esa tendencia, y realizando aisladamente obras desemejantes. Juan Ramón Jiménez propende asi a una suerte de psicologismo confesional y abreviado; Valle-Inclán gesticula su incredulidad jubilosa en versos pirueteros; Lugones se olvida de Laforgue y las metáforas formales para encaminarse a los paisajes sumisos; l'érez de Ayala ensancha en su prosa recia y palpable la tradición de Quevedo, y el cantor de *La Tierra de Alvargonzales* se ha encastillado en un severo silencio. Ante esa divergencia actual de los comenzadores, cabe empalmar una expresión de Torres Villarroel y decir que considerado como cosa viviente, capas de forjar belleza nueva o de espolear entusiasmos, el rubenianismo se halla a las once y tres cuartos de su vida, con las pruebas terminadas para esqueleto. Esto lo afirmo, pese a la numerosidad de monederos falsos del arte que nos imponen aún las oxidadas figuras mitológicas y los desdibujados y lejanos epítetos que prodigara Darío en muchos de sus poemas. La belleza rubeniana es ya una cosa madurada y colmada, semejante a la belleza de un lienzo antiguo, cumplida y eficaz en la limitación de sus métodos y en nuestra aquiescencia al dejarnos herir por sus previstos recursos; pero por eso mismo, es una cosa acabada, concluída, anonadada. Ya sabemos que manejando palabras crepusculares, apuntaciones de colores y evocaciones versallescas o helénicas, se logran determinados efectos, y es porfía desatinada e inútil seguir haciendo eternamente la prueba.

Por cierto, muchos poetasjóvenes que aseméjanse inicialmente a los ultraístas en su tedio común ante la cerrazón rubeniana, han hecho bando aparte, intentando rejuvenecer la lírica mediante las anécdotas rimadas y el desaliño experto. Me refiero a los sencillistas que tienden a buscar poesía en lo común y corriente, y a tachar de su vocabulario toda palabra prestigiosa. Pero estos se equivocan también. Desplazar el lenguaje cotidiano hacia la literatura, es un error. Sabido es que en la conversación hilvanamos de cualquier modo los vocablos y distribuimos los guarismos verbales congenerosa vaguedad. . .El miedo a la retórica—miedo justificado y legítimo—empuja los sencillistas a otra clase de retórica vergonzante, tan postiza y deliberada como la jerigonza académica, o las palabrejas en lunfardo que se desparraman por cualquier obra nacional, para crear el ambiente. Además, hay otro error más grave en su estética. Ni la escritura apresurada y jadeante de algunas fragmentarias percepciones ni los gironcillos autobiográficos arrancados a la totalidad de los estados de conciencia y malamente copiados, merecen ser poesía. Con esa voluntad logrera de aprovechar el menor ápice vital, conesa comezón continua de encuadernar el universo y encajonarlo en una estantería, sólo se llega a un sempiterno espionaje del alma propia, que tal vez resquebraja e histrioniza al hombre que lo ejerce.

¿Qué hacer entonces? El prestigio literario está en baja; los intelectuales temen que los socaliñen con palabras bonitas e inhiben su emotividad ante el menor alarde oratorio; las enumeraciones de Whitman y su compañerismo vehemente nos parecen lejanos, legendarios; los más acérrimos partidarios del susto vocean en balde derrumbamientos y aposteosis. ¿Hacia qué norte emproar la Lírica?

El Ultraísmo es una de tantas respuestas a la interrogación anterior.

El Ultrísmo lo apadrinó inicialmente el gran prosista sevillano Rafael Cansinos Asséns y en sus albores no fue más que una voluntad ardentísima de realizar obras noveles e impares, una resolution de incesante sobrepujamiento. Así lo definió el mismo

Cansinos: "El Ultraísmo es una voluntad caudalosa que rebasa todo límite escolástico. Es una orientación hacia continuas y reiteradas evoluciones, un propósito de perenne juventud literaria, una anticipada aceptación de todo módulo y de toda idea nuevos. Representa el compromiso de ir avanzando con el tiempo."

Estas palabras fueron escritas en el otoño de 1918. Hoy, tras dos años de variadísimos experimentos líricos ejecutados por una treintena de poetas en las revistas españolas *Cervantes* y *Grecia*—capitaneada esto última por Isaac del Vando Villar—podemos precisar y limitar esa anchurosa y precavida declaración del maestro. Esquematizada, la presente actitud del Ultraísmo es resumible en los principios que siguen:

1] Reducción de la lírica a su elemento primordial: la metáfora.
2] Tachadura de las frases medianeras, los nexos, y los adjetivos inútiles.
3] Abolición de los trebejos ornamentales, el confesionalismo, la circunstanciación, las prédicas y la nebulosidad rebuscada.
4] Síntesis de dos o más imágenes en una, que ensancha de ese modo su facultad de sugerencia.

Los poemas ultraicos constan pues de una serie de metáforas, cada una de las cuales tiene sugestividad propia y compendiza una visión inédita de algún fragmento de la vida. La desemejanza raigal que existe entre la poesía vigente y la nuestra es la que sigue: En la primera, el hallazgo lírico se magnifica, se agiganta y se desarrolla; en la segunda, se anota brevemente. ¡Y no creáis que tal procedijiento menoscabe la fuerza emocional! "Más obran quintas esencias que fárragos" dijo el autor del *Criticón* en sentencia que sería inmejorable abreviatura de la estética ultraísta. La unidad del poema la da el tema común—intencional u objetivo—sobre el cual versan las imágenes definidoras de sus aspectos parciales.

Escuchad a Pedro Garfias:

Andar
con polvo de horizontes en los ojos
tendida la inquietud a la montaña
y desgranar los siglos
rosarios de cien cuentas
sobre nuestra esperanza.

Y a estos otros:

Rosa Mística

Era ella
   y nadie lo sabía
pero cuando pasaba
los árboles se arrodillaban
y en su cabellera
       se trenzaban las letanías
Era ella,
         era ella.
Me desmayé en sus manos
como una hoja muerta.
      Sus manos ojivales
  que daban de comer a las estrellas
por el aire volaban
romanzas sin sonido
  y en su almohada de pasos
  yo me quedé dormido.

Gerado Diego

Viaje

Los astros son espuelas
que hieren los ijares de la noche
En la sombra, el camino claro
es la estela que dejó el Sol

de velas desplegadas
mi corazón como un albatros
siguió el rumbo del Sol.

                    Guillermo Juan

        Primavera

La última nieve sobre tus hombros
¡oh amada vestida de claro!
        El último arco-iris
hecho abanico entre tus manos.
Mira:
        El hombre que mueve el manubrio
enseña a cantar a los pájaros nuevos
        La primavera es el poema
        de nuestro hermano el jardinero.

                    Juan Las

        Epitalamio

Puesto que puedes hablar
no me digas lo que piensas
Tu corazón
                envuelve
                        tu carne.

Sobre tu cuerpo desnudo
mi voz cosecha palabras.

Te traigo de Oriente el Sol
para tu anillo de Bodas.

En el hecho que espera
una rosa se desangra.

                    Helidoro Puche

Casa Vacía

Toda la casa está llena de ausencia
La telaraña del recuerdo
pende de todos los techos.

En la urna de las vitrinas
están presos los ruiseñores del silencio.

Hay preludios dormidos
que esperan la hora del regreso.

El polvo de la sombra
se pega a los vestidos de los muros.

En el reloj parado
se suicidaron los minutos.

Ernesto López-Parra.

La lectura de estos poemas demuestra que sólo hay una conformidad tangencial entre el Ultraísmo y las demás banderías estéticas de vanguardia. La exasperada retórica y el bodrio dinamista de los poetas de Milán se hallan tan lejos de nosotros como el zumbido verbal, las enrevesadas series silábicas y el terco automatismo de los sonámbulos del *Sturm* o la prolija baraúnda de los unanimistas franceses. . .

Además de los nombres ya citados de poetas ultraístas, no hay que olvidar a J. Rivas Panedas, a Humberto Rivas, a Jacobo Sureda, a Juan Larrea, a César A. Comet, a Mauricio Bacarisse y a Eugenio Montes. Entre los escritores que, enviándonos su adhesión, han colaborado en las publicaciones ultraístas, básteme aludir a Ramón Gómez de la Serna, a Ortega y Gasset, a Valle-Inclan, a Juan Ramón Jiménez, a Nicolás Beauduin, a Gabriel Alomar, a Vicente Huidobro y a Maurice Claude. En el terreno de las revistas, la hoja decenal *Ultra* reemplaza actualmente a *Grecia* e irradia desde Madrid las normas ultraicas. En Buenos Aires acaba de lanzarse *Prisma*, revista mural, fundada por E. González Lanuza, Guillermo Juan y el firmante. De real interés es también el sagaz estudio antológico publicado en el Nº 23 de *Cosmópolis* por Guillermo de Torre, brioso polemista, poeta, y forjador de neologismos.

Un resumen final. La poesía lírica no ha hecho otra coa hasta ahora que bambolearse entre la cacería de efectos auditivos o visuales, y el prurito de querer expresar la personalidad de su hacedor. El primero de ambos empeños atañe a la pintura o a la música, y el segundo se asienta en un error psicológico, ya que la personalidad, el yo, es sólo una ancha denominación colectiva que abarca la pluralidad de todos los estados de conciencia. Cualquier estado nuevo que se agregue a los otros llega a formar parte esencial del yo, y a expresarle: los mismo lo "individual" que lo "ajeno." Cualquier acontecimiento, cualquier percepción, cualquier idea, nos expresa con igual virtud; vale decir, puede añadirse a nosotros. . .Superando esa inútil terquedad en fijar verbalmente un yo vagabundo que se transforma en cada instante, el Ultraísmo tiende a la meta primicial de toda poesía, esto es, a la transmutación de la realidad palpable del mundo en realidad interior y emocional.

Jorge Luis Borges.

Nosotros ns 151, Buenos Aires, Dec. 1921

ULTRAISM

Before beginning the explication of the brand new aesthetic, it is well to extricate the characteristic elements of the prevailing "rubenianism" and "ancecdotism," that we ultraist poets propose to take from the streets and abolish. And I am not speaking of classicism, because the concept that the majority of the classic poets had regarding lyric—that is, the weaving of versified narrations and ornate images, or the sonorous dialectic development of an ascetic intention or arrogant amorous rendition—doesn't prevail anywhere today. As far as "rubenianism" is concerned, I can already point out something significant. The initial compatriots of Ruben's [Dario] influences are stripping their work of the habitual "topoi" and subject matter that signal that tendency, and are achieving on their own dissimilar work. Juan Ramón Jiménez in this way tends towards an abbreviated confessional style of psychologizing; Valle-Inclán gesticulates his jubilant incredulity in "Pirouette-like" verses; Lugones forgets Laforgue and formal metaphors in order to focus on submissive landscapes; Pérez de Ayala enhances in his harsh and palpable prose the tradition of Quevedo, and the singer of *La Tierra de Alvargonzález* has withdrawn inside a severe silence. Given this actual divergence of the initiators, it would be fitting to insert an expression of Torres Villarroel and say that, considered as a living thing capable of forging new beauty or to stimulate enthusiasm, "rubenianism" finds itself at the eleventh hour of its life, with the final proof being its skeletal remains. This I affirm despite the numerous false counterfeiters of the art that still impose on us the rusty mythological figures and the remote ill sketched epithets that Dario lavished on many of his poems. The "rubenian" beauty is already a mature and abundant thing, similar to the beauty of an old painting, thorough and efficacious in the limitation of its methods and in our acquiescence, allowing ourselves to be wounded by its foreseen resources; and precisely for that reason, it is a finished thing, concluded, humbled and anhilated. We already know that employing crepuscular words, citations of colors and "versaillesque" or "hellenic" evocations, certain effects can be achieved, and it is foolish and useless obstinacy to endlessly try to do so.

Indeed, many young poets, those that initially resembled the ultraists in their shared tedium towards the rubenian storm, have set up a separate faction, trying to rejuvenate the lyric through rhymed anecdotes and expert carelessness. I'm refering to the simplistic writers that tend to search for poetry in what's common and ordinary, and to erase from their vocabulary all prestigious words. But they are also mistaken. To apply everyday language to literature is an error. It is known that in conversation we embroider words anyway and we distribute the verbal signs with generous vagueness

. . .Fear of rhetoric—justified and legitimate fear—pushes the
"simplistic" to a different kind of embarrassing rhetoric, so artificial
and deliberate like academic jargon, or the superfluous in thieves
Latin that is spread about for any national effort, besides there is
a graver error in its aesthetic. Neither does the hurried or panting
writing of some fragmentary perceptions nor the autobiographical
spins drawn from the totality of the conscious states and badly
copied, deserve to be poetry. With the will of a profiteer taking
advantage of the least vital pinnacle, with that continuous itch to
bind the universe and enclose it into a book shelf, comes only an
eternal espionage of the soul, that perhaps splits and "histrionicizes"
the man that does so.

What to do then? The literary prestige is low; the intellectuals
fear that they will be tricked with pretty words which will
inhibit their emotionality before the least oratorical clamor; the
enumerations of Whitman and his vehement good fellowship appear
distant to us, and legendary; the most staunch partisans out of fear
speak out in vain of collapse and apotheosis. Towards which north
shall we course the Lyrics prow?

Ultraism is one of the many responses to the previous
interrogations.

Ultraism was sponsored initially by the great Sevillian prose
writer Rafael Cansinos Asséns and in its early beginnings it was
nothing more than an ardent volition to realize novel and peerless
works, a resolution of incessant desire for excellence. This is how
Cansinos himself defined it: "Ultraism is an abundant will that
surpasses all scholastic limit. It is an orientation towards continuous
and repeated evolutions, a purpose of perennial literary youth, an
anticipated acceptance of all modules and of all ideas that are new. It
represents the obligation to go forward with time."

These words were written in the Autumn of 1918. Today, after
two years of varying lyric experiments executed by a group of around
thirty poets in the Spanish magazines *Cervantes* and *Grecia*—this last
one headed by Isaac del Vando Villar—we can set forth and limit
that expansive and cautious declaration by the master. Schematized,
the present attitude of Ultraism can be summed up in the following
principles:

1. Reduction of the lyric to its primal element: the metaphor.
2. The elimination of intermediating phrases, conjunctions and useless adjectives.
3. Abolition of ornamental flourishes, confessionalism, circumstantial reportage, sermonizing, and nebulous intellectualism.
4. Synthesis of two or more images in one, thus heightening the power of suggestion.

Ultraístic poems then, are made up of a series of metaphors, each one of which has its own suggestiveness and epitomizes an unedited vision of some fragment of life. The root similarity that exists between the current poetry and ours is as follows: in the first, the discovered lyric magnifies itself, enlarges and develops itself; in the second, it elucidates briefly. And don't believe that such procedure lessens the emotional force! "The quintessential cores work better than medleys" said the author of *Criticón* in a sentence that would be an "unimprovable" abbreviation of the ultraist aesthetic. The unity of the poem gives it the common theme—intentional or objective—over which the defining images are versed from their partial aspects.

Listen to Pedro Garfias:

> To go
> with dust of horizons in your eyes
> the restlessness extended to the mountain
> and to thresh the rosary-like
> centuries of one hundred beads
> over our hope

and to these other works:

Mystic Rose

> It was her
> and no one knew it

but when she passed
the trees genuflected
and the litanies braided
      themselves into her hair.
  It was her,
          it was her.
I swooned in her hands
like a fallen leaf.
      Her gothic hands
  that fed the stars
sent flying through the air
love songs without sound
   and on her pillow of steps
    I fell asleep.

Gerardo Diego

Voyage

The stars are spurs
that wound the flanks of the night.
In the shade, the clear road
is the wake of the Sun
with its sails unfurled
my heart like an albatross
followed the course of the Sun.

Guillermo Juan

Spring

The last snow over your shoulders
oh, beloved dressed in translucent white!
  The last rainbow
became a fan between your hands.
Look:

The man that turns the handle
teaches the new birds how to sing
    Spring is the poem
    of our brother the gardener.

               Juan Las

      Epithalamium

Since you can speak
don't tell me what you are thinking.
Your heart
       envelops
           your flesh.

Over your naked body
my voice reaps words.

I bring you the Sun from the East
as your wedding ring.

Upon the bed that waits   [*lecho* instead of *hecho*]
a red rose bleeds.

           Heliodoro Puche

      Empty House

The whole house is full of absence
The spider web of recollection
hangs from every ceiling.

In the case with glass windows
the nightingales are prisoners of silence.

There are sleeping preludes
waiting for the hour of their return.

In the darkness the dust
sticks to the cloth on the walls.

In the stalled clock
the minutes have committed suicide.

Ernesto López-Parra

The reading of these poems show that there is only a tangential conformity between Ultraism and the rest of the current aesthetics movements in the vanguard. The exasperated rhetoric and the dynamistic hodgepodge of the poets of Milan find themselves so far from us like the verbal humdrum, convoluted syllabic series, and the stubborn automatism of the sleepwalkers from *Sturm* or the tedious noise of the French unanimists [Unanimismo movement].

Besides the names of the poets already mentioned, we most not forget J. Rivas Panedas, Humberto Rivas, Jacobo Sureda, Juan Larrea, César A. Comet, Mauricio Bacarisse and Eugenio Montes. Among the writers that, sending their pledge, have collaborated in the ultraist publications, suffice it for me to allude to Ramón Gómez de la Serna, Ortega y Gasset, Valle-Inclán, Juan Ramón Jiménez, Nicolás Beauduin, Gabriel Alomar, Vicente Huidobro and to Maurice Claude. In the arena of magazines, the decennial issue of *Ultra* has just replaced *Grecia* and spreads from Madrid the ultraic norms. In Buenos Aires, *Prisma* has just been launched, a mural magazine, founded by E. González Lanuz Guillermo Juan and the undersigned. Of real interest is also the sagacious anthological study published in the ns 23 issue of *Cosmopolis* by Guillermo de Torre, the spirited polemicist, poet, molder of neologisms.

In conclusion. Lyric poetry has done nothing up till now but waver between the hunting of auditory and visual effects, and the biting desire of wanting to express the personality of its maker. The first of both efforts concerns painting or music, and the second is seated in a psychological error since the personality, the I, is only a broad collective denomination that includes the plurality of all the states of conscience. Any new state that is added to the others comes to be an essential part of the I, and expresses it: the I of the "individual" and the I of the "others" alike. Any event, any perception, any idea, expresses us with equal virtue; it's worth it to say, it can become part of us. . .Surmounting that useless stubbornness to fix verbally a vagabond I that transforms itself at each instance, Ultraism tends toward the primal objective of all poetry, that is, the transmutation of the palpable reality of the world into interior and emotional reality.

✲✲

This ultraist manifesto, "Proclama," published in *Ultra* ns 21 on January 1, 1922 was initially published in *Prisma* ns 1 in Buenos Aires in Dec. 1921 as a "mural" magazine edited by Borges and others—as such, it could be pasted onto shop windows and walls to better spread the word of *Ultraísmo*. This republication from *Ultra* is riddled with typographical errors. An excellent reproduction of the original "Proclama" from *Prisma* (a copy of which could not be found) appears in Guillermo de Torre's 1965 study *Historia de las literaturas de vanguardia* (559) and shows that many of the errors were the fault of *Ultra* editors; however, other words such as "entrañalmente," "doses," "hai," "entabillada," and "gerarquías" are from the original. I have taken the liberty to correct the punctuation errors that were shared by both versions; however, I have left the misspelled words as they appeared in *Ultra* followed by (sic). The following list of corrections are in the order they appear in the text: eliminate second "que," "diametralmente," "verdadero," "superstición," "entrañablemente," "entablillada," "dioses," "miedo" (question mark misplaced), "total," "jerarquías," "superstición," "esta," "hay," "transitoria," "Guillermo."

PROCLAMA

Manifiesto del Ultra Firmado por Jorge Luis Borges, Guillermo Juan, Eduardo Gonzalez Lanuza, y Guillermo de Torre

[Prólogo del redactor]:

Nuestro fraternal amigo y camarada Jorge Luis Borges nos envía el primer número de la originalísima revista mural Prisma, que acaba de aparecer en Buenos Aires a sus cuidados. "Hemos tirado cinco mil ejemplares—nos escribe jovialmente nuestro compañero—, con los cuales, dentro de una semana, estará empavesada la ciudad. Queremos desparramar el ultraísmo por toda la República y hemos enviado números para que sean pegados en Córdoba, en el Rosario de Sante Fe y en Corrientes. También mandamos a Chile y Montevideo. . ."

He aquí, pues, nuevas proas allende los mares dispuestas a partir y reunírsenos en el gran puerto de la última verdad. . .para partir de nuevo hacia los horizontes sueltos.

Integran el número de Prisma originales de J. Rivas Panedas, Adriano del Valle, Pedro Garfias, Isaac del Vando Villar, Jorge Luis Borges, y de los nuevos poetas ultraístas, E. González Lanuza, Guillermo Juan y Jacobo Sureda. A la cabeza de Prisma aparece una entusiast Proclama que reproducimos a continuación.

Cortemos también con "nuestros brazos como leguas" las amarras del luminico mercante cargado con el nuevo grano y cuya botadura removerá las entrañas de la hermana tierra.

PROCLAMA

Barajando un mazo de cartas se puede conseguir que (sic) vayan saliendo en un enfilamiento más o menos simétrico. Claro que las combinaciones asi hacederas son limitadas i de humilde interés. Pero si en vez de manipular naipes, se manipularan palabras, palabras imponentes i estupendas, palabras con entorchados i aureolas, entonces ya cambia diamentralmente (sic) el asunto.

En su forma más enrevesada i difícil, se intenta hasta explicar la vida mediante esos dibujos, i al barajador lo rotulamos filósofo. Para que merezca tal nombre, la tradición le fuerza a scamotear todas las facetas de la existencia menos una sola, sobre la cual asienta las demás, i a decir que lo único verladero (sic) son los átomos o la energia o cualquier otra cosa. . .

¡Como si la realidad que nos estruja entrañalmente (sic), hubiera menester muletas o explicaciones!

En su forma más evidente y automática, el juego de entrelazar palabras campeaen esaentabillada (sic) nadería que es la literatura actual. Los poetas sólo se ocupan de cambiar de sitio los cachivaches ornamentales que los rubenianos heredaron de Góngora—las rosas, los cisnes, los faunos, los doses (sic) griegos, los paisajes ecuánimes i enjardinados—i engarzar millonariamente los flojos adjetivos *inefable, divino, azul, misterioso!* Cuánta socarronería i cuánta mentira en ese manosear de ineficaces i desdibujadas *palabras*, cuánto mie?do (sic) altanero de adentrarse verdaderamente en las cosas, cuánta impotencia en esa vanagloria de símbolos ajenos! Mientras tanto los demás líricos, aquellos que no ostentan el tatuaje azul rubeniano, ejercen un anecdotismo gárrulo, i fomentan penas rimables que barnizadas de visualidades oportunas venderán después con un gesto de amaestrada sencillez i de espontaneidad prevista.

Y unos i otros señoritos de la cultura latina, gariteros de su alma, se pedestalizan sobre las marmóreas leyes estéticas para dignificar ejercicio tan lamentable. Todos quieren realizer obras apelmazadas i perennes. Todos viven en su autobiografía, todos creen en su personlidad, esa mescolanza de percepciones entreveradas de salpicaduras de citas, de admiraciones provocadas i puntiaguda lirastenia. Todos tienden a la enciclopedia, a los aniversarios i a los volúmenes tupidos. El concepto histórico de la vida muerde sus horas. En vez de concederle a cada instante su carácter suficiente i tototal (sic), los colocan en gerarquías (sic) prolijas. Escriben dramas i novelas abarrotadas de encrucijadas espirituales, de gestos culminantes i de apoteosis donde se remansa definitivamente el vivir. Han inventado ese andamiaje literario—la estética—según la cual hay que preparar las situaciones i empalmar las imágenes, i que convierte lo que debiera ser ágil i brincador en un esfuerzo indigno i trabajoso. Idiotez que les hace urdir un soneto para colocar una línea, i decir en doscientas páginas lo cabedero en dos renglones. (Desde ya puede asegurarse que la novela esa cosa maciza engendrada por la supestición (sic) del yo va a desaparecer, como ha sucedido con la epopeya i otras categorías dilatadas.)

Nosotros los ultraístas en estata (sic) época de mercachifles que exhiben corazones disecados i plasman el rostro en carnavales de muecas—queremos desanquilosar el arte. Licito i envidiable como cualquier otro placer es el que motivan las palabras eficazmente trabadas, mas hai (sic) que convenir en lo absurdo de honrar los que le venden, traficando con flacas ñoñerías i trampas antiquísimas. Nuestro arte quiere superar esas martingalas de siempre i descubrir facetas insospechadas al mundo. Hemos síntetizado la poesía en su elemento primordial: la metáfora, a la que concedemos una máxima independencia, más allá de los jueguitos de aquellos que comparan entre sí cosas de forma semejante, equiparando con un circo a la luna. Cada verso de nuestros poemas posee su v propende así a la formación de una mitología emocional i variable. Sus versos que excluyen la palabrería i las victorias baratas conseguidas mediante el despilfarro de palabras exóticas, tienen la contextura decisiva de los marconigramas.

Hemos lanzado *Prisma* para democratizar esas normas. Hemos embanderado de poema las calles, hemos iluminado con lámparas verbales vuestro camino, hemos ceñido vuestros muros con enredaderas de versos: Que ellos, izados como gritos, vivan la momentánea eternidad de todas las cosas, i sea comparable su belleza dadivosa i transtoria (sic), a la de un jardín vislumbrado a la música desparramada por una abierta ventana y que colma todo el paisaje.

JORGE LUIS BORGES
GUILLERNO JUAN
EDUARDO GONZALEZ LANUZA
GUILLERMO DE TORRE

Ultra ns 21, Madrid, 1 Jan. 1922

PROCLAMATION

Ultra Manifesto co-signed by Jorge Luis Borges, Guillermo Juan, Eduardo Gonzalez Lanuza, y Guillermo de Torre.

[Editor's Prologue]:
  Our fraternal friend and comrade Jorge Luis Borges sends us the first issue of the highly original mural magazine Prisma that has just appeared in Bueno Aires under his guidance. "We have printed five thousand copies," our colleague joyfully writes "with which, within a week,

this city will be decorated. We wish to spread Ultraism throughout the Republic and we have sent copies to be put up in Cordoba, Rosario de Sante Fe, and Corrientes. We also sent them to Chile and Montevideo. . ."

Here you have, then, new prows overseas ready to depart and reunite us in the great port of final truth. . .To depart a new towards free horizons.

The issue of Prisma includes originals by J. Rivas Panedas, Adriano del Valle, Pedro Garfias, Isaac del Vando Villar, Jorge Luis Borges, and from the new ultraistic poets, E. González Lanuza, Guillermo Juan and Jacobo Sureda. At the head of Prisma appears an enthusiastic Proclamation that we herewith reproduce.

With "our arms like tongues" let us too cut the ties of the luminous merchant ship loaded with new grain and whose launching will stir-up the bowels of the "sisterland"

PROCLAMATION

Shuffling a deck of playing cards, it's possible to line them up in a more or less symmetrical row. Of course, the combinations so achieved are limited and of meagre interest. But if instead of handling playing cards, we were handling words, powerful and stupendous words, aureoled and gold braided words, then the issue changes radically.

In their most complicated and difficult forms, we even try to explain life with these figures, and we label the shuffler philosopher. For him to deserve such a name, tradition forces him to do a "sleight of hand" trick with all the facets of life except the one on which the rest are based, and to say that the only real things are atoms or energy or something else. . .

As if reality which fundamentally twists us around needed props or explanations!

In its most obvious and automatic form, the play of weaving together words abounds in that splinted nothingness which is current literature. Poets are only busy changing the location of ornamental "knick-knacks" that the rubenians inherited from Góngora—roses, swans, fauns, Greek gods, the well-ordered and flowered ornamented landscapes—and they string together by the millions weak adjectives: *indescribable, divine, blue, mysterious!* So much cleverness and deceit in this handling of ineffective and vague words, so much arrogant fear of truly going deep into things, so much impotence in that vainglory of other's symbols! Meanwhile other lyricists, those that don't flaunt the blue rubenian tattoos, exercise a garrulous "anecdotism", and foment "rhymable" pains that, varnished with appropriate colorfulness, will later be sold as a gesture of mastered simplicity and predictable spontaneity.

So many of these young dandies of the Latin culture, gamblers of their souls, "pedestal themselves on marbled aesthetic laws in order to dignify such deplorable exercise. They all want to produce stodgy and everlasting works. All of them live within their autobiography. All of them believe in their personality, that jumble of perceptions intermingled with spattered quotations of provoked admirations and pointed "lirastenia." All tend towards encyclopedia, towards anniversaries, and dense volumes.

The historical view of life bites its hours. Instead of conceding to each instant its sufficient and total character, they place them in drawn out hierarchies. They write dramas and novels crammed with spiritual dilemmas, with lofty gestures and grand finales that absolutely stagnate life. They have invented that literary scaffolding— the aesthetic—according to which one must prepare situations and join images, and which convert what should be agile and alive into an undignified and tedious effort. Stupidity forces them to weave a sonnet in order to create one line and to say in two hundred pages what can be said in two lines. (As of now we can already declare that the novel, that massive thing engendered by the assumed "I," will disappear, as happened with the epic and other drawn out genres.)

We ultraists—in this era of cheap poetry merchants that exhibit hearts of stone and grimacing carnival masks—want to unfetter the art. Pleasure, permissible and enviable like anything else, is what motivates the effective weaving of words, but we must agree in the absurd of honoring those who sell it, dealing in flimsy sentimental dribble and antiquated traps. Our art wants to go beyond those perennial martingales and discover worldly unsuspected facets. We have synthesized poetry into its primordial element: the metaphor, to which we concede maximum independence, beyond the little games that compare within themselves things of similar form, comparing the circus to the moon. Each verse of our poems has its own individual life and represents an unedited vision. In this way, Ultraism has a propensity towards the formation of an emotional and variable mythology. Its verses that exclude the verbiage and the cheap victories obtained through squandering exotic words, have the decisive contextual quality of the wireless telegram.

We have launched *Prisma* to democratize those norms. We have "bannered" the streets with poems, we have lit your road with verbal lamps, we have lashed your walls with vines of verses: That they, hoisted like shouts, live the momentary eternity of all things, and its transitory and generous beauty be comparable to a garden, glimmering to the music spilt through an open window and which calms all the landscape.

Conclusion

Borges, El Narrador, and His "Arte Poetica"

By way of conclusion, I ask the reader to consider how much of the finest stories and novels written during the Modern Era have been described by literary critics using terms such as "poetic," "lyrical" or "musical" because the fiction writers who wrote them were once (or also) poets in their youth. Certainly, any devoted reader of Borges can detect this supposition to be true for the great *narrador* as well. The vanguard spirit led him to integrate or overlap his poetic sensibilities into the fabric of his prose. Observe the interchange between strategies Borges employs in his poetry and in his finest narratives: reoccurring themes, his characteristic metaphysical and deeply philosophical ideas, his consistent use of concise, musical language that has been called Mallarméan, an insistence on brevity, the repetition of key symbols and extensive use of figurative language. Adding on to the list perhaps is the most important element: a lifelong rejection of realistic, psychological, confessional, autobiographical fiction which proved to be the genesis of story for the majority of prose fiction writers of his generation. Borges's desire was for intelligent thought and lyrical intensity.

In Borges's *Ficciones* and *El Aleph*, certain passages occur where clearly *el poeta* is following his poetic inclinations; his highly charged poetic vision lifts the narration out of simple plot and story development. Notice in the following passage from one of his most celebrated stories, "El jardín de senderos que se bifurcan" ["The Garden of Forking Paths"], which gave his initial story collection its title in 1941 before being incorporated into *Ficciones* in 1944, how Borges's treatment of the landscape is skillfully and poetically written to seem analogous to the interior landscape of the speaker's meditation:

Bajo los árboles ingleses medité en ese laberinto perdido: lo imaginé inviolado y perfecto en la cumbre secreta de una montaña, lo imaginé borrado por arrozales o debajo del agua, lo imaginé infinito, no ya de quioscos ochavados y de sendas que vuelven, sino de ríos y provincias y reinos. . .Pensé en un laberinto de laberintos, en un sinuoso laberinto creciente que abarcara el pasado y el porvenir y que implicara de algún modo los astros. Absorto en esas ilusorias imágenes, olvidé mi destino de perseguido. Me sentí, por un tiempo, indeterminado, percibidor abstracto del mundo. El vago y vivo campo, la luna, los restos de la tarde, obraron en mí; asimismo el declive que eliminaba cualquier posibilidad de cansancio. La tarde era íntima, infinita. El camino bajaba y se bifurcaba, entre las ya confusas praderas. Una música aguda y como silábica se aproximaba y se alejaba en el vaivén del viento, empañada de hojas y de distancia. (106-107)

[Under the trees of England I meditated on this lost and perhaps mythical labyrinth. I imagined it untouched and perfect on the secret summit of some mountain; I imagined it drowned under rice paddies or beneath the sea; I imagined it infinite, made not only of eight-sided pavilions and of twisting paths but also of rivers, provinces and kingdoms. . . .I thought of a labyrinth of labyrinths, of a sinuous, ever growing labyrinth which would take in both past and future and would somehow involve the stars.

Lost in these imaginary illusions I forgot my destiny—that of the hunted. For an undetermined period of time I felt myself cut off from the world, an abstract spectator. The hazy and murmuring countryside, the moon, the decline of the evening, stirred within me. Going down the gently sloping road I could not feel fatigue. The evening was intimate and infinite. The road kept descending and branching off, through meadows misty in the twilight. A high-pitched and almost syllabic music kept coming and going, moving with the breeze, blurred by the leaves and by distance.] (93-94)

Notice, also, the parallelism he employs in the repetition of sentences with "lo imaginé" and "laberinto," a strategy Borges often employed in his prose poetry to heighten the emotional statement and force (or reinforce) the idea deep into the reader's consciousness. There is, as well, his unique choice of descriptive adjectives and poetic language rising and falling with musical rhythm—perhaps only in Spanish can this be heard, "a syllabic music" that causes the speaker's meditative and ethereal experience to stir deep within the reader's consciousness.

Taken by itself, the above passage could easily approximate the poetic achievement of *El hacedor*, that mixture of both poetry and prose, intelligence and passion, which he found so exemplary in Valéry and De Quincey. Finding oneself lost in a labyrinth—is this not the purpose of good writing? Borges might inquire. For the reader to be so seduced by both beauty and by intelligence that they lose themselves in the text? Borges certainly accomplishes this in so much of his work, as evidenced by a combination of his craftsmanship, his feeling for musical rhythm in the language, and his extremely intelligent, provocative ideas.

As this study has attempted to demonstrate, a glance at any number of his ultraísta verse and prose poems demonstrates that this same strategy was already at play during his earliest writing, such as in these lines from "Señal": "Fuimos abriendo como ramas las calles," ["We went opening the streets like branches"], or other works describing the infinite and intimate evening, the countryside, twilights and the ever prevailing moon, all of which reveal identical passages, images, music, tone of voice, as that which is present in the preceding passage from "El jardín." If readers cannot read the text in Spanish, then someone who does (preferably a native speaker) should read the text aloud so that readers might attain a greater appreciation for the skill and poetic craft involved in Borges's execution of the Spanish language.

In this sense, Guillermo Sucre writes that throughout Borges's career, he had the "capacity to shock and at the same time to seduce." He tells of how in 1933, after the French writer Drieu La Rochelle met young Borges in Argentina, he too "did not fail to perceive this aspect":

Borges, qui comprend tout, a pourtant des passions tranchantes. Il
est tout passion parce qu'il est intelligent. Un homme intelligent
n'a pas peur de ses passions, et il les sert avec cette delicatesse,
cette noblesse dans le parti pris qui le distingue du fanatique idiot.
(cited in *Borges, el poeta* 12).

[Borges, who understands everything, nevertheless, has very keen
passions. He is thoroughly passionate because he is intelligent. An
intelligent man is not afraid of his passions, and he serves them
with delicacy, with that nobility of one with strong convictions
that distinguishes him from the fanatic idiot.]

Of course, the French anti-intellectuals, among which "Borges's work
was already the object of the most passionate controversies," judged
Borges to be "too intellectual." This "implacable judgement," Sucre
goes on to suggest, was intended to neutralize Borges:

Demaisiado intelectual quería decir demaisiado frío y elaborado.
Intelectual porque era singularmente inteligente, deduce el escritor
francés; en todo caso él proponía a los regocijados antiintelectuales:
lean sus poemas. ¿No hay un lirismo generoso, una intensidad,
una secreta plenitud en ellos? ¿Acaso inteligencia y pasión no son
inherentes a la naturaleza misma de Borges? (11)

[Too intellectual meant too cold and elaborate. Intellectual because
he [Borges] was singularly intelligent, the French writer deduced;
in any case, he proposed to the delighted anti-intellectuals: read
his poems. Is there not a generous lyricism, an intensity, a secret
plenitude in them? Are not intelligence and passion inherent to
the very nature of Borges?]

Sucre believes that in Rochelle's comment exists "the most valid perspective towards the comprehension of Borges." Certainly, it is what
readers of Borges feel in his work—both the prose and the poetry—a
poet's passion for language, a storyteller's verbal talent commanded by
an intelligence that desires literature to delve into the heart of things,
both physical and metaphysical.

For a writer to see into the heart of things and then seduce readers with a "transmutation" of the thing envisioned into musical language—this "alchemic" process is the foundation of Borges's work in both poetry and prose. His is not work meant solely to delight and entertain, but to inform readers, to force them to think of infinite possibilities. Borges, in fact, declares this is the main function of poetry in his "Arte poética":

Ver en el día o en el año un símbolo
De los días del hombre y de sus años
Convertir el ultraje de los años
En una música, un rumor y un símbolo,

Ver en la muerte el sueño, en el ocaso
Un triste oro, tal es la poesía
Que es inmortal y pobre. La poesía
Vuelve como la aurora y el ocaso. (*El hacedor 141*)

[To see in every day and year a symbol
Of all the days of man and of his years,
and convert the outrage of the years
into a music, a sound, and a symbol,

To see in death a dream, in the sunset
A golden sadness—such is poetry,
Humble and immortal, poetry
returning, like dawn and sunset.] (*A Personal Anthology* 199)

Does this not hold true for his prose tales as much as for his poetry? In a collection of quotes on various themes entitled *Jorge Luis Borges: A to Z*, Borges has this to say on the subject of being a writer, not just a poet mind you, but *un escritor*:

Yo creo que todo influye en un escritor. Además, un escritor no es una persona que conozca el oficio de escribir: es, ante todo, una persona especialmente sensible a los hechos, a las cosas. Lo principal es la sensibilidad poética, lo demás es mera literatura. . .*Tout le reste est littérature*--como lo dijo Verlaine en excelente literatura--, lo demás es oficio. Y lo menos importante es el oficio; lo más importante es permanecer despierto en un. . .podríamos decirlo en inglés, an awareness of things, un estar consciente de las cosas. (88)

[I believe everything influences a writer. Besides, a writer isn't a person knowledgeable about the craft of writing: above all, he is a person especially sensitive to facts, and to things. The main thing is poetic sensibility, the rest is merely literature. . . .*Everything else is literature*—as Verlaine said of excellent literature—the rest is craft. And the least important thing is the craft; the most important thing is to remain alert with an. . .we could say it in English, an awareness of things, a conscious state concerning things.]

A "poetic sensibility" and an "awareness of things"—music and intelligence—for Borges, this is the formula for being a good writer, a fact born out over and over again in both his poetry and prose alike.

Acknowledgements

Entering USC's PhD program in 1988, I must confess that I was not the typical comparative literature scholar like most of my peers. I was, essentially, a creative writing student trying to behave like an academic. The miracle of actually finishing my dissertation is due in no small way to the poet, David St. John, who I will forever recognize as my most important mentor. He supported my proposal to write an unconventional, more "creative" dissertation—one that allowed, not only a scholarly exploration of the early writing of Borges, Faulkner and Hemingway, but also an inquiry into *creative writing* itself—how young poets transform themselves into prose fiction writers..

Thanks must also go to two other members of my committee: Beth Miller, co-chair, who first introduced me to Latin American *vanguardista* literature and the ultraistic works of young Borges. And to Gloria Orenstein, whose expertise in Anglo-American and European modernism proved invaluable to my work on Hemingway and Faulkner. I would also like to recognize Dr. Lucille Kerr of the Spanish department for having first exposed me to Borges's incredible stories from *Ficciones*—although I was not her most promising student in the explication of his strange tales.

I also owe much gratitude to the Fulbright Commission and its staff in Madrid. A special thanks goes to Patricia Zahnhiser, the program director, for her friendship, assistance and sensitive concern, which "cushioned" my labors in Spain. She was always quick to point me in the right direction to recover rare copies of the magazines I was seeking. For example, she arranged a visit to the home of Spanish poet Juan Ramon Jimenez, where I uncovered in his private collection a number of rare magazines.

I shared a portion of my residency with my father, Marcelino Padilla Ramos (1918-2010), who had agreed to join me for the first six weeks. And what a blessing that was. This book is dedicated to him, for I owe a great debt of gratitude—one that, unfortunately, I will never be able to repay. I am particularly grateful to him for his companionship in Spain and his collaboration in the translation of the poems, essays and manifestoes. His literary command of the Spanish language, his knowledge of European and Latin American history, his love for literature, his energy and enthusiasm, and his sensitive intelligence remain interwoven throughout this book. Even more, and in ways only a father-son will ever know, my father helped me to negotiate the complicated transition from life with a wife and three children back in Los Angeles to a life of scholarship and tireless research in Madrid. You might say he was the steady hand on the rudder—who helped me, in the early difficult weeks, stay on task, and who soothed my anxieties whenever waves of homesickness consumed me. Our pensión was on callé Fernando de los Ríos, in the Glorieta de Quevedo district, where I would live throughout my ten-month residency. Whenever I'm in Madrid and visit Quevedo's statue in the glorieta, I feel my father's strong, steady guidance and love.

I must acknowledge old friend, architect and Argentine literato Alfredo Fornieles, who was most helpful with the translation of Borges's "argentinisms." He, along with my colleague from SMC, Cecilia Martínez-Gil, a native of Uruguay, provided a sorely needed native's perspective to many of the terms in Borges's verse. Also, I owe much to Maureen Gates who raised our children while working fulltime during my residency in Spain. I am grateful for her patience and strength, and for her appreciation of this project.

I must recognize my late Fulbright colleague and Madrid companion, Chris Schmidt-Nowara, for his great "undercover" camera work in the *bibliotecas* of Madrid—he captured the shot of Borges's original signed version of *Fervor* (see Plates 19 and 20). Also thanks go to the rest of my posse, my tertulia friends in Madrid: Inez, Elena, Clara, Maria José, Andrew, Jake who listened to my impassioned enthusiasm for young Borges's early writing during our all-night veladas at the Café Comunista, the Café Comercial, in the Plaza Santa Barbara, at the Filmoteca, wherever we might assemble for tapas and beer, evening after evening, which made my time in Madrid so adventuresome, exhilarating, creative, and memorable.

With my dissertation complete, I was conferred the PhD in Comparative Literature by USC in May 1993. With that degree, I was able to secure a full-time professorship at Santa Monica College teaching English and Latin American Literature as well as Creative Writing. For this dream job, I will be forever grateful to the Santa Monica College hiring committee, headed by Randy Lawson and Nina Theiss, my first Department Chair, who saw my potential as both a literature instructor and a creative writer instructor.

In some way, this study was a collaborative effort, for there were those who came before me, early critics of Borges's time in Ultraism, who helped establish the parameters of my own search and gave me a clearer perspective of the Vanguardismo movement.

Guillermo de Torre, a vanguard poet and friend of Borges, wrote the earliest critical study of the vangaurdista movement which included some of Borges's poems in his *Literaturas europeas de vanguardia* (1925).

Gloria Videla, with two essays, "Presencia americana en el ultraísmo español" and "Poemas y prosas olvidades de Borges" in *Revista de Literatura Argentina e Iberoamericana* (1961), includes complete versions of "Distancia," "Insomnio," "Mañana," "Trinchera" and "S[C]ingladura" (she perpetuates the incorrect "S"); excerpts only of "Catedral," and "Himno del Mar," as well as a reproduction of the essay "Al margen de la moderna lírica." Her most thorough and important study, *El Ultraísmo* (1963), offers several more poems and essay. In 1975, Gloria Videla offers in her essay "Anticipos del mundo literario de Borges en su prehistoria ultraísta," published in *Iberoromania*, the complete versions of two previously unknown prose poems: "Paréntesis pasional," and "La llama," as well as a number of Borges's ultraist poetry. Guillermo Sucre writes perhaps the most enlightening critical work on Borges with his *Borges el poeta* (1967). Zunilda Gertel's *Borges y su retorno a la poesía* (1967) includes "Aldea [II]," excerpts of "Tranvías," "Rusia," "Gesta maximalista," "Trinchera," and discussions on Borges's ultraist manifestos, along with the essays on metaphor. Carlos Meneses discusses (with excerpts only) the early works of Borges in his essay "Los manifiestos y otros trabajos ultraístas de Borges," published in *Razón y Fábula* (1971). His *Escritores latinoamericanos en Mallorca* (1974) provides two poems whose complete versions were not previously republished:

"Poema" and "Catedral." And in his book-length study devoted to Borges's early poetry, *Poesía juvenil de J.L.Borges* (1978), Meneses reproduces complete versions of a number of Borges's ultraist poems. And Jaime Alazraki two books, *La Prosa Narrativa de Jorge Luis Borges* (1968) and *Jorge Luis Borges* (1976), were most helpful.

With regards to English studies and translations of Borges's vanguardista works, my predecessors are few. Ronald J. Christ's excellent and groundbreaking study *The Narrow Act: Borges's Art of Allusion* (1969) is essential for any study of Borges's transition from poetry to prose. J.M. Cohen in his book *Borges* (1973) includes: "Trinchera" ("Trench") and "S[C]ingladura" (which due to the spelling error he adopted from previous critics, the poem is incorrectly translated as "Day's Run of a Ship"). Thorpe Running's *Borges' Ultraísta Movement and its Poets* (1981) has been cited by a number of critics. And finally, Paul Cheselka's *The Poetry and Poetics of Jorge Luis Borges* (1987), an ambitious book indeed, attempts a discussion of all of the early poems (excerpts only) reproduced to date.

Appendix

A Chronological List of the Early Works
Published in Magazines from 1919-1926

1. Review: "Chronique des lettres espagnoles: Trois nouveaux livres," *La Feuille*, Geneva, 20 August 1919.

2. Poem: "Himno del mar," *Grecia* ns 37, Sevilla, 31 December 1919.

3. Prose Poem: "Paréntesis pasional," *Grecia* ns 38, Sevilla, 20 January 1920.

4. Essay: "Al margen de la moderna lírica," *Grecia* ns 39, Sevilla, 31 January 1920: 15.

5. Prose Poem: "La llama," *Grecia* ns 41, Sevilla, 29 February 1920.

6. Poem: "Trinchera," *Grecia* ns 43, Sevilla, 1 June 1920: 6.

7. Poem: "Hermanos," *Grecia* ns 45, Sevilla, 1 July 1920: 14.

8. Poem: "Señal," *Grecia* ns 46, Sevilla, 15 July 1920: 13.

9. Essay: "Lírica expresionista: Sintesis," *Grecia* ns 47, Sevilla, 1 August 1920: 10-11.

10. Prose Poem: "Rusia," *Grecia* ns 48, Sevilla, 1 September 1920: 11.

11. Prose Poem: "Insomnio," *Grecia* ns 49, Sevilla, 15 September 1920: 9.

12. Poem: "Poema," *Baleares* ns 121, Palma de Mallorca, 15 September 1920: 1-2.

13. Essay: "Antología expresionista," *Cervantes*, Madrid, October 1920: 100-112.

14. Essay: "Lírica expresionista: Wilhelm Klemm," *Grecia* ns 50, 1 November 1920: 10-11.

15. Review: "Vertical": Reseña de manifiesto ultraísta de Guillermo de Torre. *Reflector* ns 1, Madrid, December 1920: 18.

16. Poem: "Mañana," *Ultra* ns 1, Madrid, 27 January 1921: 3.

17. Essay: "Velada ultraísta," *Ultra* ns 1, Madrid, 27 January 1921: 3.

18. Prose Poem: "Aldea" [I], *Ultra* ns 2, Madrid, 10 February 1921: 2.

19. Manifesto: "Manifiesto del ultra": co-signed by Jacobo Sureda, Fortunio Bonanova y Juan Alomar *Baleares* ns 131, Palma de Mallorca, 15 February 1921: 1.

20. Poem: "Catedral," *Baleares* ns 131, Palma de Mallorca, 15 February 1921: 2. Republished (with revisions) in *Ultra* ns 19, Madrid, 1 December 1921: 2.

21. Poem: "Gesta Maximalista," *Ultra* ns 3, Madrid, 20 February 1921: 3.

22. Poem: "Prismas," *Ultra* ns 4, Madrid, 1 March 1921: 2.

23. Poem: "Guardia roja," *Ultra* ns 5, Madrid, 17 March 1921: 2. Republished (with revisions) in *Tableros*, ns 1, Madrid, 15 November 1921: 11.

24. Poem: "Tranvias," *Ultra* ns 6, Madrid, 30 March 1921: 2.

25. Poem: "Norte," *Ultra* ns 7, Madrid, 10 April 1921: 1.

26. Poem: "Cingladura," *Ultra* ns 8, Madrid, 20 April 1921: 3.

27. Poem: "Distancia," *Ultra* ns 9, Madrid, 30 April 1921: 2.

28. Essay: "Anatomía de mi 'Vltra." *Ultra* ns 11, Madrid, 20 May 1921: 1.

29. Poem: "Fiesta," *Ultra* ns 15, Madrid, 30 June 1921: 2.

30. Poem: "Arrabal," *Cosmópolis* ns 32, Madrid, August 1921: 622. Republished (with revisions) in *Fervor de Buenos Aires* (1923).

31. Review: "Horizontes: reseña de *Die Aktions-Lyrik--1914-1916--Berlin*" *Ultra* ns 16, Madrid, 20 October 1921: 1.

32. Prose Poem: "Casa Elena," *Ultra* ns 17, Madrid, 30 October 1921: 1.

33. Essay: "Prosistas nuevos: Critica del paisáje," *Cosmópolis* ns 34, Madrid, October 1921: 195-199.

34. Essay: "Apuntaciones criticas: La metáfora," *Cosmópolis* ns 35, Madrid, November 1921: 395-402.

35. Poem: "Ultimo Rojo Sol," *Ultra* ns 20, Madrid, 15 December 1921: 2.

36. Poem: "Montaña," *Tableros* ns 2, Madrid, 15 December 1921: 7.

37. Essay: "La lírica Argentina contemporanea: selección y notas de Jorge Luis Borges," *Cosmópolis* ns 36, Madrid, December 1921: 640-651.

38. Essay: "Ultraísmo," *Nosotros* ns 151, Buenos Aires, December 1921: 466-471.

39. Manifesto: "Proclama," co-signed by Guillermo Juan, Eduardo Gonzales Lanuza, Guillermo de Torre, *Ultra* ns 21, Madrid, 1 January 1922: 1. Originally published in the mural magazine *Prisma* (privately printed) in Buenos Aires, December 1921.

40. Poem: "Aldea"[II] *Ultra* ns 21, Madrid, 1 January 1922: 3. Republished (with added stanzas) as "Campos atardecidos" in *Fervor*.

41. Prose Poem: "Escaparate," *Tableros* ns 3, Madrid, 15 January 1922: 12.

42. Poem: "Prismas: Sala Vacía," *Ultra* ns 22, Madrid, 15 January 1922: 2. Republished (with revisions) as "Sala Vacía" in *Fervor*.

43. Poem: "Siesta," *Ultra* ns 24, Madrid, 15 March 1922: 1.

44. Essay: "Nuevos prosistas americanos, apuntaciones críticas: El cielo azul, es Cielo y es azul," *Cosmópolis* ns 44, Madrid, August 1922: 320-323.

45. Poem: "Sábado," *Nosotros* ns 160, Buenos Aires, September 1922: 55. Republished as "Sábados" (with added stanzas) in *Fervor*.

Fervor de Buenos Aires (1923), Buenos Aires, (privately printed). First book of poetry.

46. Essay: "La encrucijada de Berkeley," *Nosotros* ns 166, Buenos Aires, March 1923:359-365. Republished in *Inquiciones*.

47. Essay: "Acerca de Unamuno poeta," *Nosotros* ns 175, Buenos Aires, December 1923: 405-410. Republished in *Inquiciones*.

48. Essay: "Acerca del Expresionismo," *Inicial* ns 3, Buenos Aires, December 1923: 15-17. Republished in *Inquiciones*.

49. Poem: "Alejamiento," *Alfar* ns 36, La Coruña, January 1924: 25.

50. Essay: "La traducción de un incidente," *Inicial* ns 5, Buenos Aires, May 1924: 6-8. Republished in *Inquiciones*.

51. Essay: "Examen de metáforas" Part I, *Alfar* ns 40, La Corñua, May 1924: 385-386. Republished in *Inquiciones*.

52. Essay: "Examen de metáforas" Part II, *Alfar* ns 41, La Corñua, June 1924: 22-23. Republished in *Inquiciones*.

53. Prose Poem: "Montevideo," *Martin Fierro* ns 9, Buenos Aires, September 1924: 60. Republished in *Luna*.

54. Review: "Acotaciones: 'Prismas' (1924) por E. González Lanuza," *Proa* ns 1, Buenos Aires, August 1924: 30-32. Republished in *Inquisiciones*.

55. Prose Poems: "Jactancia de quietud," "Singladura," and "A Rafael Cansinos Assens" appear under the title Salmos in *Proa* ns 1, Buenos Aires, August 1924: 49-51. All three poems are republished in *Luna*.

56. Review: "Interpretación de Silva Valdés: *Agua del Tiempo*," *Proa* ns 2, Buenos Aires, September 1924: 24-26. Republished in *Inquisiciones*.

57. Review: "La criolledad en Ipuche: *Tierra Honda*," *Proa* ns 3, October 1924: 27-29. Republished in *Inquisiciones*.

58. Essay: "Definición de Cansinos-Asséns," *Martin Fierro*, Buenos Aires, October 1924. Republished in *Inquisiciones*.

59. Essay: "Menoscabo y grandeza de Quevedo," *Revista de Occidente* ns 17, Madrid, November 1924: 249-255. Republished in *Inquisiciones*.

60. Essay: "Torres Villarroel (1693-1770)" *Proa* ns 4, November 1924: 51-55. Republished in *Inquisiciones*.

61. Essay: "Después de las imágenes," *Proa* ns 5, Buenos Aires, December 1924: 22-23. Republished in *Inquisiciones*.

62. Review: "El Ulises de Joyce," *Proa* ns 6, Buenos Aires, January 1925: 3-6. Republished in *Inquisiciones*.

63. Review: "Omar Jaiyam y Fitzgerald," *Proa* ns 6, Buenos Aires, January 1925: 69-70. Republished in *Inquisiciones*.

64. Essay: "Ramon y 'Pombo,'" *Martín Fierro* ns 14-15, Buenos Aires, 24 January 1925. Republished in *Inquisiciones*.

65. Essay: "Sir Thomas Browne," *Proa* ns 7, Buenos Aires, February 1925: 3-8. Republished in *Inquisiciones*.

Inquisiciones (1925), Buenos Aires. First collection of essays,

66. Prose Poem: "Dualidad en una despedida," *Proa* ns 8, Buenos Aires, March 1925: 37. Republished in *Luna* and is retitled "Una despedida" in *Obra Poética 1923-1969*.

67. Poem: "Antelación de amor," *Proa* ns 8, Buenos Aires, March 1925: 38. Republished in *Luna*. Note: "Antelación de Amor" is retitled "Amorosa anticipación" in *Poemas 1922-1943*.

Luna de enfrente (1925) Buenos Aires: Proa. Second book of poetry.

68. Essay: "Sobre un verso de Apollinaire," *Nosotros* ns 190, Buenos Aires, March 1925: 320-322. Republished in *El tamaño* as "La aventura y el orden."

69. Essay: "Oscar Wilde y un poema," *Nosotros* ns 191, Buenos Aires, April 1925: 444-446.

70. Essay: "Acotación del árbol en la lírica," *Proa* ns 10, Buenos Aires, May 1925: 58-59. Republished in *El tamaño* as "Reverencia del árbol en la otra banda."

71. Essay: "El Fausto Criollo," *Proa* ns 11, Buenos Aires, June 1925: 27-30. Republished in *El tamaño*.

72. Review: "Oliverio Girondo 'Calcomanías,'" *Martin Fierro* ns 18, Buenos Aires, June 1925: 91-92. Republished in *El tamaño*.

73. Essay: "El idioma infinito," *Proa* ns 12, Buenos Aires, July 1925: 43-46. Republished in *El tamaño*.

74. Essay: "La tierra cárdena," *Proa* ns 13, Buenos Aires, November 1925: 52-54. Republished in *El tamaño*.

75. Essay: "Ejercicio de análisis," *Proa* ns 14, Buenos Aires, December 1925: 46-49. Republished in *El tamaño*.

76. Poem: "Versos para Fernán Silva Valdés," *Proa* ns 14, Buenos Aires, December 1925: 16.

77. Review: "Nydia Lamarque: Telarañas, 1925," *Proa* ns 14, Buenos Aires, December 1925: 50-51.

78. Essay: "La Pampa y el suburbio son Dioses," *Proa* ns 15 (last issue), Buenos Aires, January 1926: 14-17. Republished in *El tamaño*.

79. Essay: "Carta a Güiraldes y a Brandán en una muerte (ya resucitada) de *Proa*," *Proa* ns 15, Buenos Aires, January 1926: 26-27. Republished in *El tamaño*.

80. Reviews: "Acotaciones: Antología de la Poesía Argentina moderna ordenada por Julio Noé," *Proa* ns 15, Buenos Aires, January 1926: 51-52; along with "*Simplismo*: Poemas inventados por Alberto Hidalgo."

81. Essay: "Examen de un Soneto de Góngora," *Inicial* ns 3, Buenos Aires, May 1926: 30-33. Republished in *El tamaño*. *El tamaño de mi esperanza* (1926) 2nd collection of essays.

82. Poems: "Villa Urquiza" and "Las Palmas" both appear under the general title Dos Sonetos, *Alfar* ns 59, La Coruña, July 1926: 1.

Works Cited

Alazraki, Jaime. *Borges and the Kabbalah*. Cambridge: Cambridge University Press, 1988.

- - -. Editor. *Critical Essays on Jorge Luis Borges*. Boston: G.K. Hall, 1987.

Barili, Amelia. "Borges on Life and Death." *New York Times* Book Review 13 July 1986, national edition.

Baudelaire, Charles. *Paris Spleen*. New Directions, 1970.

Beja, Morris. *James Joyce: A Literary Life*. Columbus: Ohio State University Press, 1992.

Borges, Jorge Luis. *Fervor de Buenos Aires*, 1923. Privately printed. (note that all poems cited from *Fervor* 1923 come from this original signed edition).

- - -. "Menoscabo y Grandeza de Quevedo." *Revista de Occidente* ns 17, Madrid, November 1924.

- - -. "Sir Thomas Browne." *Proa* ns 7, Buenos Aires, February 1925.

- - -. "Ejercicio de análisis." *Proa* ns 14, Buenos Aires, December 1925.

- - -. "El jardín de senderos que se bifurcan," *Ficciones*. Madrid: Alianza, 194.

- - -. "The Garden of Forking Paths," *Ficciones*. Translated by Helen Temple and Ruthven Todd. Edited and introduced by Anthony Kerrigan. New York: Grove Press, 1962.

- - -. *Evaristo Carriego*. 1930. Buenos Aires,:Emecé Editores, 1955.

- - -. "El asesino desinteresado Bill Harrigan." *Historia universal de la infamia*. Emecé Editores, 1935, 1954.

- - -. "El enemigo generoso" *Historia universal de la infamia*. Emecé Editores, 1935, 1954.

- - -. "Dreamtigers." *El hacedor*. Buenos Aires: Emecé, 1960.

- - -. "Dreamtigers." *Dreamtigers*. Translated by Mildred Boyer and Harold Morland. Austin: Texas University Press, 1964.

- - -. "Los espejos." *El hacedor*. Buenos Aires: Emecé, 1960.

- - -. "Mirrors" *Dreamtigers*. Trans. Mildred Boyer and Harold Morland. Austin: Texas University Press, 1964.

- - -. "Ars Poética" in *A Personal Anthology*. Ed. Anthony Kerrigen. New York: Grove Weidenfeld Press, 1967.

- - -. *El otro, el mismos*. Prologue. Buenos Aires: Emecé, 1964.

- - -. *Catalogo de la exposición de libros españolas*. Prólogo. Buenos Aires: Sellecciones Graficas, 1962.

- - -. "Tres reseñas sobre Faulkner" [William Faulkner: Three Reviews"] *Borges: A Reader*. Edited by Emir Rodriguez Monegal and Alastair Reid. E.P. Dutton, 1981.

- - -. *Jorge Luis Borges: A/Z*. Edited by Antonio Ferrer. Madrid: Siruela, 1988.

Borges, Jorge Luis, Silvina Ocampo, Adolfo Bioy Casares. *Antología poética Argentina*. Buenos Aires: Editorial Sudamericana, 1941.

Borges, Jorge Luis, Guillermo Juan, Eduardo Gonzalez Lanuza, and Guillermo de Torre. "Proclama." *Ultra* ns 21, Madrid, 1 January 1922.

Bousoño, Carlos. *Teoría de la expresión poética*. Madrid: Gredos, 1956.

Calvino, Italo. "La Fortuna de Borges." *Libros* 3 de dicembre, 1992, *Diario 16*.

Caws, Mary Ann and Hermine Riffaterre, eds. *The Prose Poem in France*. New York: Columbia University Press, 1983.

Cheselka, Paul. *The Poetry and Poetics of Jorge Luis Borges*. New York: Lang Publishing, 1987.

Christ, Ronald J. *The Narrow Act*. New York: New York University Press, 1969.

Coleno, Alice. "The Meaning of Poetry." *Quarterly Review of Literature* Volume III, ns 3 (1947).

De Carlos, Maialen. "The Beginning of the American Short Story: Edgar Allan Poe." August 14, 2022. Online: byarcadia.org/post/america, May 9, 2023.

Di Giovanni, Norman Thomas, ed. and "Introduction." *Jorge Luis Borges: Selected Poems, 1923-1967*. London: Penguin Books, 1972.

Faulkner, William. Interview with Jean Stein. "William Faulkner: The Art of Fiction." *The Paris Review*, issue 12, Spring 1956.

Ferrer, Antonio Fernández. Editor. *Jorge Luis Borges: A/Z*. Madrid: Ediciones Siruela, 1985.

Fishburn, Evelyn and Psiche Hughes. *A Dictionary of Borges*. London: Duckworth, 1990.

Fredman, Stephen. *Poet's Prose: The Crisis in American Verse*. Cambridge: Cambridge University Press, 1983.

Gargatagli, Ana. "Borges traduce a Baroja: La Geuille de Ginebra. *Revista de historia de la traduccion. Núm 11* (Universitat Autónoma de Barcelona. Departament de Filologia Espanyola, 2017. Online: http://www.traduccionliteraria.org/1611/art/gargatagli5.htm.

Gertel, Zunilda. *Borges y su retorno a la poesía*. New York: Iowa University Press & Las Americas, 1967.

González Martínez, Enrique. "Tuércele el cuello al cisne..." ["Wring the Swan's Neck"]. *Twentieth-Century Latin American Poetry*. Edited by Stephen Tapscott. Texas University Press, 1996.

Horvath, Brooke. "The Prose Poem and the Secret Life of Poetry." *The American Poetry Review* September-October 1992: 11-14.

Kerrigan, Anthony, ed. Foreword. *Jorge Luis Borges, A Personal Anthology*. USA: Castle/Grove Press, 1967. Originally published as Jorge Luis Borges, *Antología personal*. Buenos Aires: Sur, 1961.

Magis, Carlos Horacio. *La literatura Argentina*. Mexico: Editorial Pormaca, 1965.

Mallarmé, Stéphane "Les fenêtres" ["Windows"]. New York: Penguin Books, 1977.

Milleret, Jean de. *Entrevistas con Jorge Luis Borges*. Caracas: Monte Avila, 1970.

Monegal, Emir Rodríguez. *A Literary Biography*. New York: Dutton, 1978.

Monegal, Emir Rodríguez and Alastair Reid. *Borges: A Reader*. New York: Dutton, 1981.

Padilla, Mario René. *Reaching Back for the Neverendings*. PSPoets, 1993; 2021.

Pratt, William. Editor. *The Imagist Poem*. Introduction. Modern Poetry in Miniature. New York: Dutton, 1993.

Scholes, Robert. "The Reality of Borges." *The Iowa Review* Vol 8. No. 3 (Summer 1977).

Smith, Barbara Herrnstein. "Poetry as fiction." *New Directions in Literary History*. Edited by Ralph Cohen. Baltimore: Johns Hopkins University Press, 1974.

Sucre, Guillermo. *Borges, el poeta*. Caracas: Monte Avila, 1967.

Tapscott, Stephen. *Twentieth-Century Latin American Poetry: A Bilingual Anthology*. Texas University Press. 1997.

Videla, Gloria. *El Ultraísmo*. Madrid: Gredos, 1963. Madrid: Editorial Gredos, 1971.

Watts, Harold H. "The Poet's Place." *Quarterly Review of Literature* Volume III, ns 3 (1947).

Whitman, Walt. *Leaves of Grass*. New York: The Viking Press, 1975.

Selected Biliography

Alazraki, Jaime. *La prosa narrativa de Jorge Luis Borges*. Madrid: Editorial Gredos, 1968.

- - -. Editor. *Jorge Luis Borges*. Madrid: Taurus Ediciones, 1976.

Alifano, Roberto. *Borges, Biografía Verbal*. Barcelona: Plaza & Janes, 1988.

Barnatan, Marcos Ricardo. *Borges*. Madrid: E.P.E.S.A., 1972.

- - -. *Jorge Luis Borges*. Madrid: Ediciones Júcar, 1976.

Bly, Robert. *Selected Poems*, "The Prose Poem as an Evolving Form." New York: Harper, 1986. New York: New Directions, 1984.

Cohen, J.M. *Jorge Luis Borges*. New York: Harper, 1973.

Cortínez, Carlos. Editor. *Borges the Poet*. Fayetteville: Arkansas University Press, 1986.

De Man, Paul. "A Modern Master." In Alazraki, *Critical Essays on Jorge Luis Borges*. Boston: G.K. Hall, 1987.

De Torre, Guillermo. *Literaturas europeas de vanguardia*. Madrid: Caro Raggio, 1925.

- - -. *Historia de las literaturas de vanguardia*. Madrid: Ediciones Guadarrama, 1965.

- - -. "Para la prehistoria ultraísta de Borges." *Hispania*, Washington, volume XLVII (1964): 457-463. Also in *Cuadernos Hispanoamericanos*, Madrid, ns 57 (1964); and in his *Al pie de las letras*, Buenos Aires: Losada, 1967.

Doyle, Raymond H. *La huella española en la obra de Jorge Luis Borges.* Coleccion Nova Scholar, Playor, 1976.

Ferrari, Osvaldo and Jorge Luis Borges. *Diálogos últimos.* Buenos Aires: Editorial Sudamericana, 1987.

Flores, Angel. *Expliquémonos a Borges como poeta.* México: Siglo Veintiuno, 1984.

Fowler, Alastair. *Kinds of Literature: An Introduction to the Theory of Genres and Modes.* Cambridge: Harvard University Press, 1982.

Freedman, Ralph. *The Lyrical Novel.* Princeton: Princeton University Press, 1963.

Houston, John Porter. *French Symbolism and the Modernist Movement.* Baton Rouge: Louisiana State University Press, 1980.

Jurado, Alicia. *Genio y figura de Jorge Luis Borges.* Buenos Aires: Editorial Universidad, 1964.

Lagos, Romona. *Jorge Luis Borges 1923-1980.* Barcelona: Edicions del mall, 1986.

Meneses, Carlos. "Los manifiestos y otros trabajos ultraistas de Borges." *Razon y Fabula* 23 (enero-febrero 1971).

- - -. "Los manifiestos ultraístas de Jorge Luis Borges." *Insula* 291 (February 1971).

- - -. *Escritores latinoamericanos en Mallorca.* Palma de Mallorca: Ediciones Cort, 1974.

- - -. *Poesia juvenil de J.L. Borges.* Barcelona: José Olañeta, 1978.

- - -. *Cartas de juventud de J.L. Borges.* Madrid: Origenes, 1987.

Monegal, Emir Rodríguez. *Borges por él mismo.* Caracas: Monte Avila, 1983.

- - -. *Borges: hacia una interpretación.* Madrid: Ediciones Guadarrama, 1976.

Pérez, Albérto Julián. *Poética de la prosa de J.L. Borges.* Madrid: Editorial Gredos, 1986.

Running, Thorpe. "Borges' Ultraist Poetry." *Borges's Ultrist Movement and its Poets.* International Book Publishing, 1981.

Shaw, D.L. *Borges: Ficciones.* London: Grant & Cutler, 1976.

Sabajanes, Beatriz Sarlo. Antología y prólogo. *Martin Fierro 1924-1927* Buenos Aires: Carlos Pérez Editor, 1969.

Verani, Hugo J. *Las vanguardias literarias en Hispanoamerica.* Roma: Bulzoni Editore, 1986.

Videla, Gloria. "Poemas y prosas olvidadas de Borges." *Revista de Literatura Argentina e Iberoamericana* 3 (December 1961).

- - -. "Anticipios del mundo literario de Borges en su prehistoria ultraísta." *Iberoromania* (1975).

- - -. "Presencia americana en el ultraísmo español." *Revista de Literatura Argentina e Iberoamericana* 3 (December 1961).

About the Author

Mario René Padilla is a tenured professor of English at Santa Monica College, where he teaches creative writing and Latin-American literature. He was born in Detroit, Michigan, and is of Mexican and Italian descent, but grew up *nevertheless* a "mid-western" kid in Columbus, Ohio. Multiculturalism and mixed-cultural identity issues are central themes in his work. His poetry and stories have appeared in *North American Review, The Antioch Review, New Letters, Alligator Juniper, The Ledge, INKWELL Magazine, Americas Review, Tulip Tree Review, Chiron Review, Atlanta Review, Westwind UCLA,* among others. His first collection of poetry, *Reaching Back for the Neverendings* (1993), was published by Red Dancefloor Press in LA. His second collection of poetry, *Blue Plums & Weeds* (2021), was published by PSPOETS in LA. His short story "Scales" won first prize in TulipTree Publishing's fiction contest, *Stories That Need to Be Told* 2020. Another story, "Le Château Poissonnier," won the same prize in 2017. Padilla won a Fulbright Award for collecting and translating the early poetry and prose of Jorge Luis Borges for his dissertation *Borges, Faulkner and Hemingway: Young Poets of Prose.* He has an MA in English from Loyola Marymount and a PhD in Comparative Literature from USC. He currently resides in Venice, CA with his wife Christine and blended family of six.

www.ingramcontent.com/pod-product-compliance
Lightning Source LLC
Chambersburg PA
CBHW020434130626
46549CB00001B/140